EYES OF THE FLEET OVER VIETNAM

EYES OF THE FLEET OVER VIETNAM

RF-8 Crusader Combat Photo-Reconnaissance Missions

KENNETH V. JACK

CASEMATE
Philadelphia & Oxford

Published in the United States of America and Great Britain in 2021 by
CASEMATE PUBLISHERS
1950 Lawrence Road, Havertown, PA 19083, USA
and
The Old Music Hall, 106–108 Cowley Road, Oxford OX4 1JE, UK

Hardback Edition: ISBN 978-1-63624-074-9
Digital Edition: ISBN 978-1-63624-075-6

A CIP record for this book is available from the British Library

Printed and bound in the Czech Republic by Finidr S.R.O.

Typeset in India by Lapiz Digital Services.

For a complete list of Casemate titles, please contact:

CASEMATE PUBLISHERS (US)
Telephone (610) 853-9131
Fax (610) 853-9146
Email: casemate@casematepublishers.com
www.casematepublishers.com

CASEMATE PUBLISHERS (UK)
Telephone (01865) 241249
Email: casemate-uk@casematepublishers.co.uk
www.casematepublishers.co.uk

Front cover: A doomed, unarmed VFP-63 RF-8 Crusader doing photo-reconnaissance over Vietnam is hit by antiaircraft fire, as jet fuel from internal tanks feeds a devastating fire that will force the pilot to eject. Above and to the rear is his F-8 Crusader escort flying target combat air patrol. (Mads Bangsø, Aircraft Profiles)

Back cover: The pilot of a VFP-63 RF-8G Crusader goes to full afterburner as he waits for the "shooter" whose hand is raised in the air in preparation for touching the deck to give the launch signal. The sailor immediately behind the shooter, sitting on the flight deck, is monitoring the current steam gauge settings to make sure all is ready for the catapult to launch that specific aircraft. The ship is the USS *Midway* (CVA-41) on its May–October 1971 Vietnam combat deployment. (USN photo via Jerry Nolan ISC)

Dedicated to all Vietnam Veterans

Contents

Acknowledgements

When I envisioned the concept of this book, I recognized the details of the stories I wanted to tell could only come from Navy and Marine Corps pilots' recollections of their missions over Laos and North Vietnam. I knew some from my work on my previous book, *Blue Moon Over Cuba: Aerial Reconnaissance During the Cuban Missile Crisis*, but I had to appeal to the broader Crusader aviator community for more help. Fighter pilots, by their nature and culture, are an insular, tight-knit fraternity. They exhibit much trust and openness among themselves when they reminisce about their adventures in the high-performance jets they flew. It was a slow build of trust and confidence building, but eventually a large number, ready to tell their stories, responded. To our benefit, photo-reconnaissance and fighter escort pilots contributed their well-written accounts from the early months of the war to the last.

Two of the most prolific resources were Lieutenant Commander Scott Ruby and Captain Len Johnson. Scott is recognized as the Light Photographic Squadron 63 (VFP-63) historian. He has extensive knowledge of the RF-8 Crusader and squadron detachments during the war. He graciously tolerated my endless stream of questions and his colorful anecdotes are sprinkled throughout the narrative. Likewise, Len, AKA "Rocky," made massive photo and written contributions that describe the progress of a photo pilot from rookie to well-seasoned fighter pilot with over 100 combat missions. His self-deprecating style and natural humor give us a sense of what a young man goes through to prove himself in an exclusive cadre of naval aviators.

Commander Andre Coltrin describes his encounters with surface-to-air missiles (SAMs), MiGs, and AAA (anti-aircraft-artillery). Most memorable is his harrowing, but sensitive, account of the tragic fire on the USS *Oriskany* (CVA-34). Another generous pilot and my friend, Commander Norm Green, from our squadron, Light Photographic Squadron 62 (VFP-62), made huge photo and written contributions to the chapter on VFP-62's only Vietnam combat detachment. Norm also provided a touching and moving memorial for his close friend, and shipmate, who mysteriously crashed at sea.

The chapter on Marine Composite Reconnaissance Squadron (VMCJ-1) would not have the depth of historical content without the late Colonel Denis "Deej" J. Kiely and Colonel Wayne Whitten USMC. Colonel Kiely generously shared his account of the first Marine augmentation detachment to VFP-63 in mid-1964, before the Vietnam War began. He was a gifted writer, with humor and humility, and showed how the Marines made extensive contributions to the photo recon effort. Additionally, I can't praise Colonel Whitten enough for providing me with research resources and his own written accounts of the progression of VMCJ-1's war effort for the years 1964–66. He was extremely generous with his time for consultation and support of this writing project. An author in his own right, he made many pertinent recommendations on how the Marine aviation story should unfold. I'm extremely grateful to both. Unfortunately, Colonel Kiely died before this book was published. Semper Fi, Colonel.

My long-time friend and mentor, Commander Peter Mersky, a prolific and highly praised aviation history writer, got behind this book early and provided guidance with his wisdom and writing experience, as well as a thorough review of the manuscript. I tested his endurance beyond all human expectation and he dutifully struggled to reinforce what writing a serious book is all about. He also generously contributed many excellent photos.

A must for a book such as this is to tell the story of the prisoners of war (POWs) and I found two aviators with exceptional stories to tell. Their shootdowns, capture and path to freedom make an exciting read. The first aviator shot down, before the Vietnam War was declared, was VFP-63 pilot Lieutenant Charles Klusmann. When (now) Captain Klusmann heard about this book project, he generously gave permission to use his captivating story of becoming a POW in Laos and his eventual escape. His memoir is so well written and interesting, it was included in the national TV documentary series *No Man Left Behind*. His wife, Ellen, became an eager and excellent liaison as I sought additional information. Additionally, his wingman, (now) Commander Jerry Kuechmann, provided his account of the shootdown and VFP-63 missions in 1964.

Finding another POW, willing to tell his story, was not easy. A number of Vietnam POWs still find the memory too difficult to review and we respect their choice. Fortunately, a generous offer came from the last VFP-63 POW, Commander Gordon Paige. His RF-8G was the last VFP-63 jet to be shot down. His fighter escort pilot, Lieutenant Pete LaChat, provided graphic details of the doomed jet's explosion after it was hit. Commander Paige's detailed account describes his life in the infamous "Hanoi Hilton" where hundreds of American pilots faced a dreadful existence. We are indebted to him.

The early years of the war, 1964–65, found naval aviators struggling to find the correct tactics to accomplish their missions. I was fortunate to find pilots of that era to help us understand that history. One remarkable VFP-63 pilot, Lieutenant Roger Crim, provided descriptive accounts and photos that illustrate the danger and value of photographic reconnaissance in the early war years. For the mid-years, 1966–67, I am grateful for the gripping account of dogfights with North Vietnamese MiG fighters from the writing of the fighter pilot, the late Captain Cole Black, who was shot down by a MiG, captured and became a POW. During that MiG vs. Crusader battle, fighter escort pilot, Lieutenant Dick Smith, adds additional insight into that thrilling event. Commander Jim Ozbirn helps us experience the dangers of facing multiple SAMs over the well-defended skies of North Vietnam. He describes the RF-8G's electronic gear that alerted pilots to SAMs and the pilot's tactics to defeat them. Also, Lieutenant Bill Kocar provides an excellent account of how his fighter escort pilot saved him from a MiG's attack by shooting it down with a missile.

The art and science of photographic interpretation is thoroughly discussed by Photo Intel Officer Lieutenant Gary Ruesling. When I first contacted him for his help, he downplayed the effort of capturing intelligence from the photography that was obtained at great risk to the pilots. With some encouragement, he produced an amazing story that illustrates why photo-reconnaissance was so important to the war planners.

Another exceptional contributor was Captain Jim Morgan, an Air Force exchange pilot with VFP-63 in 1971. From his unusual standpoint, he was able to compare the Navy and Air Force missions and jets. He also was a great editor and proofreader for a number of chapters and provided photos of his detachment.

Commander Paul Ringwood provided his story of being hit by AAA and ejecting over water. Once in the water, he faced some unusual events that make his story exciting reading. My gratitude also goes to Captain Will Gray, Commander Roy McDermid, Lieutenant Dave Leighton, Lieutenant John P Humbert, and Captain Charles Robinson for supporting stories of important events. The Thanh Hoa (Dragon's Jaw) Bridge vexed aviators for much of the war. It would not yield to heavy, continuous bombing, yet it extracted a heavy cost in men and aircraft. I thank Admiral Leighton Smith for his description of how it met its end.

There are many references to pilots ejecting from their damaged jets and Lieutenant Terry Stent helps us visualize that terror with a sequence of dramatic ejection photos.

Enlisted Sailors, Joe Nagel ADJC, Frank Bodden AZ3, Jerry Nolan ISC, provided photos and information that help explain life on board ship and flight deck action. Joe has a tremendous memory and made multiple VFP-63 detachments. Ken Killmeyer, sailor, author and historian of the USS *Forrestal* (CVA-59) Association provided dramatic photos of the *Forrestal*'s flight deck fire. Art Jorgensen PHCS provided photos and technical information on the RA-5C Vigilante. Commander Frank Peele advanced from enlisted sailor to commander. He was also a crewman/navigator on the RA-3B Skywarrior photo-reconnaissance jet and provided expert details on its missions.

I thank Lieutenant Pete Phelps for the harrowing story of the three-aircraft mid-air accident that puts us in his cockpit as it unfolds. I also used his logbook notes to describe pilot stress during the late war era. Lieutenant Phil Sherman provided excellent recon photos to help explain the work product of photo-reconnaissance.

I also give my gratitude to the National Naval Aviation Museum, Pensacola, Florida, and research assistant Jared Galloway, for the large selection of photos that help tell the naval aviation story.

My gratitude to Mads Bangs of *Aircraft Profiles* who worked with me to create our dramatic book cover. Mads captured the RF-8G aflame from an AAA hit, illustrating the danger naval aviators faced in the war.

I can't say enough about the professional staff of Casemate Publishers who accepted my manuscript and made it into the book it is. My debt of appreciation goes to: Ruth Sheppard, Felicity Goldsack, Megan Yates, Declan Ingram, Sarah Stamp, Andy Wright, and Daniel Yesilonis.

Finally, my wife Darlene gave me her early and enthusiastic support for this book's concept. From my previous book, she was well aware of the demands and frustrations that would be placed on both of us. She provided numerous proof readings that helped me develop the narrative. Most of all, she endured my obsession and isolation during the months of writing and research. I like to say, "Writing a book is like having a jealous mistress." This book would not have happened without her.

One More Roll

We toast our hearty comrades
Now fallen from the sky,
And gently caught by God's own hand
To be with Him on high,
To dwell among the soaring clouds
They knew so well before,
From dawn patrol and victory roll
At heaven's very door.
And as we fly among them there,
We're sure to hear their plea:
"Take care, my friend,
Watch your six,
And do one more roll...just for me."

Captain Jerry Coffee USN Ret.
(POW, photo recon pilot)

The Story Behind "One More Roll"
By Captain Jerry Coffee USN (Ret.)

One day, sometime in 1969, there was an air raid on Hanoi. Although we were supposed to get under our concrete "beds," I stood on mine peering through the bars on the window and into the sky. Into my view came four Air Force F-105s in perfect echelon formation as they pitched up to commence their bombing run. The air around them was filled with flak bursts and surface-to-air missile (SAM) trails. One after the other they rolled into their dives but, as number four rolled in, there was a very close burst and the plane began trailing vapor as if it had been hit. With the others, it disappeared from my view, but I immediately began to pray for number four. That evening, in my tiny cell, I composed "One More Roll," my mind on number four the whole time.

On New Year's Eve 1969, Captain Tom Storey, U.S. Air Force, and I were in the Stardust section of Hoa Lo (pronounced: wa-low) Prison. I whispered the toast I had composed, in my head, under the door to Tom. Tom was enthralled and, despite the risk of terrible punishment, insisted I repeat it several more times until he had it committed to memory. He then promised me that when the time came, and we were again free men, he would give the toast at the first "Dining-In" he attended.

After being released in 1973, Tom was assigned to the U.S. Air Force Academy. During that same year, the Academy hosted the Annual Conference for General Officers which included an official "Dining In" where the jovial clinking of glasses accompanied all the traditional speeches and toasts.

When it was Tom's turn, remembering his promise so many years earlier, he proposed my "One More Roll."

[Captain Coffee earned his Navy wings in 1959, then served three years in VFP-62 flying RF-8A photo Crusaders from USS *Saratoga* (CVA-60) and NAS (Naval Air Station) Cecil Field. During his tour he received the Distinguished Flying Cross for his low-level photos of Soviet missile sites during the Cuban Missile Crisis in October–November

1962. He then served three years in RVAH-3, training photo-reconnaissance pilots in the RA-5C Vigilante, and then deployed to Vietnam with RVAH-13 aboard USS *Kitty Hawk* (CVA-63).

On February 3 1966, his RA-5C Vigilante was shot down over North Vietnam and he was held as a prisoner of war (POW) for the next seven years. The remains of his reconnaissance navigator, Lieutenant Robert T. Hanson, were returned to the U.S. on November 3, 1988]

Foreword

I came to VFP fairly late in my Navy career, but I enjoyed a great time and got to know many photo-reconnaissance aviators, including those who saw combat over Vietnam. I served two lengthy tours in VFP-306, the Navy's penultimate Crusader squadron, as the squadron air intelligence officer. I've written four books on the Crusader, both fighter and reconnaissance variants as well as the occasional magazine article.

Thus, I can write with confidence and appreciation for what former PH2 Ken Jack has done for our community with the skill and knowledge he could only have gained with the experience of serving as one of us in a VFP unit.

The author includes interesting seldom-discussed details of the specific light-photo mission. His accounts of photo and electronic reconnaissance are also rare and give the reader a new knowledge of how the early air war in Southeast Asia was conducted, definitely a new type of reporting in all the literature on Vietnam.

"Unarmed and Unafraid" and "Eyes of the Fleet" were the legendary mottos of the special fighter pilots who flew a special variant of what was in their time perhaps the most dangerous and capable naval jet fighter in the world. Its fighter version had its own claim as "Last of the Gunfighters." The photo pilots' only "weapon" was their service-issued pistol strapped either to their chest or hip. Yet, they launched in all types of weather or sea state to fly their vital missions over some of the most dangerous, most highly defended real estate in the then-50-year history of military aviation. More than a few never returned to their carrier or were captured to suffer years of the terrible incarceration as a prisoner of war.

Ken Jack's efforts in writing this first-time full-length biography of one of the Navy's most highly decorated combat squadrons in a perplexing and often unpopular war sheds new light on the men and their aircraft.

Peter B. Mersky
Commander, USNR (Ret)
VFP-306, 1975–1983

Preface

As a newly-hatched Navy photographer (photomate) fresh out of photo school, I first saw (then) Lieutenant Jerry Coffee in the photo shack on my VFP-62 squadron's flight line. Pilots would often stop there prior to going on their photo-reconnaissance training missions. As a kid, I would glue together wooden or plastic model aircraft, but there he was, a real fighter pilot in his G-suit, .38 cal. pistol with rows of tracer bullets strapped across his chest, holding his helmet and face mask with the VFP-62 film-strip logo painted across the top. He looked daunting. I was soon going to be a part of United States Naval Aviation and a detachment to the fleet.

Time went by for the both of us. I made two VFP-62 detachments to carriers, the last being as lead photomate on board USS *Forrestal* during the Cuban Missile Crisis. Following my discharge in 1963, I worked for a year to accumulate money for college, then started my freshman year at Penn State University.

With my Navy memories behind me, I took on my new life's challenges. Then, one day, passing by a television in the Student Union, a video of prisoners in striped, filthy uniforms being paraded down a street in Hanoi caught my eye. They were obviously U.S. prisoners of war (POWs). As I watched I saw someone familiar. The man, fearful of the jeering crowds, very tired looking with his head down in obedience to his captors, was Jerry Coffee. There was no mistake about it. Today, writing this, I still get goose bumps thinking about that chance event.

At the same time, anti-war protests were at our campus, as everywhere in the country. My roommate, also a Navy veteran, and I watched them with seething anger. Joe couldn't restrain himself and cussed, "What idiots!" The long-haired, disheveled draft-dodgers were protesting a war I knew little about, but one that had put a good man doing his duty to his country, an officer I knew, into a North Vietnamese prison. I struggled with that incongruity of the sixties for years, but as more was learned about our government's decisions during that period, I began to question: "Oh God, were *they* right?" Many of their tactics were disgusting, particularly their disrespect to the military, but should we all have challenged the bloodbath of Vietnam more?

This book is about those who took another path: U.S. naval aviators, some in their early twenties, like the protestors, but photo-reconnaissance pilots, arguably the bravest of the brave—flying unarmed supersonic jets over the dangerous skies of Southeast Asia. While my name is on the cover of this book, many pilots and veterans contributed to the content. In the following pages, their stories, many written in their own words, put the reader into the cockpit as they describe the thrill, terror, and sacrifices made to obtain the needed photographic intelligence to prosecute the war more effectively. For those who died in the service of their country, their memorials in the following chapters detail the ultimate sacrifice they made, but also the pain and loss suffered by their families. For me, I wrote them with moist eyes and shallow breath.

The aftermath of the September 11, 2001, Al-Qaeda attack brought with it a renewed and sincere public outpouring of appreciation and support for the military that has remained and been well received by those who served. These days, when I wear my jacket with *Forrestal* aircraft carrier patch, or my squadron cap, someone usually expresses their gratitude; it is always humbling. The most memorable was at the grocery store checkout counter when a small, six-year-old boy tugged at my sleeve, looked up at me with very sincere eyes, and gave his confidently expressed, "Thank you for your service." He was supported by his two slightly older brothers while his mother watched in approval. It was a true Norman Rockwell moment—one you see frequently in small-town America. However, we veterans also know the large gap that exists between our military-life experiences and those who did not serve. For veterans, it is most difficult to explain our intimate encounters with death and the impact it made on us. Today, Post Traumatic Stress Disorder haunts those with the most gruesome experiences. Veteran suicides are too common.

This book's goal is to help explain what "the price of freedom" means through the stories of heroism and sacrifice, exemplified by Navy pilots—those who survived or were rescued, missing in action, prisoners of war, or killed in action. For the missing in action, searches for their remains continue, only through their nation's willingness to pay any price, to find and return them to their families for a hero's burial decades later. That too is part of this story. Finally, we tell the sad story of those who became POWs and endured torture, solitary confinement, the harshest living conditions, and returned at war's end. Today, some still refuse to discuss those haunting memories. Others, in their advanced years, have generously shared with us what "Duty, Honor, Country" means.

I and those who contributed to this book hope our stories help the reader appreciate what it means to be a member of the United States military and why we owe them an enlightened debt of appreciation. Vietnam veterans have waited too long for their nation's understanding, gratitude, and respect. We citizens owe it to their memory, and future veterans, by taking on our citizens' responsibility and obligation to understand better the wars our country wages. It is imperative to require any president to honor the constitution and get congressional approval for all wars. Had Presidents Kennedy, Johnson, and Nixon followed that requirement, the Vietnam Veterans Memorial Wall in Washington, D.C., with 58,318 names inscribed on it—and this book—would not exist.

Introduction

Light Photographic Squadron 63

In the early years following World War II, the U.S. Navy had a small number of combat-experienced photo pilots attached to carrier air wings, but there was no standard syllabus or specialized training for replacement naval aviators. One of the favorite aircraft configured with a camera was the F4U-4/5P Corsair, a fully armed fighter with a single camera mounted aft of the wing. With guns, the pilot could shoot back if attacked. Ironically, its manufacturer, Vought, would later design and build the F8U-1P (later designated RF-8A in 1962) Crusader, the photo-reconnaissance aircraft this book celebrates.

On January 20, 1949, a dedicated photographic-composite squadron, VC-61, was established on the West Coast to provide carrier-based photo-reconnaissance. It flew a variety of propeller-driven aircraft, including the F8F-2P Bearcat and F4U-5P Corsair, until it got its first photo-reconnaissance jet, the F9F-2/5P Panther, in mid-1951. Soon after, it received the more advanced F2H-2P Banshee that had three cameras, all of which could be rotated by a switch in the cockpit. Importantly, it had a viewfinder in the cockpit that gave the pilot a complete view of the ground beneath his aircraft and the ability to center his pictures exactly. The quality and quantity of photographs increased accordingly. The Banshee was the answer to a photo pilot's prayers. Powered by two Westinghouse J34WE2 turbojet engines, it had tremendous versatility thanks to its 600mph top speed and service ceiling in excess of 40,000ft. In July 1956, VC-61 was re-designated Light Photographic Squadron 61 (VFP-61) and acquired the F9F-6/8P Cougar that provided even more performance and capabilities.

Finally, in September 1957, VFP-61 received its first F8U-1P supersonic Crusader. The aircraft had vastly improved photographic capabilities and speed. The Navy had been working with aerial camera manufacturers and that effort resulted in smaller and

F9F-8P Cougars of VFP-61, Detachment G, off USS Lexington *(CVA-16), circa 1957. The F9F-8P preceded the RF-8A Crusader. Note the two oblique camera windows in the nose area. (National Naval Aviation Museum, Pensacola, FL)*

An F2H-2P Banshee of Composite Squadron 61 (VC-61) off the carrier USS Essex *(CVA-9) in 1955. (National Naval Aviation Museum, Pensacola, FL)*

more capable cameras that could easily fit into a fighter's cramped confines. Advanced electronic equipment made possible well-focused photos taken from low-to-high altitudes and high speeds. Also important for a reconnaissance jet, it had what aviators call "long legs"—larger fuel capacity than the fighter version. On July 1, 1959, VFP-61 was re-designated Light Photographic Squadron 63 (VFP-63). It was colloquially referred to as "Eyes of the Fleet." On the East Coast, a similar evolution resulted in VFP-62; it was referred to as "Fightin' Photo."

The RF-8A/G Crusader

In 1953, Chance Vought Division of United Aircraft received the Navy contract to design and build the first XF8U-1 Crusader. The Navy was seeking a supersonic fighter for its fleet of aircraft carriers. On March 25, 1955, the XF8U-1's test pilot felt confident enough on the maiden flight that he broke the sound barrier. Later Vought would win the Thompson Trophy for the jet's speed and the coveted Collier Trophy for its innovative design and development in 1956—the first fighter recipient in the 73-year history of the award. Finally, it was the winner of the first Certificate of Merit from the Bureau of Aeronautics. Its impressive speed was made possible by the Pratt & Whitney J57 turbo-jet engine with an afterburner pushing it to Mach 1.2+ (Mach 1 is 767.27mph). The afterburner injects raw fuel into the hot exhaust gas, generating 16,600 pounds of thrust and a significant boost in speed. Vought celebrated aviators who exceeded 1,000mph in the aircraft by providing them a pin and certificate that welcomed them into the "Thousand Miles-Per-Hour Club"—a right-of-passage so to speak. Aviators say that, with later advanced engines, they were able to achieve Mach 1.8+.

Among the Crusader's innovative design features was a variable incidence wing, which could be raised seven degrees by an internally self-locking hydraulic jack. In the raised position, the wing provided more lift for takeoff and landing. Due to the wing design, repositioning the wing provided excellent visibility for the pilot during the landing approach. However, the wing in its raised position also posed a danger to maintenance crews—it was a two ton "head cracker." Like all aspects of working around potentially dangerous equipment, safety rules are often written in blood. There were several fatalities due to the wing being lowered while on the ground and safety procedures not being followed.

A VFP-63 RF-8A comes in for a recovery on the USS Midway *(CVA-41) in the Tonkin Gulf (circa September 1968). Note the wing in the raised position, wheels and tail hook lowered, and camera bays two and three oblique and vertical windows. (Robert L. Lawson Collection, National Naval Aviation Museum, Pensacola, FL)*

Naval Aviation, a Dangerous Profession

Death comes quick and unforeseen in naval aviation, especially when at war. Working on an aircraft carrier flight deck is considered one of the most dangerous occupations. Everyone is taught to "keep your head on a swivel"—Navy-speak to be alert, watch your step, and keep an awareness of your position and surroundings at all times. It also means looking out for your shipmates. After the jets were started, their air intakes could suck a man into the engine's rotating blades. We would stand to the side of the gigantic Crusader's intake—giving it the moniker "The Gator"—warning anyone from walking into it. VFP-62 Aviation Machinist Mate Jets (ADJ) John Dwyer, tells his horrific story of such an accident:

> I was the assigned Aviation Machinist on the flight deck for our detachment. Our RF-8A always used burner [afterburner] for launching and my position was between the catapults [cats] and forward enough to make eye contact with the pilot so when he would go to burner, I would give a quick look for fuel venting and good burner, then give the thumbs up. On this launch, on the starboard cat, when he (Tal Bagget) went to burner the nose kicked left and the launch crew came to the inboard side to push the jet back in line with the cat.
>
> On the third try the Flight Deck Chief went close to the intake to motion his guys to get in the cat walk [a narrow passageway off the flight deck], while at the same time the pilot went full power and got the "five-sign" to go into burner. Then, the plane had a massive compressor stall. The pilot pulled power and opened the canopy and motioned me up. He said, "Something went down the intake!" The jet was pushed to the number-one elevator and I went down the intake

> and found the Chief draped over the engine cone. There was nothing I could do and came out and got some lights.
>
> A doctor asked if there was any way to see in and we went to the left wheel well and I removed the 4-inch cover where the inlet temperature probe went and the doctor was able see him. Three guys went in and were able to remove him by making a three-man chain, holding each other's feet, and all being pulled from outside. I think the three who went in were ADJ2 Al Bellavance, Randy Lusby and Bud Moore. This was just off the East Coast in December 1958 or January 1959 on USS *Franklin D. Roosevelt* (CVA-42). The Chief was transported to the hospital where he died that night. He was soon to retire.

On my first day on the VFP-62 flight line, the chief petty officer gave us a familiarization tour. He pointed out the camera bays we would be working with, how to climb up to the cockpit, the knife-edged trailing wing surface to avoid, and the dangers of the jet's tailpipe. When we got to the massive man-eater intake, he warned us to "not get close to the intake," and illustrated with the above gruesome story. Chief Blake was a jolly, short, Southerner and with his southern drawl warned, "Men, when that aircraft was taken to the hangar deck, it bled for days." Thinking back on that, it was the chief's dramatic way to get our clueless attention.

We photomates were required to be by the aircraft during each launch. The purpose was to gain flight deck experience. On critical missions, such as during the Cuban Missile Crisis, the last prelaunch check was for the pilot to turn on each camera and the photomate would check for proper shutter operation. We bypassed the forward-pointing camera station because it was under the intake. On recovery of the photo jets, we often practiced drills to time how fast we could get photographic film from the cameras, rush it to the ship's photo lab, develop it, and get the processed film to the photo intelligence officer for interpretation.

VFP-62 pilot Lieutenant Commander Newby Kelt being rescued after a flight deck accident. His not-fully deployed parachute can be seen, as well as the plume of water (at right) where his RF-8A hit the water. The circle of water is caused by the rescue helicopter. (Cmdr. Newby Kelt)

The author on the flight deck of the USS Shangri La *(CVA-38) circa 1961. Note the size of the RF-8A's intake. The aircraft's moniker was "The Gator." Maintenance crewmen wear green. A-1 Skyraiders are seen in back. (Kenneth Jack)*

The most frightening dangers on the flight deck were turning propellers that could slice you into pieces and engine exhaust blasts that could blow you down the flight deck into danger or, God forbid, overboard. Prior to launch, the carrier is turned into the wind to create extra wind across the deck to enhance aircraft lift off. Our dungarees would flap in the wind and sometimes you could lean into it and not fall. Jet blasts could threaten aircraft as well. On April 16, 1963, on board USS *Enterprise* (CVAN-65), VFP-62 officer-in-charge Lieutenant Commander Newby Kelt's RF-8A was on the angled deck's catapult and was downed by a plane captain for an oil leak. He was directed to maneuver his aircraft forward to the elevator to be taken to the hangar deck for repairs. Several A-4 Skyhawks were preparing for launch and at least one was at 100 percent power. The A-4s' jet blasts caught the RF-8A broadside and it started to slide on the slippery deck. The pilot couldn't stop, either by steering the nose wheel or applying brakes. Aviation Machinist Mate Peter Wallace tried desperately to use a wheel chock, but it was too late. The doomed aircraft went over the side as the pilot ejected. A low-level ejection during that time was most often fatal. Fortunately, his parachute opened and he hit the water, still attached to his seat. The ship's captain immediately ordered a violent turn to port to distance the carrier's fantail away from the floating jet and pilot. He was rescued by the ship's guard helicopter and sustained some injuries but returned to flight status after some days in sickbay.

In war, of course, there are bombs, rockets and missiles everywhere. On July 29, 1967, during its first combat deployment to the Vietnam War, the first supercarrier, USS *Forrestal* (CVA-59), was in the South China Sea. During launch operations, a Zuni rocket was accidentally fired by a voltage surge when an F-4 Phantom's engine started. The rocket flew across the aft flight deck, slamming into an A-4 bomber's fuel tank which ignited a massive fire, quickly causing a chain reaction of more explosions and generating tremendous heat that set off 1,000-pound bombs, fuel, and other ordnance. Pilots, including the late Senator John McCain, had to escape from their cockpits, some jumping into the flames. The massive fire and explosions melted gigantic holes in the thick-steel deck. Burning fuel poured through the gaping holes into VF-74's sleeping quarters directly below, killing many. The search and recovery teams said the bulkheads were cherry red.

The carrier was in mortal danger. With the fire raging out of control, fire crews were mowed down by the blasts and replaced by others. Some were blown into the ocean, others jumped to avoid the inferno. Some that survived the fall to the ocean 70 feet below were rescued by escort destroyers or helicopters. In all, 134 sailors and officers were killed and many others injured.

While in my senior year in college, I saw *LIFE* magazine's cover of the devasted flight deck. It reminded me that my 1962–63 VFP-62 detachment had our maintenance compartment directly beneath the area of major fire and explosions. Seeing the devastation and burned aircraft gave me a flashback to my bootcamp experience of learning how to

USS *Forrestal* (CVA-59) *fire damage as search and rescue teams search compartments below the flight deck. (Ken Killmeyer)*

The USS Forrestal *(CVA-59) fire in the Tonkin Gulf on July 29, 1967 caused intense heat and destruction from exploding 1,000-pound bombs. Crew members were killed in compartments beneath the flight deck and recovery teams faced great danger. This photo shows that teamwork and bravery. (Ken Killmeyer)*

USS Forrestal *fire teams battle the flight deck inferno. (Ken Killmeyer)*

Forrestal *fire fighters shrouded in steam from a hot spot being doused with water. Teamwork is part of the training and that is shown here in this dramatic photo. (Ken Killmeyer)*

battle an oil-fed fire in a simulated, dark, smoky-ship compartment. I remembered the old salt instructor warning us, laconically, "Men, fire is the only thing the United States Navy fears."

Navy fighter pilots are a unique breed. At sea, they launch into flight, night and day, in all sorts of weather, with the assistance of a steam-powered catapult and have a brief, fast ride to the edge of the flight deck, traveling at about 125mph (an unnamed pilot described it as "The most fun you can have with your clothes on"). Only then, they gained control of their aircraft. Many pilot deaths occur around the ship. There are multiple mechanical or pilot failures that can put him (there were no female pilots in the sixties) into the water where survival has a probabilistic outcome. We once had a VFP-62 Crusader lose lift after launch and skim the water, but miraculously managed to pull up. On return, maintenance crews had to clean salt water from the wheel wells. Once in flight, the fighter pilot has many skilled tasks to perform: controlling a supersonic jet, navigating to the target, accomplishing his mission, surviving enemy defenses and flying the aircraft—sometimes with battle damage—back to the ship where the greatest of all dangers awaits—landing aboard a moving and rolling carrier deck. The latter separates Navy pilots from all other military aviators. The Crusader was notoriously difficult to land aboard ship. U.S. Air Force exchange pilots assigned to a Navy squadron quickly gained respect for naval aviators.

A VFP-63 Det. 31 RF-8G engaging the barricade on board USS Bon Homme Richard *(CVA-31) on May 24, 1968. This aircraft was repaired and, on July 22 1972, was hit by AAA; Lt. Cmdr. Gordon Paige ejected and became a prisoner of the North Vietnamese. (Robert L. Lawson Collection, National Naval Aviation Museum, Pensacola, FL)*

All hands prepare the crash barrier for an emergency landing. (National Naval Aviation Museum, Pensacola, FL)

A pilot's eye view of the emergency landing barrier. (National Naval Aviation Museum, Pensacola, FL)

Lt. Dick Nelson's VF-194 F-8E Crusader experienced a landing gear failure and he had to make an emergency barricade landing on board USS Ticonderoga *(CVA-14) in 1968. He was returning from a combat mission escorting VFP-63's Lt. Bill Kocur who took these dramatic photos with his photo-Crusader. (Via Frank Bodden AZ3)*

Lt. Nelson's F-8 rolling towards the barricade at over 100 mph. This device has saved many ejections, salvaging expensive aircraft and saving pilot's lives. The landing gear problem was not due to combat action. (Lt. Bill Kocur via Frank Bodden)

The F-8 engages the barricade and comes to a rapid stop. Lt. Nelson was not hurt. (Lt. Bill Kocur via Frank Bodden)

When a multi-million-dollar jet experiences a serious mechanical problem with its landing gear, flight controls, tail hook, or low-fuel state, and can't make a normal recovery, a decision may be made to avoid an ejection and make an arresting barrier recovery. All hands quickly erect a sturdy, nylon strap barrier across the flight deck to "catch" the distressed aircraft. It is amazing to watch a 30–50,000-pound jet, flying about 130mph, perform a controlled crash into the barricade and come to a quick stop. Pilot and aircraft are saved to fly another day.

VFP-63's Crusaders were flown by fighter pilots trained to execute their flight plan to the target and retrieve the assigned photo intelligence. Unlike the fighter version of the Crusader, the RF-8A/G had no weapons and was totally defenseless except for the skill of the pilot and its blazing speed. A favorite boast of photo pilots was "Unarmed, Unescorted, and Unafraid." However, most admit the unafraid part was a bluff. As for the unescorted part, the presence of North Vietnam MiG jets necessitated fighter escorts to be assigned for their protection.

Death can come to an aviator before being catapulted. After our jets had launched, I was walking towards the carrier's island and stopped to watch the launch of a VF-103 F-8 Crusader, piloted by Lieutenant (junior grade) Walt Davis, on the waist cat (catapult on the angled deck). The jet was positioned and the pilot pushed the throttle to 100 percent power. What followed was a slow-motion nightmare I'll never forget. I knew something was wrong, but my brain couldn't comprehend the impending danger. Slowly, the doomed Crusader coasted to the end of the deck, tipped forward, then disappeared. My last sight of it was its tail going over the deck edge. The impact may have dazed the pilot and he sank with his aircraft. I remember once encountering him in a passageway. He was very young, Hollywood handsome, and gave me a friendly smile and greeting as I stood by in deference to his rank. Scenes like this are what many veterans experience and take into civilian life and never discuss. Pilot Gene Conner, from VF-103, explains the cause of the accident:

> The F-8 used a launch pendant vice a bridle. The pendant hooked to the aircraft over a short bar/pin between two somewhat rounded flanges that were part of and below the aircraft keel. Those flanges were not completely flat on the bottom surfaces but were machined to a small fairing along the bottom.
>
> The launch was initially normal. Part way down the cat one of the flanges broke and the pendant separated from the aircraft. We found some debris on deck and an engineering analysis showed that machining the flanges with those small fairings allowed localized abnormal stress patterns and cracks to set up. The fix was simply to grind off the fairings and dye check the flanges. It was a depressing investigation on which to work because it seemed that the old fickle finger of fate had sealed the result the instant the cat fired. However, at least we found the cause and the fix worked. If the small number of debris had not remained on deck, it might have been a mystery until perhaps it happened again.

VFP-63 was the West Coast Navy squadron assigned the responsibility of providing photo-reconnaissance (recon) detachments to many attack carriers during the Vietnam War. It did so from 1964 to January 8, 1973. It was a large squadron home-based at NAS [Naval Air Station] Miramar, San Diego, California, and had about 500 men. The squadron carries the distinction of having the most combat deployments of any squadron.

Unlike complete squadrons with a dozen or more aircraft and about a hundred men deploying to the carrier, VFP-63 sent a detachment of four pilots, one or two photographic interpreters (PIs), three jets, chief petty officers, and a crew of about 25–40 enlisted men to maintain the aircraft. It was the Rodney Dangerfield (a comedian who feigned being a loser) of the air wing—it got little respect, or so it seemed at times. Because of its size, the detachment didn't warrant a senior officer-in-charge. My first detachment had a lieutenant. Often it was a lieutenant commander. After deployment its aircraft were often the last to fly off and return home. The crew didn't get the choice berthing compartments and we had less clout with the ship's various departments and carrier air wing commander. With all these indignities, it had one of the most crucial of missions: getting pre-and-post strike photographic intelligence for planning attack missions and bomb damage assessment (BDA). The photos would give the all-important photo interpreter the ability to find the anti-aircraft defense locations to be eliminated or avoided to save pilot lives. The photos also gave fighter and attack pilots visual cues to familiarize them with the target. They were a major component of the pilot briefings and gave crucial information and guidance to senior mission planners.

The Art and Science of Photo Interpretation

Pilots and fleet commanders conducting strikes against a target are not able to determine the effectiveness of their bombing missions without bomb damage assessment provided by photo-reconnaissance. Admiral James L. Holloway III, participating in a forum discussing the effectiveness of *Rolling Thunder* to accomplish U.S. objectives, provided the following insightful analysis of the value of photo interpretation:

> I'm an old veteran, so what I give you are my impressions, which you historians can clean up—my impression was and I think the folklore at the time was that the Navy pilots coming back from their strikes on [World War II] forces were claiming so many hits on the cruisers and the carriers that the BDAs, which were only available when the pilot landed, were inaccurate. At that time the intelligence officer said, "What happened?" And the pilot said, "Oh, I put a 1,000-pounder right down the stack." And he probably thought he had, but to be honest with you, you're looking over your shoulder dodging Zeros and flak at the time so that kind of BDA was not very accurate.
>
> ...Photo interpretation is not just looking at the rubble, but trying to determine what is functional [emphasis added]. For example, you can have a power plant that has been beaten up pretty badly with all the windows blown out. But is that generator still working inside and that takes quite a bit of collateral photo interpretation to see if there is evidence that there is still power being put out. On the other hand, there could be a building that looks almost undamaged, but you have destroyed its function inside because it was perhaps a function that required a lot of people or a lot of very specialized equipment. I've taken too long to answer your question, but I see BDA improving in quality and its usefulness to the commander and that you're just not counting the bricks that are in that half-acre. You're trying to determine and tell the commander whether the function of that target has been interrupted, and if so, is it restorable[2] [emphasis added].

The photographic squadrons were unique in a carrier air wing. They did not bring death and destruction to the enemy, at least not directly. They brought back photographic intelligence that would facilitate the planning and evaluation of the bombing campaigns. Many specialists were involved with getting that intelligence to the decision-makers. First, photomates had the responsibility to install and maintain the cameras and electronic components in the RF-8's four camera bays. Camera bay one was a forward firing camera (most often a KA-45 5-inch format camera) under the intake giving the pilot's eye view of the target area. Aft of the cockpit was bay two, which originally had an oblique camera on the port (left) side, a vertical camera and oblique camera on the starboard (right) side. Photos from those three cameras provided so-called horizon-to-horizon coverage of a wide swath of terrain underneath the aircraft. Later, VFP-63 replaced the three cameras

The KA-45 5-inch format aerial camera. Note one-of-two film canisters on the right and the power cables on top. This camera is usually mounted in camera bays one, three, or four. (Kenneth Jack)

with a KA-66 panoramic camera that utilized a rotating prism device in front of the lens to produce lateral horizon-to-horizon coverage. It combined all the features of vertical and oblique photography in one camera system and was generally used for low level reconnaissance. Further aft on the port side was camera bay three with a KA-53 frame camera and, on the starboard side, bay four. Both bays could support a large variety of cameras and some configurations could be in the vertical position or rotated to different angles by the pilot in the cockpit. Some configurations included the panoramic KA-68 in bay four. Air-to-air photos were shot from bays three and four and the pilot could center the target by an optical device mounted on the canopy rail.

The electronic components that controlled the RF-8G's cameras were crucial to obtaining well focused photos of objects whizzing by underneath an aircraft capable of supersonic speeds. When you read pilots flew over their targets at 600 knots and low altitude, that means the cameras were taking photos at a very fast rate. To obtain this photography, two requirements had to be accomplished. First, to control the proper rate of exposures, the electronic components took inputs of the aircraft's speed and altitude and provided appropriate signals to the cameras that responded with a complicated

A photomate prepares to install a camera film magazine in this RF-8G of VFP-63 at NAS Miramar in 1969. Photomates were the camera technicians and without their knowledge and skill the intense photo-reconnaissance effort performed throughout the war would have been impossible to sustain. Note the small viewfinder window on the nose cone. (Cmdr. Peter Mersky)

A VFP-63 photomate installing camera brackets in camera bay four. Note the jet's piping and cables share the same space as the cameras. The photo was shot from bay 3. (Cmdr. Peter Mersky)

sequence of events for each cycle. Each photo frame had to have the correct *overlap of coverage* the photo interpreters needed. The overlap of coverage required from one photo to the next was 60 percent. This overlap provided the photo analysts, using stereoscopic viewers, a pseudo-stereo (three-dimensional) view of the ground images. In essence, each object on the ground was captured from a different angle on adjacent photos, similar to how human eyes create three-dimensional impressions of the world around us.

Secondly, the images of the objects on the ground had to be focused (not blurred) regardless of any changes in altitude or speed of the RF-8. The process to accomplish that was known as "image motion compensation" (IMC).[i] In the camera, the light-sensitive roll of film was connected to supply and take-up reels. On each cycle, an unexposed section was moved to a location behind the lens, waiting for the next picture to be taken.

For each new photo, the camera performed the following sequence of events to accomplish the proper overlap and IMC—made possible by amazing technology: (1) apply a vacuum to the light sensitive film to flatten it against a metal frame; (2) open the camera's shutter to let reflected light from ground objects, strike the film while, *at the same time,* move the film in the *opposite* direction of flight at the *correct speed* to compensate for the ground target's movement; (3) close the shutter to end the exposure; (4) release the vacuum; and (5) advance the film to the next frame. Of course, that all happened very quickly. Most camera damage resulted from the excessive demands placed on it. Fortunately, the ship's photo lab usually had a camera repairman.

The camera's controlling electronic boxes contained early examples of integrated circuits and solid-state components (there were no vacuum tubes) that would be essential to the future innovations of computers, satellites, and cell phones. This miniaturization of electronic circuits and cameras enabled them to be fitted into the small confines of a fighter jet. Considering the hard landings and stressful situations fighters encountered, the equipment was very reliable.

Part of the photomate's job was to keep the camera bay windows clean. The Crusader was notorious for hydraulic fluid leakage that dripped across the vertical camera-bay and scanner windows. We griped about that mundane task but joked, "If the enemy could develop a SAM (surface-to-air missile) sensitive to hydraulic fluid, there would be no Crusaders in the sky." At the end of a flight, photomates retrieved the film from the cameras and rushed it to the ship's photo lab for developing (a chemical process). The lab had special developing equipment capable of handling rolls of film hundreds of feet long.

---

i IMC is dependent on the speed and altitude of the RF-8G. The pilot could manually dial them in; or a special optical scanner looking at the ground could calculate it automatically (not always reliably); or the pilot could synchronize the ground movement to grids in his viewfinder centered on his instrument panel. The viewfinder was a marvel of optics and electronics.

The resulting product from the development process was negative images (black and white reversed). The photo interpreters (PIs) could use the negative images but often wanted a positive image to analyze. If so, a second process provided a new duplicate copy strip of positive images that were in normal visual tones of black and white.[ii] Additionally, paper prints of the images could be made. Rolls of this final product were then provided to the photo interpreters in the classified Photo Intelligence room. On a photo detachment there were one or two PI officers and one or two enlisted Photographic Intelligence Specialists (PT or later IS). The PIs and PTs were the important middlemen in the photo intelligence endeavor. They viewed the hundreds of feet of images after each mission. PIs prepared reports, interfaced with the ship's Intelligence staff and the Carrier Air Wing Commander, and briefed and debriefed the photo and escort pilots.

Lt. (j. g.) E. H. Haffey and J. C. Shokitano PT2 examining mission film in the VFP-63 Det. B Photographic Intelligence Room on board USS Hancock *(CVA-19), circa 1967. They are comparing film details with points on a map (under Haffey's hand). The film is rolled across the light table from the round reels. The newspaper on the table is* Stars and Stripes, *the armed forces periodical. The headline reads, "AF, Navy Pilots Down 3 MiGs." "N. Viet Has Rejected 28 Peace Bids: [Sec. of State] Rusk." (Capt. Len Johnson)*

Photo interpretation is an art and a science. Photo interpreters are trained to look for hints that point to hidden information. A well-trained PI or PT can tell the difference between a housing development and a military installation at a glance (military sites were often in civilian areas). The placement of vehicles, the number, size and organization of tents, the existence of cables running between buildings, the existence—or absence—of security fences and gates, and the shape and placement of storage tanks provide clues the PI can turn into knowledge.

A PI can determine from the depths of tracks in the mud what kind of truck made them and how heavy the load was. Disturbances of the earth could point to underground installations. Infrared film (sensitive to heat radiation rather than light) could show objects that had been moved or detect camouflage from vegetation; trees or vegetation

ii This was not always done immediately: Positives were run only if requested. The negatives were clearer and the PI could receive them sooner. On Yankee Station, speed was always the emphasis and we didn't need a lot of detail. Detailed PI work was always left for the Intelligence folks "upline" from us—Lt. Gary Ruesling.

that had been cut to cover objects emitted different levels of heat radiation than naturally growing plants, thus exposing hidden objects.

The job was tedious, and hours could be spent looking for signs of new activity: a car parked near a peasant's thatched shack will attract attention—they would strain to spot all major movements of men and any slightest change would come under suspicion. To facilitate this the PI would often go back to look at previous days' coverage of the same area and compare them for changes. He also used the shadows of objects to gain information and for that reason photo missions were often flown in the morning or afternoon when the shadows were at their most pronounced. PIs were also trained in architecture and engineering; the layout of objects is important for it can tell a PI what a building is used for. He can tell what is going on inside by the position of buildings and wings, entrances and loading platforms, the shape of roofs, the position of smokestacks, or their absence, the position of windows, or their absence, and the material of the buildings and roofs. He can even tell in which part of what building each operation is being performed.

These techniques, along with years of experience and training, make PIs essential to the intelligence endeavor. Their track record provides the confidence in their analyses, which in turn produces the hard evidence that makes aerial photography such a valuable intelligence tool.

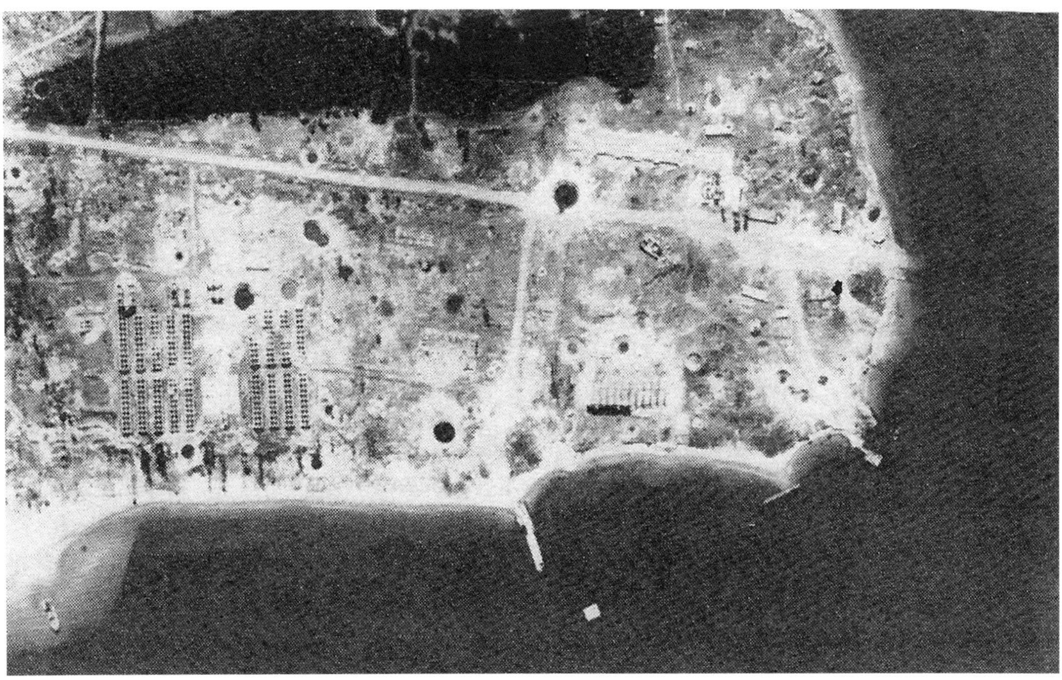

The Quang Khe ferry point lies idle on January 29 prior to the bombing pause during the Tet holiday truce. North Vietnam massively stepped-up supplies to troops in the South, as shown in the accompanying photos. (Capt. Len Johnson)

Quang Khe, in the southern part of North Vietnam, became a focal point for transshipment of war supplies towards the DMZ. A few days earlier, this river port was inactive. On the second day of the truce, it came alive. This VFP-63 photo by Lt. Len Johnson shows the estuary of the Song Giang River bustling with river craft unloading light cargo ships offshore. The shoreline is jammed with supplies in baskets, boxes and bags. Recon also spotted Soviet-built K-61 amphibious vehicles for first time. (Capt. Len Johnson)

In an enlarged view of Quang Khe, Soviet-built K-61 tracked amphibious cargo carriers are seen for the first time as they move across the beach in resupply activities. A good example of the value of photo recon. (Capt. Len Johnson)

A VFP-63 post-strike photo taken by Lt. Len Johnson on March 26, 1967. Three destroyed bridges are shown. Later photo missions revealed a pontoon bridge in place to restore traffic. Note bomb craters on local facilities. (Capt. Len Johnson)

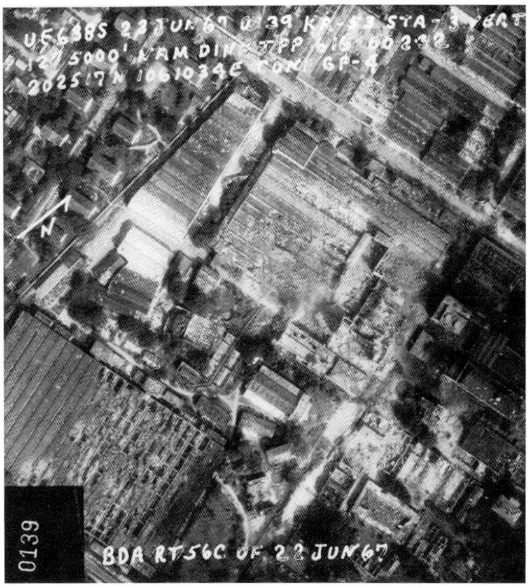

A June 22, 1967 VFP-63 BDA photo of the Nam Dinh manufacturing area. PI notation indicates the photo was taken from 5,000 feet. (Capt. Len Johnson)

A BDA photo of the NVN Kep MiG airbase on May 26, 1967. This photo records the PI's annotations showing MiG 17s (open circle), undamaged (U/D), high damage, light damage, even a MiG with tail pulled. PIs used special optical devices to gather this detailed information. This photo intelligence is used for restrike bombing missions. (Capt. Len Johnson)

Besides the official mission, pilots would also take dramatic aerial photos of the ship and air wing aircraft. We photomates took advantage of our access to the ship's photo lab and made copies for the cooks in the mess hall. Besides obtaining donuts for our maintenance compartment, we could get repair parts in expedited fashion. The Navy has a term for this skullduggery: cumshaw.

Pilots loved the Crusader's challenges and its speed. Down through the years, pilots found flight maneuvers to reach Mach 1.8 (1,381mph)—well into the forbidden red-line zone. Just in time for the Vietnam War, the RF-8A was remanufactured in 1965 as the RF-8G, giving it surface-to-air missile radar detection capability, airframe improvements, attachments for under-wing pylons, and an improved engine that attempted to compensate for the additional weight. Pilots still saw a drop in speed at low altitudes and finally the P-420 engine replacement, with 2,000 pounds increased thrust, gave "speed of heat" performance as the pilots like to say. VFP-63 pilot, Commander John "Lightnin" Davison, fondly remembers the Crusader. "I flew Vigis [RA-5C Vigilante, see Chapter 8] and A-4s as well—all fun. But I don't think there is a pilot alive who flew F-8s who won't say that it was the most fun to fly—I considered it to be the Harley Davidson of airplanes." However, the Crusader had a dark side as Captain Ron Knott describes the love and fear that surrounded the Crusader:

> The pilots that flew this supersonic machine loved her with a passion, having both admiration and respect for the jet. The Crusader was unorthodox. This sleek fighter commanded the respect of all

> that were fortunate enough to take her screaming through the skies at the speed of heat. This bird would kill you as quick as an enemy missile if you didn't stay within her performance envelope. She was a touchy thoroughbred that demanded fair treatment. With the latter, she would give you awe-inspiring performance. But just lead her onto the forbidden path and she would throw you into eternity very quickly. Many F-8 pilots were handed the fate of death because of this temperamental beast.

The squadron enlisted aircraft maintainers loved it as well. In the early 1960s, those of us who were lucky enough to witness a high-speed Crusader flyby from a carrier's flight deck know how difficult it was to see its approach from a distance. A bit stealthy, it blended in well with the horizon, sea, and sky, even when you knew it was coming. The high-positioned knife-edged wings were nearly invisible from the front and when you finally saw it, you couldn't help being mesmerized—the mind had nothing to compare it with; the long, sleek profile, with its prominent shark-like vertical tail, streaking momentarily abeam the ship, outracing the roar of its engine, gulping thousands of pounds of air each minute. Then, the ear-shattering sonic boom followed by an abrupt vertical climb, standing on the afterburner's translucent fiery plume, while performing a perfect eight-point roll. Still visible, the RF-8A clawed through the air with supersonic shock waves glowing above the wings. Then, it was gone. Even after 60 years, the memory of it is still vivid—always producing goose bumps—evoking the pride we had in this most beautiful of man-made machines and the aviators who flew it.

Captain Will Gray, VFP-63 pilot, sums up his feelings about the Crusader, particularly the photo-bird:

> If you have to go to war, the Crusader was right for the job. Fast, maneuverable, easy on the fuel, and a bit stealthy—its heart was the J-57 engine, reliable and forgiving. The Crusader was hard to land aboard ship and very difficult to max perform in air combat, but for flat-out running in the world of the photo pilot, it was a real sweetheart. With the droops up in a descent, followed by a good shove from the hard-lighting afterburner, the airspeed spun up toward 700 knots indicated like a video game, only this was real. Only the high-speed fighter pilot knows what it feels like to be running at high speed. You can feel the power.

VFP-63 Det 2 RF-8G 622 (Bu. No. 144617) on the port bow cat on board USS Coral Sea *(CV-43), early 1980. A nice view of a burner catapult launch. (Jerry Nolan ISC)*

CHAPTER 1

1964–66: VMCJ-1 Photo-Reconnaissance and Electronic Countermeasures

Marine Composite Reconnaissance Squadron 1 (VMCJ-1) was known for being the "Eyes and Ears" of the First Marine Aircraft Wing (1st MAW) with its RF-8A Crusaders being the eyes and the Korean War-era EF-10B Skyknight's electronic sensors as the ears. The Marine Corps had a robust history of providing photo-reconnaissance and electronic surveillance during the Cold War, and on occasion augmented Navy RF-8A recon squadrons. In October–November 1962, its East Coast sister squadron, VMCJ-2, augmented VFP-62 during the Cuban Missile Crisis. They provided five pilots, four RF-8As, and maintenance personnel. They flew, both lead and wing positions, with VFP-62 during the low-level photo missions over the Soviet medium-range ballistic-missile sites in Cuba. For their skill and bravery, the Marine pilots received the Distinguished Flying Cross and, along with VFP-62, the squadron was awarded the Navy Unit Commendation.

Before and during the Cuban Missile Crisis, VMCJ-2 operated around Cuba capturing electronic signals and was credited with one of the first intercepts of Soviet early-warning radar in Cuba. The squadron also monitored the build-up of the Soviet-designed radar-controlled surface-to-air missile (SAM) defenses in the months before the crisis. No ground-based radar could search the sky without being monitored and recorded by the Skyknights' electronic countermeasures (ECM) "black boxes."

While VMCJ-1 was primarily stationed at land bases, its RF-8A pilots were carrier qualified for deployments with the Navy, but most of the enlisted maintenance and photo technicians had never served at sea. I remember one Marine fighter squadron coming aboard USS *Shangri La* (CVA-38) in 1961 for carrier qualifications (CARQUAL). It was very apparent they were Marines. They dressed sharper—"squared away" in Navy parlance—and the enlisted officer greeting followed military regulations more rigorously than we. For instance, when a pilot came to the flight deck to man his aircraft, he was greeted with a sharp salute from the enlisted plane captain.[iii] I don't remember seeing that being rigorously followed by their Navy counterparts.

Retired Brigadier General Art Bloomer served three tours with VMCJ-1, the last as its commanding officer when it was decommissioned in 1975. He describes the squadron's early history:

> Three VMCJ squadrons were established to support our three active-duty Marine air wings (MAW). We actually had another, VMCJ-4, that supported our Reserve Air Wing, the 4th MAW. During the Korean War, the 1st MAW was deployed from MCAS [Marine Corps Air Station] El Toro to Korea. It had two recon squadrons, VMC-1 for Electronic Reconnaissance and VMJ-1 for Photo Recon…the VMC and VMJ squadrons were combined into Composite Squadrons and gave rise to the designation of VMCJ. I believe the first VMCJ squadrons had F9F-8P photo-Cougars and F3D-2Q electronic recon birds. Prior to that, the VMC had the propeller-engine AD-5N for electronic recon and VMJ had the F2H-2P Banshees as their photo aircraft.
>
> VMCJ-1 supported 1st MAW and was commissioned at MCAS El Toro California on July 31, 1958. It was the last of the three VMCJs to standup and remained at El Toro when VMCJ-3 deployed to Japan in August 1958. Under the leadership of Lieutenant Colonel Albert James, who took command on August 31, the squadron transitioned to the F8U-1P (re-designated RF-8A in 1962) photo-reconnaissance aircraft and the F3D-2Q (re-designated EF-10B) ECM aircraft before departing CONUS [continental U.S.] to relieve VMCJ-3 in November 1959. The squadron took the new photo jets with them to Japan, but took custody of VMCJ-3's ECM aircraft at MCAS Iwakuni Japan. It would remain forward deployed to MCAS Iwakuni until the start of the Vietnam war. Thereafter, each fall, the squadron's personnel would be replaced by a cadre from VMCJ-3 under the leadership of a new commanding officer. The RF-8A pilots in each deploying cadre had undergone CARQUALs and maintained their proficiency during their year-long deployment. It would be the spring of 1964 before VMCJ-1 was tasked to provide a photo recon detachment to a carrier in the Pacific.
>
> From November 1959 until April 1965 the squadron continued to fly the *Sharkfin* electronic reconnaissance missions with the EF-10Bs, under the National Peacetime Aerial Reconnaissance Program, that were begun by VMCJ-3 in 1958. These missions not only made vital contributions to the intelligence community on our Pacific adversaries during the Cold War, but provided invaluable training for the aircrews in a radar-signal environment similar to what the squadron would face in Vietnam.[1]

Colonel H. Wayne Whitten USMC (Ret.), a Naval flight officer and EF-10B electronic counter-measures officer (ECMO), provides a summary of VMCJ-1 organization in the years of the war:

> In 1964 the situation in Indochina was heating up and long before the Tonkin Gulf incident, VMCJ-1 began to provide RF-8A detachments to Task Force 77 [TF-77] carriers augmenting the Navy's VFP-63. They began flying missions over Laos during that secret war and continued to

iii A plane captain is usually a junior enlisted person, but he has the huge responsibility of looking after the aircraft. He keeps the jet clean and before launch goes through the safety checks with the pilot. Long hours are part of his daily routine, especially on board ship. One of his duties is to sit in the cockpit and ride the brakes in case the aircraft has to be moved. In recognition, only he and the pilot get their names stenciled on the side of the aircraft.

support TF-77 operations over North Vietnam until December 1965. The squadron lost its first RF-8A in combat on August 13, 1965 when Major P. A. Manning's aircraft from USS *Coral Sea* (CVA-43) was hit by AAA [anti-aircraft artillery] on a photo run and losing fuel was forced to eject over water where he was recovered. [See Chapter 3 for more details.]

In the Spring of 1965, the Joint Chiefs of Staff [JCS] authorized the *Rolling Thunder* bombing campaign against selected targets in North Vietnam. The historic first U.S. Marine Corps (USMC) combat mission employing active ECM or jamming [thwarting] enemy radars was conducted by EF-10Bs on April 29, 1965, in support of a U.S. Air Force (USAF) strike mission. Another first occurred on July 27, 1965, when four of VMCJ-1's EF-10Bs supported a massive USAF strike against one of the newly identified SAM sites near Hanoi. From that point on until the end of the war the focus of the squadron's ECM support was against the SA-2 SAMs and associated radars.

On March 18, 1966, the squadron lost its first EF-10B and crew to enemy action, when 1stLts McPherson and Davis's aircraft was shot down by a SA-2 missile northwest of Vinh. Before departing Vietnam, the squadron would lose four other EF-10Bs and crews to accidents or unknown causes.[2]

1964: VMCJ-1 Augments VFP-63's Detachments on Task Force 77 Carriers

On May 22, 1964, VMCJ-1 First Lieutenant Denis "Deej" Kiely was stationed at MCAS Iwakuni in Japan and rudely awakened by a squadron member. He was told, "Get in your flight gear and get ready to launch." In the ready room he and four other pilots were assigned their Crusaders. In a 2014 article, retired Colonel Kiely described how "he didn't learn his destination from the division lead, Captain Russ French, until airborne and did not get more information on the purpose of the flight until they landed at NAS (Naval Air Station) Cubi Point in the Philippines. Upon landing, the Marine pilots met a Navy lieutenant commander and learned they all were going to fly to *Kitty Hawk*, led by Lieutenant Commander Bill Lott, officer in charge of VFP-63 Det. C on the carrier."[3]

The Navy's first modern aircraft carriers began with the USS *Forrestal* (CVA-59), the first supercarrier, named after the first Secretary of Defense James Forrestal and commissioned in 1955. *Forrestal* was followed by USS *Saratoga* (CVA-60), USS *Ranger*

VMCJ-1's F3D-2Q, the predecessor of the EF-10B electronic warfare jet. (USMC photo via Colonel Ed Love)

A VMCJ-1 RF-8A taxiing to the active runway. Note the raised wing and combat sortie markings of cameras on the fuselage. (Robert L. Lawson Collection, National Naval Aviation Museum, Pensacola, FL)

VMJ-1 (predecessor of VMCJ-1) saw a lot of action in the Korean War. An F2H-2P Banshee pictured on the ground in Korea on May 15 1953. Note the number of combat missions recorded on the fuselage. (National Naval Aviation Museum, Pensacola, FL)

USS Kitty Hawk *(CVA-63) was commissioned in 1961. In this photograph taken the following year, the destroyers* USS McKean *(DDR 784) and* USS Harry E. Hubbard *(DD 748) steam alongside the carrier. The massive size difference from the 27C carriers is substantial. (National Naval Aviation Museum, Pensacola, FL)*

(CVA-61), and USS *Independence* (CVA-62), all known as the Forrestal-class carriers. Afterwards a new generation, USS *Kitty Hawk* (CVA-63) along with the USS *Constellation* (CVA-64), evolved with further advancements and set the stage for the first nuclear-powered carrier, USS *Enterprise* (CVAN-65), launched September 24, 1960. All of these modern carriers saw duty in the Vietnam War.

The supercarriers were larger than the earlier Essex-class carriers in every way. *Kitty Hawk*'s length was 1,068.9ft vs. 880ft; the air wing had approximately 75 aircraft; and the ship had about 4,500 personnel aboard. Its size allowed the operation of the Navy's larger aircraft such as the RA-5C Vigilante (discussed in Chapter 8). It also had better living accommodations, including air conditioning throughout the ship, and, most importantly for the pilots, it was easier to land aboard.

Seen here as a major, and the operations officer and XO of VMFA-122 in 1973, Denis Kiely flew some of the war's earliest photo-reconnaissance missions as a member of VMCJ-1 on board USS Kitty Hawk *(CVA-63). He later transitioned to the Marine's F-8E and F-4 Phantom II fighters, flying many in country close-air-support missions with VMF(AW)-235. (Cmdr. Peter Mersky)*

In March 1964, full-scale fighting broke out in Laos when North Vietnamese and Pathet Lao forces attacked across the Plain of Jars—literally a plain where there were ancient, massive stone jars. By mid-May, the communists had taken control of the strategic region, bringing an end to the shaky coalition government. President Lyndon B. Johnson's administration, just six months old, reflected the national fear of communism and endorsed the prevailing "falling domino" theory that if one Southeast Asian country fell to communism, they all would—it had to be contained. There was no formal war mandate in Southeast Asia (SEA), only CIA clandestine operations. However, VFP-63 and VMCJ-1 pilots would soon be flying photo-recon missions off aircraft carrier decks supporting Operation *Yankee Team* (the campaign against the North Vietnamese infiltration of Laos). Their

Demonstrating how huge aircraft carriers are, this photo shows USS Midway *(CVA-41) in drydock, circa 1980. Note the gigantic propellers and rudders compared to the men working and climbing the stairs out of the drydock area. (Stephen Miller PH2 USN)*

photographic film provided valuable intelligence otherwise unattainable. That intelligence supported an armed interdiction campaign to thwart the infiltration of North Vietnamese troops and supplies into South Vietnam (SVN). American foreign policy was "dipping its toe" into a conflict that would become part of the Vietnam War. Colonel Denis Kiely's witty and detailed article is excerpted here to tell VMCJ-1's involvement:

> The time for greater pressure on the communists had arrived. The violation of Laotian neutrality by North Vietnam became a problem that required both, proof and once having documented that, a "graduated response" meant to dissuade Ho Chi Minh from further aggression by an American show of resolve. With Prince and Prime Minister Souvanna Phouma's approval, the United States proceeded to plan for low-level reconnaissance of eastern Laos to ascertain the degree of communist army (NVA) build-up. U.S. reconnaissance efforts, both USAF and U.S. Navy, commenced on May 22, 1964.
>
> Once aboard the *Kitty Hawk*, the Navy tried to figure out where to put us. After some shuffling around, the air group found spaces for us and the business prompting our presence occupied our time. We had yet to really know what the mission was, except that it involved a rather large number of photo birds, both VAP-61 (Heavy Photographic Squadron 61), RA-5Cs from Guam, RF-8As from VFP-63 Dets. C and E and five birds from VMCJ-1 (one spare would be kept at NAS Cubi Point).
>
> CAG-11 had put almost all its attack and one squadron of fighters (VF-114) ashore, keeping the "Old Nicks" of VF-111, aboard and clearing the deck for the photo birds. After I trapped [landed], I still had no idea what we were going to be doing, the sight of a damaged RF-8A convinced me it would be serious business. The VFP-63 bird had been badly hit that day, but managed to make it back to the ship. VFP-63's Lieutenant Chuck Klusmann had been the pilot who did a great job to bring the bird back. On June 6, he would not be so lucky [see next chapter].[4]

What's surprising about Colonel Kiely's account is how *Kitty Hawk*'s air wing had been drastically altered. All attack and fighter squadrons, with the exception of VF-111, had been sent to NAS Cubi Point. It is clear *Kitty Hawk*'s entire mission was to support Operation *Yankee Team* photo-reconnaissance missions. The Marines merged into the Navy RF-8 recon operations. Their RF-8As were still equipped with the original-equipment, Chicago Aerial camera systems, which the Navy partially replaced with VFP-62-developed cameras, used first in the combat environment of the Cuban Missile Crisis. Colonel Kiely gives us good insight into the planning for the missions and that included survival advice if shot down, including the chilling warning, "there was no rescue plan." He continues:

> Fits and starts characterized the next couple of days. We manned aircraft only to be told to stand down on several occasions. Nonetheless, we managed a few areas fam [familiarization] flights before being sent far into the Plaine de Jarres. Our Navy hosts had prescribed that each Marine should fly wing on a Navy pilot before conducting flights on our own. That seemed quite reasonable until we noticed differences in our methods of mission execution. We had trained long and hard to conduct our recon missions very low and very fast (100–200 feet and 450–500 knots) using our 70mm format Chicago Aerial Systems (CAX) cameras to their limits. The Navy, however, had abandoned the 70mm format system in favor of the 4.5-inch format KA-45 cameras. They conducted their runs differently, at higher altitude, 2,500–3,000 feet, and at a slower airspeed and had little confidence in the 70mm film because they claimed it lacked good resolution.

Message traffic during the period was heavy, though dissemination was reserved to a higher level. We still didn't know precisely what the mission was. No matter, First Lieutenant Xandy Carter and I got together and began to plan how we would conduct missions; photo pilots were taught to be good navigators because they either went in alone, or led a flight to a target. Noting the prevailing weather of the Plaines area, we planned to commence our reconnaissance from a point at the westward bend of the Mekong River, figuring headings from that point to any of a number of known sites of interest. Our effort soon would pay dividends.

One evening, an A-3 came aboard carrying a rather old fellow wearing wash khakis and the leaves of an Army major. We were told he'd been in the Far East for many years, having served in the World War II China, Burma, India Theater, and was an authority on escape and evasion. He told us there was no rescue plan for us should we go down, but we might be picked up by Air America[iv] helicopters, though—the Navy—had no communication with them and Air America had no idea of what we were doing, where or when. In short, rescue would be a long shot. His advice was, "Don't bail out, but ditch your aircraft and stay near it; you may be spotted more easily." Ditch an F-8! Where had this guy been? With that helpful hint I tuned him out, hoping I wouldn't get shot down. By morning he was gone.

The last week in May was taken up with missions that involved counting junks in the Gulf and area reconnaissance of routes in the Plaine. I had started flying on the 25th and we Marines were getting into the swing of things. Amid all that were the constant "man-up" and "stand down" orders coming, apparently, from very high up. In the meantime, we were flying and getting more comfortable with shipboard operations.[5]

VMCJ-1 Pilots Make Their First Mission Over Laos

Two VMCJ-1 pilots, originally scheduled as wingmen to VFP-63 leads, ended up making the first missions over Laos due to a mechanical problem with a VFP-63 jet and confusion on the part of the launch officer. In his discussion, Colonel Kiely describes navigation difficulties during that era of flying. They soon learned how hostile their reception would be when they encountered AAA. See the footnote to picture the "as planned" launch cycle.[v]

On June 3 I was scheduled for a flight into the Plaine on the wing of Lt. Cmdr. Bill Lott. I had thoroughly studied my chart to various sites and felt well prepared. We would take with us two A-4s as tankers. They would top us off passing Tchepone and return to the ship. As back-ups for us, Lieutenant Jerry Kuechmann of Det. C and First Lieutenant Xandy Carter were manned, started and ready. Lott and his tanker were on the bow cats, I and my A-4 on the waist. Off we went. Immediately after launch we were to stab the tanker [try to plugin] to check for a good transfer; if there was a problem, a spare tanker would launch right behind us. As it unfolded, the tankers were okay, Lott's aircraft lost a generator and he had to abort the mission. On the deck having seen us launch, the yellow shirts [flight deck officer] directed Kuechmann to the elevator, just as Lott's aircraft lost

iv The CIA's private airline operating in Laos during the Vietnam War.

v The plan was for VFP-63 Lieutenant Commander Lott to launch with his A-4 tanker followed by VMCJ-1 First Lieutenant Denis Kiely and his tanker. Kiely and the two tankers launched. On the other cats, Lott lost his generator and pulled off the cat. Kiely and two A-4 tankers were in the air waiting for Lott. On the cat, First Lieutenant Xandy Carter was launched and VFP-63's Lieutenant Jerry Kuechmann was pulled off the cat.

Aerial refueling requires high-level skills as seen here as a VFP-63 Det. 19 RF-8G from USS Hancock *(CVA-19) refuels from a VA-55 A-4 in January 1970. In the distance, two other RF-8Gs refuel from a second A-4. (Robert L. Lawson Collection, National Naval Aviation Museum, Pensacola, FL)*

its generator. What to do? The cat officer, seeing Xandy ready to go, motioned him to the cat and fired him off. At that point Pri-Fly suddenly realized that there were two Marine lieutenants airborne with no adult supervision. They issued a recall. We gave them the old "Say again?" a couple of times, then pressed on. We were confident, but our Navy friends could see only disaster. Captain Drayer in Pri-Fly assured the Air Boss that all would be well; we Marines knew what we were doing, and I was a qualified section leader. With that, all settled down to a tense wait.

To that point, the weather over northern Laos and the Plaine had been mostly poor, resulting in several missions unable to bring back any useful photos. One flight got lost and wandered into North Vietnam. Fortunately, the flight exited the area without incident. It caused all hands to study the area more closely, finding good landmarks in order to stay oriented.

We reached Tchepone, topped-off our fuel and said bye-bye to the tankers. I headed for the start point at the Mekong's bend. Ahead to the north, the weather was almost solid overcast with tops around 10,000 feet. After selecting one of our headings to the northeast corner of the Plaine, we cruised along at about 20,000 feet, playing the time-distance[vi] game to reach the first site. Xandy, in loose trail, called attention to the black puffs that had popped up between us; we were taking some fire. Both new to such, he and I were fascinated by it. I started evasive maneuvering. The bursts followed my moves. We continued jinking until the fire ceased. Moments later, I spotted a hole in the overcast and we commenced a steep descent, breaking into the clear at about 2,000 feet.

Quickly checking my chart, I figured we were just south of a place called Ban-Ban. After a right turn, I spotted what turned out to be Sam Neua nearby. It was time to get real-low, real-fast, and look for a road or other targets. I picked out a road that came out of Ban-Ban…We were right on the deck, and in places, looking under the jungle cover that shaded the road. I was taking photos like mad. At one point, I noticed something dead ahead, and triggered my KB-10A forward-fire camera. It turned out to be a guy on what appeared to be a road grader. I boomed over him at 450 knots… We started picking up a barrage fire of tracers coming from the area, having no choice but to blast through it. The area was christened "Lead Alley." We roared by at high speed and never took a hit.

Our next target was an airfield just south of Xieng Khouang. We turned northwest, following another road catching a convoy of Pathet Lao trucks and a tank headed south. By that time, we were bingo [low on fuel] and headed back to the ship. When the Air Intelligence officers (AIs) and photo interpreters looked at the film, they were excited. It even got an "Atta boy" from the CARDIV Rear Admiral William Bringle. It was the first mission that had produced results and the film was fired off to Washington.

Concern about hostile fire was growing; several of us had been shot at, and with no real rescue capability in place, the powers that be considered armed escorts, something that had been prohibited previously.[6]

vi It was basic piloting to use a compass and second-hand clock to time each leg of the flight plan.

On reading this account, Commander Jerry Kuechmann remarked, "Colonel Kiely's account is correct. I was really mad at the Air Boss for sending me down to the hangar deck too soon. The Marines got some great photos on that flight."

Shootdowns Increase and Changes Come to Yankee Team *Recon Tactics*

On June 6 1964, Lieutenant Chuck Klusmann from VFP-63 was shot down, captured and escaped (see the following chapter). American jets were starting to accumulate losses as Colonel Kiely's article describes:

> With that, CINCPAC [Commander-in-Chief, Pacific] ordered armed escorts for the photo birds, ushering in the first step toward armed conflict. And on June 8, one of the F-8 escort pilots, Commander Doyle Lynn, commanding officer of VF-111, was shot down and rescued the following day. The USAF retaliated with a strike hitting targets with 750-pound bombs, rockets, and 20mm cannon. With that a nervous Prime Minister Souvanna Phouma demanded that no further American air operations be conducted over Laos. The effort came to a dead stop. It was not until June 14 that the Americans persuaded him to allow a resumption of reconnaissance flights.[7]

According to Colonel Kiely, changes came to *Yankee Team* tactics:

> The Joint Chiefs of Staff issued instructions that reconnaissance flights were to be done above 10,000 feet, a job for the RA-3Bs [VAP-61], with RF-8A flights approved on a case-by-case basis.
>
> *Kitty Hawk* departed Southeast Asia; VFP-63 Det. C and VMCJ-1 transferred to *Constellation* [CVA-64] on June 8 [where no reconnaissance was done], then cross-decked to USS *Ticonderoga* (CVA-14), joining Air Group Five. *Yankee Team* operations resumed July 19.[8]

August would bring the first fatality and historic events would expand the air war into North Vietnam. Colonel Kiely summarizes VMCJ-1's history in late 1964:

High oblique of USS Bon Homme Richard *(CVA-31) in the South China Sea. (National Naval Aviation Museum, Pensacola, FL)*

A VFP-63 Det. B, USS Ticonderoga *(CVA-14), RF-8A (Bu. No. 145641) refueling from a VAQ-130 Det. 3 KA-3B tanker, July 30, 1964. (Robert L. Lawson Collection, National Naval Aviation Museum, Pensacola, FL)*

> Due to the Tonkin Gulf incident [August 2 1964—see next chapter], reconnaissance missions continued but were beginning to take a back seat to other combat operations. VMCJ-1 pilots and personnel were relieved in November by a new cadre from the States. Unfortunately, having suffered no accidents or combat damage or losses since its arrival aboard *Kitty Hawk*, on May 22 the squadron suffered its first loss November 10 as Captain Darrell Bloom was killed in a mid-air collision with a Navy A-4 Skyhawk.
>
> For almost six months, VFP-63 and VMCJ-1 had bounced from *Kitty Hawk* to *Constellation*, to *Ticonderoga*, back to *Constellation*, again to *Ticonderoga*, then to USS *Bon Homme Richard* (CVA-31). VMCJ-1 would keep augmentation detachments aboard a series of carriers until 1966.
>
> The accomplishments of VFP-63 and VMCJ-1 detachments were remarkable, considering the constant turbulence caused by VMCJ-1 shuffling from carrier to carrier, and the ups-and-downs of rudder orders straight from Washington. Not until late in the game did most of us know exactly where all that effort would lead us, or how deeply we'd become enmeshed in the Asian conflict.[9]

Colonel Wayne Whitten explains the organizational changes for 1965:

> The end of VMCJ-1's one-year assignments of its personnel to MCAS Iwakuni Japan came at the end of each year. Lieutenant Colonel O. W. Corman had led a cadre from VMCJ-3 at MCAS El Toro California into MCAS Iwakuni at the end of October 1964 and took command of a reconstituted VMCJ-1. Two of his RF-8A pilots and a 14-man maintenance team from his advance party had picked up the commitment to augment VFP-63 detachments supporting *Yankee Team* operations over Laos.[10]
>
> With a replenished crew, during the period December 1–26, 1964, VMCJ-l Detachment A remained in a standby status both at MCAS lwakuni and at NAS Cubi Point. Day and night refresher carrier landings were accomplished on December 19 aboard USS *Hancock* (CVA-19). On December 27 the detachment flew aboard *Hancock* to remain in an operational status attached to VFP-63 Detachment L until January 18, 1965.[11]

1965: A Year of Escalating Combat Missions and Transition for VMCJ-1

The beginning of 1965 found the Navy still struggling to meet its photo-reconnaissance commitments in the effort to stem communist aggression in Laos and South Vietnam. Laos in particular was a theater where infiltration of men and material flowing down the Ho Chi Minh trail required significant photo-reconnaissance resources.

With the approval from the Gulf of Tonkin Resolution (see Chapter 2), the air war expanded into North Vietnam. This meant VMCJ-1 would continue to provide augmentation detachments to VFP-63 in multiple aircraft carriers as the demands for photo-reconnaissance increased. The account that follows details the many short-duration VMCJ-1 deployments between land and sea and carrier-to-carrier movements that made it possible. A deployment to and off a carrier requires great effort: moving all the aircraft, maintenance tools, supplies, equipment, pilots and maintenance crew is a logistical challenge, especially when detachments are shuffled around constantly. Once on-board ship, the maintenance crew has to hand-carry that heavy and bulky equipment to various work places in the ship, all the while enduring the tropical heat. Also of no small effort was the difficulty finding their way around a strange ship's labyrinth of passageways and getting used to life aboard ship. It would be VMCJ-1's way of life for the following year.

January–March 1965: VMCJ-1 Rolling Thunder *Operations Begin*

In February 1965, President Lyndon B. Johnson approved Operation *Rolling Thunder*, permitting combat missions in North Vietnam to start in March. For VFP-63 and VMCJ-1, it would mean new targets and increased danger from AAA, SAMs and MiG fighters. For the first time, damage to aircraft resulted from more sustained combat missions into heavily fortified North Vietnam. The following declassified excerpts from Top Secret operations reports detail the Marine participation in the intense air war in Vietnam:

> As a result of the shootdowns in 1964 and subsequently ordered by the JCS, the assigned altitude for *Yankee Team* photography was 10,000 feet without exception. Under no circumstances was the pilot to deviate from this altitude even if mission accomplishment had to be sacrificed. On numerous occasions cloud cover precluded good photography. However, during the *Yankee Team/Barrel Roll* missions, the photo aircraft were allowed to descend below 10,000ft, but then only to 4,000 feet AGL in order to obtain accurate bomb damage assessment [BDA] photography. No low-level high-speed photo mission was assigned. [However, those flight restrictions were not strictly enforced in 1965 and zeal for mission completion meant aircraft hits increased as a result].
>
> During January both VMCJ-1 Det. A and VFP-63 Det. L continued to fly *Yankee Team* recon missions from *Hancock*, including five-night missions. On January 6, First Lieutenant K. J. Sienicki flew the first VMCJ-1 combat mission of 1965, a BDA flown at 4,000 feet, to determine the results of a strike on a northern Laos target under the newly authorized *Barrell Roll* program.[vii] The operational commitments for this operating period concluded on January 18 when VMCJ-1 Detachment A departed *Hancock* and remained in a standby status at NAS Cubi Point.[12]
>
> The VMCJ-1 operations officer, Major J. J. Mitchell, led the next deployment aboard *Coral Sea*, with 1stLt. John "Pappy" Dodson on February 13, under the operational control of VFP-63 Detachment D. At that point, the only strikes against North Vietnam (NVN) targets were in retaliation for Viet Cong attacks against American forces in South Vietnam. That was about to change in a big way as the Johnson administration authorized sustained strikes against NVN targets under *Rolling Thunder* on March 2. *Blue Tree* was the nickname for the related reconnaissance missions. F-8 fighter escorts were assigned and kept a visual on the RF-8As. On one occasion they served to back up a claim by 1stLt. John Dodson that he was the first reconnaissance pilot to record a NVN truck kill. On a low-level road reconnaissance mission, he was flat-hatting along a highway at 100 feet and 500mph when he saw a NVN truck heading towards him and as he bored down on it, he noticed the driver swerving in an attempt to stop. In a panic the driver abandoned the truck as it left the road and crashed. It was Pappy's 13th mission and his troops painted a truck instead of the customary camera on the side of his aircraft. His story about eliminating a truck was written up in the April 25, 1965, edition of *TIME* magazine. *TIME*'s summary of the incident was, "So far as known, Dodson is the world's only photo-recon pilot to put an enemy truck out of action."[13]

The following operations reports excerpts show the variety of VMCJ-1 missions (South Vietnam, North Vietnam, and coastal activity recon) and a year-long pattern of deployments to and from carriers:

---

vii Code name applying to U.S. armed reconnaissance and prebriefed air strikes against infiltration routes and facilities in Laos. Small bombers would follow intelligence or own surveillance to eliminate infiltration.

For a second time in two months, the VMCJ-l detachment departed *Coral Sea* on the 4th of March, pursuant to Commander Task Force 77 [CTF-77] instructions, and proceeded to NAS Cubi Point in a standby status for possible call to the *Ranger* or *Hancock* in the event of special operations. Eleven days later, on March 15, the detachment returned to *Coral Sea*. On March 19 an operation consisted of four phases with each phase involving strikes on military targets in North Vietnam. On the 22nd a mission consisting of coastal reconnaissance of South Vietnam was flown by 1stLt. John Dodson. The object of the flight was to find unfriendly shipping activity and to photograph all the coves and inlets for possible hiding places.

No tactical flights were flown on the 23rd of March due to practice being conducted for an air show for Prime Minister Quat of South Viet Nam and Ambassador Maxwell D. Taylor the next day. [Yes, we can stop a war for a VIP visit!]

On the 29th of March a maximum effort strike was conducted against the military installation and radar site at Back Long Vi Island. The attack was the most intensive effort thus far by *Coral Sea*. Attack aircraft included six A-3B aircraft loaded with four 1,000-pound bombs each, releasing their ordnance from 15,000ft guided by their own radar. It was the first recorded drop by A-3B aircraft in combat. In addition, eight A-4E, ten A-1E, eight F-8D, and eight F-8C aircraft were utilized in the strike. The ordnance consisted of 500 and 1,000-pound bombs, Zuni rockets, napalm and 20mm cannon. Repeated runs were made and the target was under bombardment for one hour and fifteen minutes. Ground fire was intense throughout the attack and consisted mostly of automatic 12.5mm with some quad 37mm. The target damage was extensive and secondary explosions took place in the middle of the island when some ammunition revetments were hit. There were five primary targets consisting of the radar antenna, communications shack, barracks area, administration building and antenna yard. Additionally, six secondary targets consisted of concrete buildings scattered throughout the island. Midway through the strike photo runs were made at 500 feet down the length of the island by Major Mitchell and First Lieutenant Dodson flying in formation in order to increase the coverage and split the fire.

After the A-4E aircraft completed their runs a final photo run in which the VFP-63 det Joined in with the two VMCJ-l pilots. Photo coverage was excellent utilizing the KA-56 Panoramic Camera, forward firing KA-58s, 30- and 15-degree oblique KA-45s. Coverage indicated extensive damage to all primary targets and complete destruction of the radar and communications building. The heavy ground fire was fairly accurate. First Lieutenant Dodson, following in trail of Major Mitchell, saw many tracers pass just behind his aircraft. 1stLt. John Dodson's aircraft sustained a 12.5mm hit in the vertical stabilizer just forward of the pneumatic control package [a vulnerable and critical location]. Three other aircraft were shot down during the raid.

During this operating period, from February 13 to March 31, VMCJ-l detachments logged a total of 103 flight hours and made 49 arrested landings, 15 *Yankee Team* missions, weather reconnaissance and cyclic operations. VFP-63 Detachment D flew a total of 29 *Yankee Team* photo missions.[14]

April–June 1965: VMCJ-1 Electronic Warfare Operations Move to Da Nang

The following excerpts from the declassified April–May 1965 VMCJ-1 operations reports help us understand the growing number and variety of photo missions VMCJ-1 was conducting during this period, including: targets of opportunity, *Yankee Tree* (Laos), *Rolling Thunder* (North Vietnam), *Blue Tree* (NVN roads and military build-up), river boats, and many bomb damage assessments. Also, important to note is the increase of *Rolling Thunder* missions over North Vietnam, including a significant number of night photography missions which will be discussed in depth in Chapter 3. This increase in tempo meant VMCJ-1 RF-8As were receiving more AAA damage from the air defenses near their targets. Additionally, the pattern of cross-decking to carriers increased as operation requirements changed. It demonstrates the difficulties associated with being an augmentation detachment to VFP-63. It is worthy to note most of the missions were flown by two pilots.

Also, of significance during this period is VFP-63's discovery of the first SAM site near Hanoi and VMCJ-1 electronic warfare (EW) EF-10Bs being sent to Da Nang to conduct electronic countermeasures operations to neutralize the SAM threat. This new phase of operations became a most important contribution to the air war effort over the following years.

VMCJ-1 Detachment A remained aboard *Coral Sea* for the period April 1–14. The majority of missions were BDA. Detachment B arrived aboard *Hancock* April 18, Easter Sunday. In May, photo pilots met more hostile fire with a VMCJ-1 RF-8A damaged and losing another on June 1, flown by a VFP-63 pilot who was shot down and killed (see Chapter 3). Also, difficult night photo missions were flown. As the story unfolds, Major Manning will accumulate an increasing number of hits.

> On April 28 Major Manning launched on a special damage assessment sortie to photograph five boats dead in the water and a sixth beached, apparently heavily damaged. Over the target, he received six small arms hits, one rupturing his main fuel cell and another ingested into the engine—both critical areas [Hit #1]. The aircraft was safely recovered and received extensive over-haul damage repair.
>
> On April 30 First Lieutenant Hoyt Wayne Young flew BDA photographs for *Rolling Thunder 13C*, a strike against the ammunition dumps at Phu Qui, North Vietnam.
>
> [Continuing their pattern of hop-scotch migrations] Detachment B from *Hancock* transferred at sea to *Coral Sea* on May 3; men and equipment were transferred by helicopter. The two RF-8As were flown aboard by Major Manning and 1stLt. Hoyt Young.
>
> On May 5, 1965, 1stLt. Hoyt Young flew a target of opportunity reconnaissance mission in conjunction with *Rolling Thunder 13C* along routes between Vinh, and Thanh Hoa, NVN. He obtained excellent coverage of hydro-electric facilities, bridges and railroad cars. Heavy fire was received from the Thanh Hoa dam area.
>
> On May 6 1stLt. Hoyt Young flew another target of opportunity mission for *Rolling Thunder* photographing bridges and minor rail marshalling points. Major Manning flew a night reconnaissance mission in the Vinh-Thanh Hoa area obtaining excellent night photography of a lumber mill and several vehicles.
>
> On May 8 Major Manning flew BDA for *Rolling Thunder* strike on Vinh airfield. The mission was flown at 500 feet with a KA-56 pan camera and *flying down the runway* [emphasis added]. Antiaircraft fire was very heavy however no damage was incurred. [It is worthy of note that one VFP-63 RF-8A (Lt. W. B. Wilson) from *Midway* was destroyed over the same target earlier in the day, see Chapter 3 for details].
>
> On May 10 1stLt. Hoyt Young flew a *Yankee Team* mission photographing selected portions of, routes 8, 12, and 23 between Mu Gia Pass and Nepe Pass in Laos. Weather prevented significant coverage. Major Manning flew a target-of-opportunity photo-reconnaissance mission in conjunction with *Rolling Thunder* 140. A new POL [petroleum, oil, lubricants] storage facility was photographed near Phu Qui in North Vietnam.

On May 11 Major Manning flew another target of opportunity mission as *Rolling Thunder*, road construction was photographed in the Bon Chieng area. 1stLt. Young flew a night BDA mission on the river near Than Hoa.

On May 21 Major Manning flew a *Blue Tree* mission to photograph the Dong Phong Thuong bridge just north of Thanh Hoa, a radar site near Quang Ke and the Route 1 bridge in the town of Dong Hoi. The mission altitude was specified at 500 feet. Major Manning received two direct hits in the main fuel cell of his aircraft while in his photo run on the first target, the Dong Phong Thuong bridge [Hit #2]. The rate of fuel loss was such that he would have been unable to return to *Coral Sea* or reach a friendly airfield. He elected to continue his mission, receiving heavy fire over Dong Hoi, but received no further damage, and then rendezvoused with an A-3D tanker just off his last target. The tanker provided 500 pounds of fuel enabling Major Manning to return to *Coral* Sea arriving with 2,000 pounds of fuel.

The 13 enlisted members on the detachment embarked aboard *Bon Homme Richard* on May 22, 1965 [another carrier change for the detachment]. On May 27 Major Manning and 1stLt. Hoyt Young were released from TF-77 and departed for NAS Cubi Point that evening. On May 28 [replacement pilots] Major Mitchell and First Lieutenant I. J. German recovered aboard the *Bon Homme Richard*.

On June 1 a VMCJ-1 aircraft, flown by VFP-63's Lieutenant Commander Frederick Crosby was destroyed photographing the Dong Muong Thong [sic] bridge at 200 feet altitude and 530 knots. The aircraft was seen to roll 120° and strike the ground, exploding on impact. Lt. Cmdr. Frederick Crosby went in with the aircraft [see Chapter 3].[viii]

June 6, 1965, 1stLt. I. J. German flew a BDA mission for *Rolling Thunder 17C2* which was a recycle of the strike on the port facilities of Than Hue just south of Vinh. Excellent photographic coverage was obtained utilizing a KA-53 at 10,000 feet. Heavy 37mm and 57mm fire was received, however no damage was inflicted.

On June 16 Major Mitchell and 1stLt. I. J. German departed the *Bon Home Richard* and recovered aboard *Oriskany* [CVA-34]. Seven enlisted were hi-lined[ix] to the USS *Pyro* (AE 24) for further hi-line transfer to *Oriskany*. The enlisted transfer was completed June 18 [another carrier change].

On June 19 Major Mitchell flew a new mission covering the choke points at Mu Gia Pass and Nepe pass. Heavy 37mm fire was received at an altitude of 3,000 feet while photographing a bridge. No damage was sustained.[15]

After reading the summary of sorties (one aircraft mission) above, it is easy to see how busy the photo detachments were and how dangerous the missions were becoming. For the period April–June, VMCJ-1 detachments flew 128 sorties and made eight sea-to-land, land-to-carrier, and carrier-to-carrier movements.

---

viii This incident demonstrates that aboard ship the VMCJ-1 and VFP-63 pilots would occasionally fly the other's RF-8As when necessary.

ix "Hi-lined" is a daring transfer of men from one ship to another while both sail close and parallel. A rope is shot from one to the other followed with strong cables connecting both. A man in a dangling "chair" is hoisted across the water separating the ships. It takes expert seamanship of both ships' captains while the transported person gets the ride of his life.

VFP-63 RF-8G ready to launch from USS Bon Homme Richard *(CVA-31) in 1965. Note the "Eyes of the Fleet" logo on the raised wing and the hold-back cable under the fuselage. (Cmdr. Peter Mersky)*

An A-4 (top left) launches from USS Oriskany *(CVA-34) during flight operations in the South China Sea, July 19, 1968. (Robert L. Lawson Collection, National Naval Aviation Museum, Pensacola, FL)*

VMCJ-1 Electronic Countermeasures Aircraft Join a New Phase of the War

Colonel Whitten provides the following summary of VMCJ-1's early ECM operations:

> Soon after initiation of *Rolling Thunder* the Navy and Air Force were faced with a rapid buildup of radar-controlled AAA and newly identified SA-2 surface-to-air missile sites. At this time, none of the American aircraft was equipped with SAM radar-warning receivers and there was no radar-jamming support aircraft available. An urgent order came to deploy VMCJ-1 EF-10B Skyknights to Da Nang, Republic of Vietnam [RVN]. Lieutenant Colonel Wes Corman led a detachment of six EF-10Bs to Da Nang with his staff on April 17, 1965, where the squadron headquarters would remain until 1970. The EF-10Bs were quickly assimilated into TF-77 and U.S. Air Force (USAF), 2nd Air Division's daily frag order providing threat warning and ECM support for their strike and reconnaissance aircraft against North Vietnam's air defense radar nets. They would be joined by six USAF RB-66Cs and a few antiquated Navy AD-5Q propeller-driven aircraft that constituted about one third of the total American Electronic Warfare force.

USS Franklin D. Roosevelt *(CVA-42) replenishes fuel at sea. In addition, ordnance, food stores and personnel can be "high lined" with similar rigging. This requires superior seamanship from both ships' captains, especially in rough seas. (Stephen Miller)*

The Marine aircrews were no strangers to Soviet and Chinese radars having flown numerous missions around the periphery of these adversaries over the previous six months. However, as yet there had been no intercepts of the SA-2's Fansong target-tracking and missile-control radars. VMCJ-1's EF-10Bs conducted the first tactical employment of active ECM or jamming against enemy radars on April 29th flying in support of a USAF strike on NVN targets.[16]

When a Soviet made SA-2 SAM site under construction outside of Hanoi was discovered on April 5 by VFP-63's Det. D, flying from *Coral Sea*, it added a whole new dimension to the NVN air defense environment. This discovery led to high-level discussions, all the way up to the White House, on how to deal with this new threat. The president rejected a strike against the site, fearing the killing of Soviet advisors. Ironically, this echoed a similar response from President Kennedy when he fended off similar requests during the Cuban Missile Crisis in 1962. The major difference, however, was that the United States was at war with North Vietnam. By the end of the war, the NVN had constructed 56 SAM sites. The first casualty of an SA-2 was on July 24 1965 when an Air Force F-4C Phantom II was shot down 40 miles northwest of Hanoi. The first Navy aircraft shot down by a SAM was an A-4 Skyhawk from the USS *Midway* (CVA-41) on August 11 1965, "mandating a retaliatory strike, the first in the history of tactical air operations. All six VMCJ-1 EF-10Bs would take part in this historic operation. From that point on, the focus of VMCJ-1's EF-10Bs would be to warn strike and recon pilots of impending SAM attacks and to jam the SA-2 target tracking radars."[17]

August 1965 Photo-reconnaissance Resumes with More RF-8A Losses

July 1 found VMCJ-l photo Detachment A embarked aboard *Oriskany*. No flight operations were conducted. On July 2, the detachment was released to NAS Cubi Point to remain in a standby status while *Oriskany* moved south to conduct operations in support of I Corps. A month-long period of inactivity for VMCJ-1 Detachment A occurred.

This summary of August photo-reconnaissance operations shows that most missions flown were in support of *Rolling Thunder*. It also shows that in August concern over

SAM sites was getting the attention of the admirals; photo and EW surveillance were stepped up to confront the threat. VMCJ-1 pilot Major P. Manning was hit by AAA, ejected, and rescued [Hit #3, see Chapter 3]. It also shows how lost and damaged photo-jets were making aircraft availability a new concern.

The following illustrative excerpts from Top Secret Marine Corps operations reports give a sample of VMCJ-1's tactics and missions down to the level of detailing the cameras used. This is of interest because it demonstrates how the air-intelligence mission planners were selectively specifying the correct camera suite to match the intelligence desired. The first excerpt shows the Marines were now using Navy cameras. When necessary, two RF-8As were flown in section (lead and wing) formation to maximize the coverage, mirroring VFP-62's tactics over Cuba. Additionally, on important missions, it provided assurance of coverage if camera failure occurred in one RF-8A. Importantly, the mission reports demonstrated to Marine superiors that the dangerous missions were being flown by an experienced, competent and reliable military organization:

> On August 4 Detachment A was aboard *Coral Sea.* A strike on the Vinh Army Barracks was conducted on August 11. Major Mitchell and First Lieutenant Sienicki flew BDA in section and excellent results were obtained using KA-53 panoramic [horizon-to-horizon] cameras.
>
> The first operational flight during this period was conducted on August 12. First Lieutenant Sienicki flew route 2607/156 which was a photo recce (reconnaissance) of targets of opportunity from the DMZ[x] to 19-00°N. Satisfactory coverage was obtained showing various bridges and roadways under construction.
>
> On August 13 Major Manning and 1stLt. K. J. Sienicki launched on special recce missions in North Vietnam to locate and photograph a possible SAM missile site believed to be in the area. Major Manning elected to approach the area at low-level commencing his run-in just north of Thanh Hoa. First Lieutenant Sienicki's low-level run-in was to begin over Hon Me Island and to approach the suspected area from the southwest. Shortly after commencing his run, Major Manning was hit by flak and was forced to eject in the vicinity of the SAR [Search and Rescue] destroyers. Ejection and subsequent rescue were successful, but moderate to severe back injuries were sustained. First Lieutenant K. J. Sienicki encountered no flak but was unable to obtain photo coverage of his assigned search area due to low hanging clouds over the mountains west of the suspected SAM area. Other *Coral Sea* aircraft continued the mission of searching for this new suspect SAM site. During operations three strike aircraft were destroyed and one was severely damaged but managed to recover aboard ship.
>
> There were no flight operations for VMCJ-l conducted on August 14. VFP-63 Det. D flew two sorties, both BDA for an attack on the Vinh Army Barracks and Supply Depot. With the loss of PP 920,[xi] VFP-63 Det. D had no operational RF-8A aircraft as PP 924 remained below deck in maintenance status. Both VMCJ-l aircraft, RM 16 and RM 17, constituted the only RF-8A aircraft in an "up" status aboard *Coral Sea.* [This highlights the dangerous missions' impact]

x The Demilitarized Zone spanned 60 miles, and was 1-mile-wide, north of the city of Hue adjacent to the 17th parallel.

xi PP is the tail code for VFP-63 Photo and 920 is the nose number indicating the particular RF-8A in the squadron. RM is the tail code for VMCJ-1.

A C-1A Trader COD (carrier onboard delivery) aircraft assigned to VR-30 over the Pacific in 1969. The COD delivered personnel, important supplies and, most importantly, mail for the crew. (National Naval Aviation Museum, Pensacola, FL)

Major Mitchell arrived aboard by COD[xii] as a replacement for Major Manning on August 16. No VMCJ-1 operations were flown on this date.

On August 19 Major Mitchell flew a special low-level recon of the Nam Dinh area, penetrating the low altitude SA-2 envelope of Sites One and Three in a search for suspected additional sites in that area. The flight was conducted between 500 feet and 5,000 feet at an indicated airspeed of 600kts [approximately 720mph]. Good area coverage was obtained with a forward firing KA-45 camera, CAX tri-met in station two and KA-45 in the 15degree oblique position. [Low altitude with the KA-45 camera gets excellent pre-strike photos]

First Lieutenant Sienicki, on August 21, flew BDA for a strike on the Thanh Hoa Barracks.

On August 22 the *Coral Sea* steamed south proceeding to Dixie Station. Trouble in the ship's number 3 engine necessitated this shift to southern waters. It was believed that temporary repairs could be completed while on Dixie station and that the ship could again steam north.

VMCJ-1 Detachment Alpha remained aboard. However, on August 23, Major Mitchell flew aboard *Oriskany* to supplement an *Iron Hand* mission. The mission was a three-wave strike against a suspected SAM site, just east of Kep Airfield, 30 miles northeast of Hanoi. Damage was inflicted on the target however photos later revealed the complex to be a heavy gun emplacement rather than a SA-2 site. Six A-4s were hit but all managed to return safely.

From August 24–30 a total of 34 in-country BDA missions were flown of which VMCJ-1 flew 13. While on Yankee Station from August 12–22 a total of 32 photo sorties were flown, of which VMCJ-l flew 11. Combat readiness was affected to a moderate degree by the crash of an RF-8A aircraft shortly after take-off [at Da Nang] on August 22. The aircraft was destroyed but the pilot ejected successfully. Combat readiness in all other areas remains high.[18]

August Electronic Countermeasures Missions increase in North Vietnam

The U.S. military was caught off guard when the Soviet SA-2 SAMs were found in North Vietnam by VFP-63. Command officers rushed orders to VMCJ-1 to move its EF-10Bs to Da Nang to mitigate the new threat to Navy, Marine and Air Force aircraft. Marine Corps declassified documents provide this chronology:

During August VMCJ-l EF-10B aircraft conducted electronic counter measures against fire-control radars[xiii] in the Vinh, Thanh Hoa and Nam Dinh areas in North Vietnam in support of 17, 2nd Air Division, and 15 Seventh Fleet, *Rolling Thunder* strikes, with three additional missions conducted

---

xii COD stands for Carrier Onboard Delivery, a two-engine propeller aircraft that transported supplies, personnel, parts and, most importantly, mail for the crew.

xiii Fire control radar was used to accurately aim anti-aircraft artillery at moving targets.

in support of 2nd Air Division strikes (Operation *Left Hook*) on SA-2 missile sites on the 9th, 11th and 31st of August.

The strikes on August 9th and 11th were unsuccessful due to the sites having been vacated[xiv] during the interim between site location and a combination of tactical ELINT [Electronic Intelligence], photo-reconnaissance and strike execution. VMCJ-l participation on these two missions involved a passive/active ECM role, consisting of missile radar detection, strike aircraft warning, and then electronic jamming of the emitter. The strike against a SA-2 site on the 31st was considered a success from an Electronics Warfare point of view in that the site was located purely by tactical ELINT—the missile radar having been stimulated into emitting by other reconnaissance and tactical aircraft penetrating the general area. With the strike force having been launched within a short subsequent time interval (in this case about two hours), the missile site was visually located by the strike force, but only one strafing run was accomplished. VMCJ-l participation on this mission was limited to launching on the strike phase from a ground alert status and conducting electronic jamming[xv] against the missile radar under attack.

In addition to the above missions twenty-three tactical ELINT missions (*Iron Hand*) in North Vietnam were conducted in support of 2nd Air Division, the majority of which were for collection and location of SA-2 missile associated radar emissions.[19]

September–December 1965 Photo-Reconnaissance and Electronic Warfare

September was a continuation of reconnaissance targeting SAM sites in heavily defended North Vietnam, resulting in the shootdown of a carrier air wing commander who became a famous POW. In addition, a VFP-63 RF-8A was hit and damaged, while another VFP-63 pilot, Lieutenant (junior grade) Robert Rudolph, was shot down and killed in action (see Chapter 3).

VMCJ-l Det. An aircraft and pilots shifted to *Oriskany* on September 1. Major Mitchell flew in a three-plane *Iron Hand* mission the afternoon of arrival. The mission was a SAM recon in the Haiphong to Hanoi area and was flown at 50 feet and 500kts Until the IP (initial point) just northwest of Haiphong then the aircraft popped up to 1,000 feet for all photography. The three aircraft separated and flew different routes after reaching the IP (retirement was made at 600-plus kts). Lieutenant Commander Thalman, officer in charge of VFP-63, Det. G aboard *Oriskany*, was hit by small arms fire and diverted to Da Nang.

Maj. Mitchell again flew Rt. 9 in the Tchepone area of Laos on September 8. First Lieutenant Sienicki flew BDA for an *Iron Hand* mission north of Thanh Hoa. He was in company with Lt. (j. g.) Robert Rudolph of VFP-63. Their flight was called into an area on Highway 1 about 25 miles north of Thanh Hoa to photograph some trucks that had been attacked by the A-4 strike group. As the two RF-8As entered the area at 1,000 feet and 600kts they encountered extremely heavy 37mm and light-automatic fire. VFP-63's Lt. (j.g.) Robert Rudolph's aircraft was hit and seen to roll inverted and immediately plunged into the ground.

On September 9 Major Mitchell flew BDA for a combination strike on the Thanh Hoa bridge and SAM hunt, however the mission was aborted because of weather. Commander James Stockdale,

xiv The North Vietnamese moved their mobile radar-controlled SAMs and AAA frequently.

xv Electronic jamming caused the defense radar to lose "lock-on" with its target, thus defeating the system.

Carrier Air Wing (CVW-5) Commander and his squadron commanders, including future Medal of Honor recipient Cmdr. James B. Stockdale (seated far right), pictured on the flight deck of the carrier Ticonderoga *(CVA-14). On August 5, 1964, CVW-5 participated in Operation* Pierce Arrow*, the first U.S. air strikes against North Vietnam. Standing (far right) behind Cmdr. Stockdale is Lt. Cmdr. Don Hegret, officer in charge, VFP-63 Det. B. (National Naval Aviation Museum, Pensacola, FL)*

Carrier Air Wing Commander, was shot down just south of Thanh Hoa and is believed to have been captured.[xvi]

On September 11th, VMCJ-l Det. A's RF-8As departed *Oriskany* and returned to Iwakuni. The flight was made non-stop from Point Yankee utilizing in-flight refueling from an A-3 Tanker approximately 140 miles out from the carrier. During the operating period from September 1 to September 10, 1965, VMCJ-l Detachment A flew a total of 13 photo missions. VFP-63 Detachment Golf flew 14 photo missions.

On September 12, VMCJ-l Detachment A was reconstituted with a new group of men [It was the final VMCJ-1 RF-8A detachment]. This det proceeded to Cubi Point on September 27 and reembarked aboard *Oriskany* on September 29. Veteran pilots First Lieutenant Young and First Lieutenant Dodson joined the same day. They would be relieved in mid-October by Captain Michael Gering and First Lieutenant Alton Butler who was on the advance party of the incoming cadre from VMCJ-3.[20]

A VFP-63 Det. G RF-8A (Bu. No. 146825) with a VMF-212 F-8E on USS Oriskany*'s Elevator #3. This jet was lost with pilot R. D. Rudolph on September 9, 1965. Notice the yellow "Cherry Picker" crane permanently on the flight deck for lifting heavy objects. (USN Photo via John McKenna)*

A Time of Transition for VMCJ-1 Photo and EW Operations

Major changes were coming for the role VMCJ-1 would play in the war and Colonel H. Wayne Whitten helps us understand the course of the war going forward:

By September the last of VMCJ-1's photo assets were moved from MCAS Iwakuni to Da Nang as shore-based RF-8As, and at that point, were fully committed to supporting and expanding daily intelligence requirements of the Third Marine Amphibious Force (III MAF). First, the Third Marine division and later elements of the First Marine division were supported, as ground operations expanded throughout I Corps, the northern most military region of South Vietnam. Unlike reconnaissance missions over NVN and Laos, there were no MiG or SAM threats in South Vietnam

xvi Commander Stockdale became a prisoner of war in the "Hanoi Hilton" and, due to his rank and leadership, became a high-profile propaganda source for NVN. His leadership earned him the Medal of Honor when he returned home.

and ground fire was limited to small-caliber automatic weapons usually from known hot spots controlled by the NVN-backed Viet Cong rebels. VMCJ-1's RF-8A aircraft were not allowed to obtain photo coverage of targets in the DMZ or northward into NVN under the division of operational responsibility between COMUSMAV and CINCPAC [Commander, U.S. Military Assistance Command, Vietnam and Commander-in-Chief, Pacific respectively]. Air Force tactical reconnaissance aircraft, on the other hand, were allowed to fly missions throughout the Southeast Asia area of operations.

Lieutenant Colonel Francis Opeka brought his cadre to Da Nang on October 13, 1965, and assumed command of the reconstituted VMCJ-1. His was known as the "war cadre" as it was the first to serve a full tour in combat. Soon after arriving in country all Marine tours were extended for a 13th month, although their replacements were scheduled to arrive as originally planned in October 1966. The plan was to bring two new aircraft to the war effort in the fall of 1966—the RF-4B Photo-Phantom II [see Chapter 8] to replace the RF-8As and the EA-6A Electric Intruders [a direct conversion of the standard A-6 Intruder airframe, with two seats, equipped with electronic warfare equipment] to replace the EF-10Bs. But one more year of service lay ahead for the EF-10B (although it would turn out they would remain in a secondary EW role for three more years) and both fulfilled that operational need in spades.

The VMCJ-1 commitment to augment VFP-63 ended on December 18, 1965, with the return of Marine RF-8As from *Bon Homme Richard*. Captain Michael Gering flew the last Marine RF-8A combat mission from an aircraft carrier.[21]

1966: VMCJ-1 Operations in South and North Vietnam and a Change of photo-Jets

With the start of a new year, VMCJ-1 no longer had carrier commitments and the RF-8As, flying from Da Nang, were restricted to below the DMZ, but the EF-10Bs were conducting active and passive ECM and ELINT (Electronic Intelligence) in the north. The passive ECM listened while the active ECM interfered with and suppressed (jammed) the NVN radar emitters. The ELINT missions were part of the *Iron Hand* operations and were focused on the location and collection of fire control radar emissions.

A Marine Corps VMCJ-1 RF-4B Phantom II landing at NAF Astugi, Japan, circa 1968. Note the parachute deployed to retard speed and oblique camera window near the number "16" on the nose. (Saburo Inoue)

A VMCJ-1 EA-6A Electric Intruder used for electronic countermeasures against North Vietnamese AAA and SAM radars. The bulge on the tail houses the antennae for the ALQ-86 ECM Receiving System and the first attachment under the wing is an ALQ-76 ECM jamming pod. These are the two main ECM systems in the EA-6A configuration. Also note the large in-flight fuel probe. (USN Photo)

They were very busy. In the period January to September 1966, they had a monthly average of 150 ECM, 43 ELINT, and 151 RF-8A sorties. The EF-10Bs contributed to the safety of Air Force and Navy strike pilots by jamming the enemy fire control radars. In July the commander of Carrier Task Group 77.6 congratulated VMCJ-1 on the effectiveness of its ECM support.

At the same time, the RF-8As were meeting their III MAF and Seventh Fleet photo commitments. In July, it used and processed 41,303 feet, or 8 miles, of film. A number of those sorties produced strip-maps for the ground troops.

On one occasion the EF-10Bs and RF-8As were employed in a mutually supporting combat role—a counter-radar operation near the DMZ. Colonel Whitten describes how that unfolded:

> In mid–August 1965 we were directed to begin nightly surveillance of the Demilitarized Zone to detect threat radars that might be emplaced near the demarcation line separating South and North Vietnam. The DMZ was supposedly a neutral sanctuary overseen by an international commission. The EF-10Bs were for the first time going to be employed in support of ground operations albeit indirectly. It seems that American interdiction efforts along the Ho Chi Minh trail extending from NVN through Laos into South Vietnam had thwarted NVN invasion attempts and they decided to make a direct attack through the DMZ. Their plan to infiltrate a division-sized force through the DMZ and initiate a surprise attack on the Marines defending the South Vietnam's upper two provinces in mid-July was discovered and rebuffed. General William Westmoreland, Commander US Military Assistance Command Vietnam, felt they would resume their attacks, perhaps in conjunction with renewed efforts through Laos. He had convinced the JCS to give him authority to initiate Operation *Tally Ho*, an air interdiction campaign in the border area up to 30 miles north of the DMZ. The commanding general 1st MAW had beefed up his fixed wing and helicopter operations supporting the ground Marines along the DMZ and was understandably concerned the North Vietnamese would bring in radar-controlled AAA or establish a SAM site in the area under cover of darkness threatening these vulnerable assets.
>
> So, with that we began to fly DMZ patrols each night. We flew boring race track patterns back and forth along the DMZ for two and a half hours until relieved by another EF-10B. After a week or so with no intercepts, I finally picked up what we later identified as a Cross Slot, a Chinese variant of a Soviet surface-search and short-range gap-filler radar, just north of the DMZ. Puzzlingly, it only radiated at night so we dutifully included it on our post-mission reports for several days. The commanding general 1st MAW took notice and became convinced the radar was posing a threat to his air operations south of the DMZ. On the night of August 23, we were tasked to determine the location of the radar to the best of our abilities. My EF-10B, piloted by First Lieutenant Gail "Subs" Sublett, was joined by another so that both ECMOs could work together in recording lines of bearing to the radar for post-mission analysis. We also made homing runs against the radar signal and with the assistance of a nearby Air Force Sky Spot tracking radar were able to fix its location within a circular area of probability less than 1 mile.
>
> The general wanted to get confirming aerial photos of the radar site and wasn't happy to learn existing policy didn't allow VMCJ-1 RF-8s to go north of the DMZ under Marine control, meaning the mission was to go to the Air Force. But there was another solution, unbeknownst to 7th AF, the EF-10B had a K-17 belly camera that could get those pictures if tasked. That proved easy as 2ndLt. Jim Doyle, our liaison officer at 7th AF, managed to get a special EF-10B reconnaissance mission added to the schedule and Subs and I got the nod to fly it.

We arrived in the area to find the weather was good and proceeded to fly a two-or-three-line mosaic [map] at five thousand feet over the coordinates we had determined the night before. Subs then asked if I was up to making a low-level pass to see if we could get a visual on the radar. I agreed as the weather was so clear I thought we had a good chance of picking it up. Subs then rolled in rocking the wings just above the treetops. Looking out I was shocked to see rows of manned antiaircraft weapons and a few helmeted soldiers running for their lives from the ugly American attack plane. Several make-shift structures were in sight but no radar. Suddenly, we took a hit that sounded like an artillery shell going off. Subs pulled up sharply and luckily there were no red lights on the instrument panel. Deciding that discretion was the better part of valor we decided to get back to Da Nang with our film. On the way home we discussed whether we should have made the last pass with our 20mm guns blazing but agreed we had pressed our dumb lieutenants' luck far enough.

Safely back in Da Nang we discovered we had been likely hit by a 12.7mm or larger round that went right through the nose ra-dome and exited with a fist-sized hole about eight inches in front of the windscreen. As our film was being downloaded, Subs and I tried to answer questions from the maintenance officer as to how we were hit by this relatively small caliber weapon while at five thousand feet. We were saved from an inquisition by the skipper when Jim Doyle called saying that 7th AF wanted to have our film readout in Saigon and debrief the aircrews. So, Subs and I jumped into another EF-10B and flew down to Saigon where we later learned we did get the radar on film albeit not with targeting quality. Doyle did his liaison magic again and for the first time got approval for our RF-8s to get higher resolution coverage to assist in strike planning.

On September 2 our operations officer, Capt. Mike Gering, led a pair RF-8As on a successful pre-strike reconnaissance mission. Their film revealed not only the Cross Slot radar but a built-up area with numerous secondary targets. The next morning Marine Air Group-11 (MAG-11) sent a strike force of F-4B Phantoms and F-8E Crusaders in to takeout the radar and numerous collateral military targets. Our RF-8s returned for BDA and confirmed a successful strike that knocked out the radar and destroyed several buildings and gun emplacements. All hands received atta-boys, but as far as I know, no one received anything other than points toward another air medal.

Two camera stations can be seen in the nose cone area of this Marine Corps' training squadron, VM-3, RF-4B Phantom. Marine photo recon squadron, VMCJ-1, transitioned from RF-8A Crusaders to the RF-4B in October 1966 to support marine ground operations. (National Naval Aviation Museum, Pensacola, FL)

VMCJ-2 "Playboys" (note bunny on tail) display their (top to bottom) EA-6A, RF-8A, EF-10B, and RF-4B. (National Naval Aviation Museum Pensacola, FL)

The successful *Tally Ho* missions were a fitting swan song for VMCJ-1's RF-8A combat service as they were retired less than a month later. This was a somewhat of a high-water mark for the EF-10Bs as well. They were relegated to a supporting role with arrival of the new EA-6A Electric Intruders in October 1966. The Marine RF-8As were replaced in October 1966 with the new RF-4B Phantom [see Chapter 8], this after eight-years of service with the VMCJs. The follow-on cadre also brought in the EA-6A Electric Intruder, the nation's first purpose-built tactical EW aircraft. Meanwhile the EF-10Bs remained heavily committed to supporting both Air Force 2nd Air Division and Navy TF-77 air operations over the heavily defended areas of NVN. The EF-10Bs would continue to serve for three more years but relegated to a secondary role.[22] Five EF-10Bs were lost during combat operations during the Vietnam War.

CHAPTER 2

1964: VFP-63 Photo-Reconnaissance Over Laos and First Prisoner of War

On November 1 1963, Vietnam's autocratic and unpopular President Ngo Dinh Diem and his younger brother and advisor, Ngo Dinh Nhu, were executed by ARVN (Army of the Republic of Vietnam) officers, ending months of Buddhist protests and public unrest. While optimistic for new leadership, American officials felt shame for any involvement. Almost three weeks later, on November 22 1963, President John F. Kennedy rode in an open-top limousine by the Texas School Book Depository at Dealey Plaza in Dallas, Texas. At 12:30 pm, several bullets, from an inexpensive Italian Carcano Model 91/38 infantry rifle, struck the president in the neck and head and made Lyndon Baines Johnson the 36th president of the United States. With that, the new president inherited the U.S. military advisory role in Vietnam. For him and the nation, the dark storm clouds of Vietnam loomed menacingly over the horizon and would envelop his presidency and all of us for the next decade.

The American commitment to Vietnam "began as far back as 1950 with President Truman's decision to help the French to retain their hold over Indochina, was designed to prevent Chinese Communists expansion into Southeast Asia."[1] This fear, known as the "domino theory" held that, if the communists succeeded in Vietnam, Laos and Cambodia, the rest would fall as well. This theory was conceived by those who did not understand the history of Vietnam fighting enemy invaders for hundreds of years. Nevertheless, it held high influence over American foreign policy in the region.[2]

By the end of President Eisenhower's term, "he was troubled less by the growing insurgency in Vietnam than by a mini-crisis in adjacent Laos, where the Soviet Union had stepped in to take advantage of a confused civil war…and cautioned the newly elected President John F. Kennedy, that 'Laos was the key to the entire area of Southeast Asia,' and might require the introduction of American combat troops."[3]

As discussed in Chapter 1, the U.S. Navy's 1964 reconnaissance role over Laos was in support of Operation *Yankee Team*, dedicated to hampering North Vietnamese infiltration into South Vietnam via Laos. VFP-63 had detachments on six aircraft carriers during this period. From October 17, 1963 to July 20, 1964, VFP-63 had Detachment C on board the USS *Kitty Hawk* (CVA-63), augmented by VMCJ-1's detachment. This chapter concentrates on VFP-63's 1964 combat missions, which would conclude with a congressionally authorized Vietnam air war.

The following memoir, *The Price of Freedom* by Captain Charles Klusmann, describes VFP-63's first missions and losses in Laos and is provided here in its entirety with the approval of the author. He vividly describes his harrowing experiences that typified the dangers of flying unarmed-photo missions for nearly a decade. He would become the first of six VFP-63 prisoners of war.

The Price of Freedom

By Captain Charles Klusmann

The First VFP-63 Shootdown of the Vietnam War

The air war in Southeast Asia began in May of 1964. The U.S. Government had been requested to provide [a] show of support to the Royal Laotian Government. No one had flown over North Vietnam, and the air war in the south was still in the early stages of getting organized. The request of the Laotian Government would provide the catalyst which would lead to the most intensive air war ever conducted by anyone. The beginnings were relatively minor on a world-wide scale, but the events were very real for the few involved in carrying out the missions.

Aboard *Kitty Hawk*, the cruise was coming to an end. The ship had deployed in September 1963, and was soon due to head home. While cruising off of Okinawa, she received orders to proceed to a geographic point about 100 miles east of Da Nang off the coast of South Vietnam. This point was to be designated 'Yankee Station.' In route [sic], there was considerable discussion regarding how the show of support for Laos was to be implemented. The options being considered ranged from an air group fly-over of a large number of aircraft, commonly referred to as a 'group grope,' to a fly-over of six-to-eight fighters and bombers, and finally with a fly-over of two unarmed reconnaissance aircraft. Fortunately for a number of pilots, the last option was selected.

The first mission was flown by Lieutenant Commander Ben Cloud, the recce [photo-reconnaissance] team officer in charge, and myself flying two RF-8A Crusaders. It was approximately 500 miles from the carrier to the target area and was within range of the aircraft and would provide about 20 minutes at low altitude to get some good photo coverage. No inflight refueling was planned. The flight went well and we were flying over the Plain des Jars separately to improve coverage, but still within sight of each other.

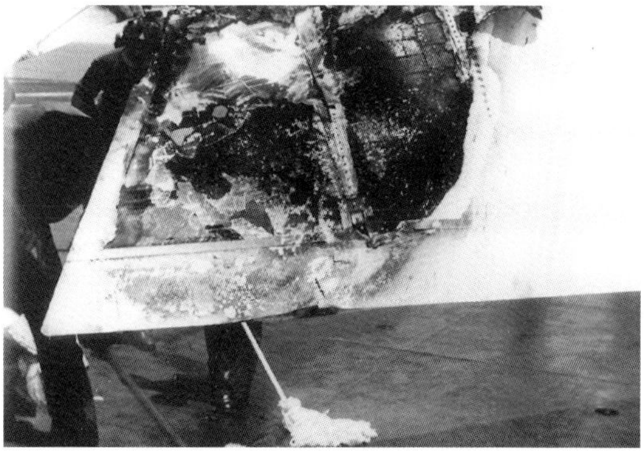

On May 21, 1964, "Corktip 918", flown by Lt. Charles Klusmann, was hit over Laos. The fire and blast from the 37mm and 23mm flak put holes in the wing and droops, allowing fuel to pour out. This was rapidly ignited by more 37mm hits, the resulting fire burning for 20 minutes before going out as Klusmann climbed to 42,000ft. He then recovered safely back aboard USS Kitty Hawk *(CVA-63). (Cmdr. Peter Mersky)*

Ben then called out that he thought we were being shot at. I had seen nothing yet but noticed some white puffs around the aircraft, then some red [tracer] streaks coming up from the ground. About that time, several red lights came on and I noticed fuel pouring from the left wing.[xvii] Ben told me when to turn to avoid the AAA [anti-aircraft artillery] as it started to track up my tail. There were a number of these breaks to get away from the area of intense AAA and by the time I was clear of the area, the left wing was on fire at the wing fold area. We decided that it was time to head home and scramble for altitude in the hopes that the fire would go out. We got to 40,000 feet and after about 20 minutes the fire did go out. On the way back to the ship, I saw pieces of aircraft flying off the wing, but Ben said not to worry. After all, it wasn't his plane. The flight back to the ship was a bit tense. I had lost considerable fuel from the hits in the wing and was trying to figure if I had enough gas to make it back to the ship. We saw some contrails heading toward us from the West and called for some fighter cover from the ship. The contrails turned out to be some USAF aircraft who were checking us out because they didn't know about us either. Weather was great and I started an idle descent from 42,000 feet toward the ship. Emergency lowering of the landing gear and raising the wing worked OK and I recovered on a straight in with about 600 pounds of fuel. Almost enough for one more pass if needed, but I wouldn't want to try it. Once on deck, I saw that the left-wing fold was a mass of melted aluminum and the top of the left aileron was burned away. There were holes all over the aircraft but it would live to fly again about 18 months later.[xviii]

---

xvii The RF-8A had fuel tanks in the wings.

xviii The reader will remember VMCJ-1's Colonel Kiely describing this RF-8A upon his arrival on the *Kitty Hawk*. For him, it was a foreboding of the dangers of the missions over Laos.

More Reconnaissance Missions and the Shootdown

The reconnaissance missions would continue, both day and night, for the next several weeks. Many requests, from the ship's Captain and the Seventh Fleet admiral, were made for these reconnaissance flights to be provided with armed fighter escorts. They were all denied.

The flying was difficult. Nothing changed with regard to the rules of the game. We still had no escorts and no-good SAR plans in case a pilot had to eject over this area. This continued until early June. We had been deployed for more than eight months and were due to rotate back home. We had only one more mission remaining and that was on the 6th of June. 'Piece of cake,' I thought. We fly this mission and will be on our way home tomorrow. Little did I know!

I was assigned to fly this last mission with Lt. Jerry Kuechmann that dreadful day. The launch was normal. Jerry and I proceeded toward the target by flying down along the Mekong and taking a heading for the Plain of Jars. As we were approaching the target area the AAA got really intense and I took some hits in the wing. I was losing a lot of fuel from the hits.

I called Jerry and said, 'Pull up; we're getting out of here!' During the pull up, I took a good solid hit on the fuselage. This was the first time, out of four times being hit, that I could actually feel the impact of the ammunition. I somehow knew that I was in deep serious trouble. The plane was climbing and flying very fast, but I was losing my flight controls. The RF-8A has a fully powered hydraulic system and I was losing this precious fluid in a hurry. In just a couple of minutes the controls system froze. I had to get out of the airplane, or die in it.

I called Jerry and said, 'Adios.' I actuated the ejection system. The ejection was a violent ride. Fortunately, the parachute opening was as advertised, but I was floating down into enemy territory.

I took my body inventory and noted that all the parts seemed to be properly attached and in working order. GREAT! I saw my plane crash in a ball of fire not too far away. I sure hated to lose that aircraft. I could hear a lot of shooting from the ground. It dawned on me that I was their target. I could hear bullets whizzing by my body. Thank goodness I was not hit. I was about to land into a really deep ravine. The ground was coming up very fast. There was only one tree in the clearing and I was heading directly for it. I landed in the top of the tree and fell to the ground, making a very hard landing.

My right hip, knee, and foot were badly wrenched. I could hardly stand up. I did manage to wedge my foot in a bush and pulled until something popped. That procedure helped and the pain somewhat subsided. I surveyed the situation and gathered my survival gear. I had to get out of that area quickly because I knew the enemy was coming after me.

Jerry remained circling overhead until his fuel got low. After he departed it got very quiet. I started walking up the hill. The grass was high and I was leaving a significant trail that could be noticed easily by the enemy. I couldn't walk very well due to my injuries. I could only half crawl and half drag myself through the rough terrain.

Soon I heard another aircraft. I jumped with joy when I spotted a helo *Courier* aircraft overhead. There was no radio in our survival package to communicate with the SAR pilot. There was only an electronic beeper that would automatically send out a distress signal. I assumed that it was working and hoped that the battery would last for a long period. In addition, I set off a smoke signal to let the pilot know my exact location. This probably let the bad guys know where I was as well. When I signaled the plane with my signal mirror, they spotted me immediately. The pilot responded by rocking his wing and revving up his engine. I thought, 'Great! Now at least, someone knew I was alive.'

Two additional aircraft, a C-123 and a *Caribou*, soon joined the helo. I was almost sure that these aircraft were from Air America [CIA operated].

Jerry later confirmed that after the first MAYDAY (distress) call; Air America responded with, 'Where are you and what do you need?'

Aviators, like seamen, are quick to respond when one of their clan is in trouble. These aircraft remained overhead for a couple of hours. I still had not seen, or heard any of the ground troops during this period.

Finally, I heard the sound of helicopters in the distance. I thought for sure that I would be rescued in no time. I confirmed my position with them by my signal mirror. Then I crawled up a small hill, to a clearing on the ridgeline, to make my rescue much easier. Soon the H-34 helicopters approached my position. I was to learn later that Tom Moher flew the first helo that started in after me. (I will always be grateful for the heroic effort of all the pilots and crewmen who placed themselves in danger during all my rescue attempts.)

As the first helicopter started toward my position all hell broke out with intense ground fire from the enemy. They were trying to knock the chopper out of the air. It seemed like gunfire was coming from everywhere. Tom pulled up and struggled to get away from the hostile area. (I later learned that his co-pilot was hit in the head and the helicopter had more than eighty hits from the enemy.) Then the *Caribou* made a low pass for ground fire suppression. Crewmembers in that airplane were shooting and throwing out hand grenades on the bad guys. This was particularly exciting since one of the grenades went off about 15 feet from me. The ground troops responded with more gunfire during these fly-bys.

In spite of the enemy's barrage of bullets, Bill Cook, the second helicopter pilot, started in to make an approach for me. As he flew near, it became very obvious to me that there was no chance for a safe rescue. If he continued his crew would be injured or killed. I did not want other people hurt that were trying to rescue me. These guys had pulled out all the stops and made every possible effort to liberate me. I really appreciated their heroic effort, but I could not let them continue and be slaughtered. I signaled them to leave the area. This of course placed me in a very lonely and desperate situation.

My world, as a Jet Pilot, had changed and was changing very fast that deplorable day. I prayed!

The Capture

Within a short time, I could see the Pathet Lao troops closing in on me from all sides. They were all heavily armed with automatic weapons. I only had my trusty .38 handgun for defense. Needless to say, they captured me. My hands were tied behind my back and a noose was tied around my neck. Then they took me to a nearby small village. They noticed that I couldn't walk very well so they untied my hands and made a crude crutch to assist me in walking. It was almost dark when we reached the village. I was offered some rice, cooked greens, and a small can of stewed pork. It was not tasty, but it was all the nourishment I had for a while.

The next morning, after a sleepless night, I was taken to a nearby cave. I was kept there most of the day. During that day a T-28 aircraft made bombing raids on the village. This old Navy trainer aircraft didn't do much damage and no one seemed too concerned about the raids. I assume that Laos pilots were flying these aircraft.

In late afternoon we started walking toward the village of Xieng Khouang. It took us three days to get there. After arriving, I was given a bucket of water to clean up a bit. My hotel for the night was one of the infamous tiger cages. They tied me down and latched the door. The following day, I was loaded into a truck and we headed toward the Plain of Jars.

All of a sudden, the sky was filled with United States Air Force F-100 Super Sabre fighter-bombers. The guards looked very apprehensive and I was quietly cheering for the Air Force. They hid me under an old farmhouse during the raid.

After the raid we continued on the journey. We walked through the Plain of Jars for a while. Then they headed us into the mountains past Khang Khay along Route 7, finally arriving in a small village. The next day I met the 37mm AAA crewmembers who were given credit for shooting me down. They were heroes and I was the caged enemy. I was on display, in a tiger cage, for all who cared to observe me. (I will never like going to a zoo again to see caged animals!)

That night I was taken to a high-ranking civilian. I think he was Prince Souphanouvong.[xix] There was an officer in uniform who spoke English and acted as the interpreter. He became my interrogator and indoctrinator for the next couple of months. His name was given as Captain Boun Kham. He claimed to be a Laotian, but I believe he was North Vietnamese. Nothing much came of that meeting and I never saw the prince again.

They then moved me to an area of small huts. I was placed in a small room in a hut that had no windows, a dirt floor, walls of mud plastered over woven bamboo, and a

xix Former President of Laos, supporter of Ho Chi Minh and joined the Indochinese communist movement.

thatched roof. Furnishings consisted of a few boards between logs for a bed, a mosquito net, grass mat, blanket, a metal table and chair, a cup and a canteen. The guards that captured me stayed in the other part of the hut 24/7.

The daily routine was much the same each day. I would be escorted to a latrine nearby and then down to a stream to wash-up. The morning and evening meals usually consisted of a small bowl of rice, some soup, and some boiled greens. Occasionally the guards would share some of their food which was a fiery sauce made with fish, salt, and roasted peppers. Occasionally they would have a raiding party on nearby caves to catch rats. They also caught stray dogs. They would then cook these creatures into some kind of stew and call it a 'special meal.' Yes, I ate it. I made up my mind that it was T-bone steak. In a situation like this one will eat whatever he can get to survive. I went from 175 pounds to 125 pounds in a very short time.

The interrogator came nearly every evening. He was more interested in talking about politics than in seeking military information. He was well informed about the military and said that they knew what they needed to know. He had a copy of a book similar to *Jane's All the World's Aircraft*. He also had a very recent copy of the CINCPACFLEET [Commander-in-Chief, Pacific Fleet] organization manual. I wondered how he got a copy of that classified document? This document listed all the U.S. Navy ships. It also listed all squadrons aboard each ship, and who was in command of each unit. He said that he knew that my ship, *Kitty Hawk*, had passed through the Bashi Channel north of the Philippines on a particular night in May while en route to Vietnam—he was correct on the date!

This all seemed a bit incongruous to be sitting in a mud-walled hut, deep in the jungle, with only a kerosene lantern for light, and listening to him talk about world politics. His primary effort, I later determined, was to get something for publicity purposes, and political influence.

He frequently mentioned that the radio had announced that I had been killed in the crash and that no one knew that I was alive. He said that I could write letters, but later said that he couldn't deliver them for one reason or another. He suggested that I make a radio broadcast, just to let everyone know that I was alive and being treated well. I replied with reference to a well-known phrase about the probability of frigid temperatures in Hades. He never asked again. He did continue to encourage me to write a letter to the prince requesting my release.

I was constantly bothered by diarrhea. Sometimes it was not so bad and other times it was very severe. I had a serious attack with fever that lasted about two weeks. This left me very weak and unable to concentrate. The guards kept a fire going in the hut and the smoke caused me to cough almost continually. This lasted the entire two months that I was in solitary confinement.

In my weakened condition and after considerable coercion, I wrote a brief note asking to be released. My letter was rejected. Then I was compelled to sign a dictated letter.

I did not have the strength to resist and was not coherent at the time. I really didn't comprehend what I was writing. Days later the interrogator proceeded to read the letter that I had written to the prince. I was shocked and mortified at what was in the letter. Only then did I realize that they had set me up. That was a big mistake on their part, because from that moment on, I was determined to escape, or die trying.

About a month earlier I had tried to escape by digging under a wall. That is when I discovered that they had driven bamboo stakes about three feet deep around my room. This was their way of making it impossible for me to dig out. I would find another way out of that POW camp. The false letter, they tricked me with, gave me more willpower to get back at them by escaping.

A few days later I was moved to another prison compound about a half mile away. On the way there we passed a two-story wood frame building with many antennas on the roof. I recognized the building. I had taken photographs of it on an earlier photo mission. This let me know exactly my location, in that foreign country, and would be very helpful knowledge in my escape.

The new POW location was in a group of buildings that was isolated from the main road. It was, in fact, the location of Pathet Lao Headquarters. The building they put me in was long and divided into three rooms. They placed me in a small room in the center part of the building. There was a three-foot gap between my building and a barbed wire fence. I had access to that area. There was another barbed wire fence about five feet beyond the first one. The area between the fences was filled with matted barbed wire making an escape impossible, so they thought.

Soon they placed about thirty-five Laotian prisoners in the other two rooms. I had learned a few words of Lao, but my communication ability was very limited with these new prisoners. One of them had worked in Vientiane and had an English/Lao dictionary. This really helped us in communicating with each other.

The Great Escape

About a week after the new prisoners arrived, one of them approached me about the possibility of trying to escape. At first, I was somewhat apprehensive about this fellow. I pretended not to know where we were. Then he proceeded to draw a map in detail about our location. The map was very accurate so I began to have trust in him.

Over a period of several weeks, we discussed the escape plan and where we should go, once we got out. After much planning we decided that our best escape route would be through the two fences. We activated a plan to work the nails loose that held the barbed wire to the posts. Wiggling the nails for hours freed them so they would easily slip out of the post. The inside fence did not take long to convert for our purpose. However, the outer fence was much more difficult.

We were occasionally allowed to wash our clothes in a nearby stream. They allowed us to hang our wet clothes on the outer fence to dry. When we did that, we managed to work on the nails of the outer fence as well. We took our own good time and were very deliberate where we hung our clothes. This frustrated the guards, but they did not have a clue why we were so slow.

Eventually, we were ready to give it a try. There were six Laotians who intended to go out with me. The group was large but we all had a right to make a go of it. My escape partner was Boun Mi. The conditions were just right. It was about 9pm on a dark rainy night and the guard had gone to his shelter to get out of the rain.

I changed into the dark trousers and shirt that we were given. I asked God for help and guidance. Then I eased around to the rear of the building where we had loosened the nails. The guards were busy talking. Boun Mi gave me the signal to go. I raised the wire and crawled under the loosened section. I was out of the compound in seconds as planned. We had about two hundred feet to go to a tree line to hide from view. Boun Mi was right behind me. Two others quickly joined us. We were concerned about the others. One of our group said he would wait for the others and join us later. We never saw him again, nor do we know what happened to the others who had planned to go.

The three of us worked our way around some Russian built tanks that were being guarded. We then had to cross a wide clearing in order to get to the mountains covered with trees. We dashed across the clearing and made it to the woods safely. We found a well-worn trail and followed it for several miles. We stopped for about twenty minutes waiting on the others. They never came. We had to keep going. It was still very dark and we needed to travel as far as possible before daylight.

After daylight we saw a farmhouse at the upper end of the valley. The third man in our group wanted to try to get some food from the farmers. I had a very uneasy feeling about this endeavor. I told Boun Mi that we needed to take cover and watch him approach the house. My gut feeling was correct. In just a few minutes he emerged from the house with his hands tied and a rifle at his back. He had walked into a guerrilla outpost. Soon a large group of soldiers were heading our way with the intent to re-capture the escapees.

This caused us several hours of excitement as we fled through the forest. The soldiers did fire some shots in our direction, but I don't think they ever actually saw us. We managed to double back on our course and lose them. We made the decision to never approach anyone unless we were positively sure that they were friendly.

The remainder of our trek was just pure drudgery, going up over one mountain and down the next. The terrain was very rugged and steep. It was slow going for sure. I prayed for strength to continue. It came. Surely the 'Unseen Hand' was watching over me. I didn't want to ask for too much, so I prayed for God to get me over the next hill and I would climb the following hill on my own. It worked. We ate bamboo shoots, corn stalks, sweet potatoes, wild berries and fruit that we found along the way. Finding water to drink was not a problem since this was the rainy season.

Lt. Charles Klusmann and fellow POW Boun Mi at the Mao village where they ended their escape and celebrated with friendly Laotians. (National Naval Aviation Museum, Pensacola, FL)

Lt. Charles Klusmann arriving at Udorn, Thailand air base. (National Naval Aviation Museum, Pensacola, FL)

Lt. Charles Klusmann greeted by enthusiastic reporters on his trip back to the U.S. (National Naval Aviation Museum, Pensacola, FL)

Leaches were one of the worst pests that we had to tolerate. They seemed to be everywhere. When possible, we used animal trails to make travel easier. We had to stop occasionally to remove the leaches from our bodies. They were drinking way too much of our precious blood. They would always go back to the same wound and start feasting again. This caused some very bad wounds on our bodies. Our motivation kept us going even though our capabilities were lagging.

Three days later we were crossing a high mountain. All of a sudden, we heard voices coming from a small hut. We were very cautious. Boun Mi indicated that they were friendly forces. I wasn't so sure and wanted to keep going. He indicated that he was so sure that he would go in by himself. He agreed for me to watch from a safe distance. As he approached the small hut two men came out with guns and met him. They talked for a few minutes. Then I noticed that they shook his hand and lowered their guns. Boun Mi turned and waved for me to join them. I did.

We had reached an outpost of the village of Baum Long, or better known as Site 32 to Air America. A man was dispatched to the village to telegraph the authorities about our

Back in the cockpit following his return to the States, Lt. Klusmann prepares for his first flight. Note the rocket-jet fittings on his shoulder straps and the V-ring on the right strap which served as a hook-up point for a rescue helicopter's hoist. (Cmdr. Peter Mersky)

Lt. Klusmann indulges in a little self-portraiture during a hop in June 1964. Note the large butterfly release on his oxygen mask. These rather cumbersome devices were replaced by bayonet fittings that slid into the helmet and locked and could be pulled out again in one motion. The large yellow and black ring behind his head is the handle for the ejection seat face curtain. (Cmdr. Peter Mersky)

Details of typical aviator flying gear of the mid-1960s are shown in this view of Lt. Klusmann climbing into his Crusader. Besides the brown flight boots—black boots did not arrive until 1967—we can see the two leg-restraint garters above and below the knees, and a large survival knife pocketed in his G-suit on the outside of his left leg. (Cmdr. Peter Mersky)

arrival. After a short rest we walked the last two kilometers of our ordeal to the village Baum Long.

At Baum Long we received a very warm welcome. We were given food and treatment for the many cuts, scratches, and leach bites that we acquired along the ordeal. About an hour after we arrived, I heard the sound of an aircraft. The villagers hurried us toward the landing site.

It was a very emotional moment for me when I saw the airplane land. This was truly the sound of freedom at last. I heard an American voice calling my name. Terry Burke, who was one of the CIA representatives, greeted me as a long-lost brother. He helped me up to the aircraft where I met Dr. Jiggs Weldon and pilot Lloyd Zimmerman. After a few pictures were taken they flew us back to Udorn. It was hard to believe. My prayers had been answered. I was finally on my way to true freedom.

About two months later, we learned from intelligence sources, that the two men, who initially escaped with us, were recaptured and executed. This let us know, 'That the price of freedom is never free.'

To quote an anonymous inscription on a wall of the Hanoi Hilton: "Freedom has a taste to those who fight and almost die for it, that the protected will never know."

A Wingman's Perspective

Commander Jerry Kuechmann gives some insight into what VFP-63 missions were doing in early 1964 and Lieutenant Klusmann's shootdown:

> Our photo missions on the *Kitty Hawk* prior to going to Yankee Station consisted of beach and island recce, some of them very long range. We had missions to photograph disputed islands between Indonesia and the Philippines, where we would fly to Cubi Point with a A-3B Skywarrior tanker, refuel, fly to the disputed islands, refuel from the A-3B, photograph the islands, return to Cubi Point and refuel again, and then return to the ship. I did the Nightmare Bombing Range near the DMZ in Korea using a A-3B tanker when the *Kitty Hawk* was near Scarborough Shoals in the South China Sea, a six-hour flight.
>
> We would also do bridge level runs of the shoreline leading into ports the ship would visit for the ship's navigator to use. Also, we would act as bogies for the fighters to intercept and at night we would just burn gas to stay proficient for night landings. If a Russian spy trawler was in the area, we kept making visits trying to get photos of its uncovered antennas. We did do a night photo mission in the Plain of Jars and northeast Laos (Lt. Cmdr. Ben Cloud and myself) using two A-3s and their radar to get us to the proper area. We did get some antiaircraft fire, but it was well behind since the flares had an 8-second delay—the first night combat mission for the RF-8, I believe. Cloud cover prevented getting good photos of anything interesting.
>
> I never flew again into Laos after Klusmann's shootdown. With the detachment officer in charge, Lieutenant Commander Ben Cloud, en route to Washington and Lt. Klusmann gone, I was busy running the det and taking care of the Marines [VMCJ-1], so I didn't get scheduled again.
>
> When we flew the road-recce missions we often changed lead so we could not be considered as just an escort. Often the road turned sharper than we could at 500ft and 575kts. In this case the second aircraft would position himself to swing wide and turn in, to pick up the road on the new heading, while the first aircraft finished that part of the road and then would swing in behind, what was the second aircraft. We would repeat this at each sharp turn in the road. Thus, it was just by chance that Klusmann was leading when he was hit.
>
> When I got the Air America aircraft on the radio, after the shootdown, they asked if we were the Crusaders that had flown past them earlier. I told them yes. When I gave them Klusmann's position and asked them to take over the SAR, they said, "Wow, that is a hot spot—close to a division in that area. We are dumping our cargo and going to that position."
>
> After landing on the *Kitty Hawk*, I was met by a ship's Marine when I got out of the aircraft and escorted to the Flag Bridge where several O-6 officers [Navy captains] started questioning me as I entered. Vice Admiral Tom Moore interrupted them, asked me if I wanted some coffee and had one of the O-6s get me some. He then asked me what happened. I was pretty nervous, because he had talked to us before we took off and the last thing he said was, "Do not get shot down." When I finished, he pointed to an A-3 on the waist cat [angled deck catapult] and said, "Get in that A-3, fly to Laos and find your friend." I did, without ever getting even a sip of the coffee.

A VFP-63 Det. D RF-8G (PP 920 Bu. No. 146832) refueling from a VAH-2 A-3B. Both squadrons were on board the USS Coral Sea *(CVA-43), 1964–65.*

The A-3 pilot was shocked when the ship told him to follow my directions and I said we were going to Laos. He said he was going to Cubi Point and had no navigation information on Laos. I said I did and since I knew the A-3 burned twice as much fuel as a F-8, I also knew his fuel requirements. When we got back to the ship it was dark, so I got to experience a night landing in an A-3. Not fun, but after sitting in a cockpit for about eight hours and 15 minutes without any food or water, I was ready to get out.

The A-3 mission was useless, but it was not thought to be when we launched. However, Secretary of State Dean Rusk and Secretary of Defense Robert McNamara decided it was alright to abandon a Navy pilot, that they had sent into Laos, had the flights of F-8s and A-1s en route to provide close air support recalled, and thus made our efforts in the A-3 worthless. I'll let you guess what I think of those two.

When we got back from that cruise, I was the back-up pilot for several dets, but I didn't have enough time left in the squadron to make another full deployment. I did deploy to Vietnam twice with VF-211 in the 1968–71 timeframe and was the commanding officer of VF-211 assigned to the *Hancock* [CVA-19] when it evacuated Saigon in 1975. I flew 189 combat missions total between VFP-63 and VF-211.

Tonkin Gulf Incident and Congressional Declaration of War

On July 30 1964, USS *Maddox* (DD-731), recently outfitted with electronic surveillance gear and 17 technicians to operate it, was cruising the Tonkin Gulf offshore the North Vietnam coast. Captain John J. Hetrick was adhering to orders to get no closer than 8 miles. His ship's mission was to collect electromagnetic signals from North Vietnamese radar installations. His ship's presence was starting to draw attention from the North Vietnamese. On August 2 "the destroyer's skipper encountered hundreds of North Vietnamese junks and fearing they may be armed sounded a general quarters alarm—a condition that prepared for combat. He spotted three communist patrol boats and later reported, 'The next thing we knew, they came out at us.' He ordered his crew to commence firing if the craft came within ten thousand yards."[4]

The North Vietnamese pursued the *Maddox* and it opened fire. "Two of the patrol boats launched a torpedo each at the *Maddox* but missed. The third, its weapons pumping away, sped directly at the destroyer to discharge its torpedo, which turned out to be a dud. Hetrick's gunners hit one of the craft as three needle-nosed Crusader jets from *Ticonderoga* (CVA-14) arrived overhead to strafe the other enemy boats. To a *Maddox* crew member, radarman James Stankevitz, 'it was, like trying to swat mosquitoes with a big fly swatter.'"[5]

Along with the fighters, one of the "needle-nosed" Crusaders was of the photo type, a VFP-63 RF-8A, from the *Ticonderoga*. Lieutenant (junior grade) Bob Kay flew low over the disputed sea looking for evidence of a battle. He is quoted in a 2004 article, "Instead of the telltale aftermath of a sea battle, Kay saw nothing in the waters around the *Maddox* and the *Turner Joy*."[6] Nor did his cameras find any evidence, adding more doubt to the event that triggered an escalation to the Vietnam War.

In response, President Johnson, ordered a strike by American naval aircraft, including VFP-63, against four North Vietnamese patrol boat bases and an oil depot. In his book, Secretary of Defense Robert McNamara writes, "Some elements of Congress and the public believed the Johnson administration deliberately provoked the attacks in order to justify an escalation of the war and to obtain, under a subterfuge, congressional authority for the escalation. Does this have any merit? None at all."[7] Down through the decades, many still remain skeptical. The Congress passed the Tonkin Gulf Resolution on August 7 1964. McNamara asks in his memoir, "Was the Johnson administration justified in basing its subsequent military actions in Vietnam—including an enormous expansion of force levels—on the Tonkin Gulf Resolution? Answer: Absolutely not. Although the resolution granted sufficiently broad authority to support the escalation that followed, as I have said, Congress never intended it to be used as a basis for such action, and still less did the country see it so."[8]

By late 1964, 23,300 U.S. advisors were in South Vietnam and 225 killed in action. It was a clear indication of South Vietnam's inability to defend itself, even with American training and logistical support.[9]

A VFP-63 Det B RF-8A PP 931 landing aboard USS Ticonderoga *(CVA-14), July 30, 1964. Target practice sled in wake. (Robert L. Lawson Collection, National Naval Aviation Museum, Pensacola, FL)*

USS Ticonderoga *(CVA-14), May 9, 1964. (Robert L. Lawson Collection, National Naval Aviation Museum, Pensacola, FL)*

An F-8 on the elevator on board USS Ticonderoga *(CVA-14), circa 1963–64. Note wing folded and in up position. Also note the slight fence around the elevator to "guard against" falling to the hangar deck. (Joe Nagel, ADJC.)*

VFP-63 Det. B, USS Ticonderoga *(CVA-14) party in Hong Kong in 1964. Sitting row two L–R: Braska PH1, Lt. Ron Ball, Lt. Cmdr. D. Hegret, officer in charge, Lt. (j. g.) R. Kay, Lt. (j. g.) E. Miller, and M. Gallant (standing "P" on sleeve). Det. B photographed the Tonkin Gulf attack area in August 1964. (Joe Nagel, standing with hat upper-left)*

CHAPTER 3

1965: VFP-63 Support of Operation *Rolling Thunder* Begins

"Speed is life and random flying helps a lot, too."

—CAPTAIN WILL GRAY USN (RET.)

In late 1964, President Lyndon Johnson was fending off increasing pressure from his advisors and Joint Chiefs of Staff (JCS) to expand the air war, but he was wary of drawing China and the Soviet Union into the conflict and getting more deeply involved with the incompetent and corrupt government of South Vietnam. His instincts were telling him to find an honorable exit, but his concern for the safety of the increasing American military ground presence, the continuing insertion of North Vietnam troops into the south, and bolstered by the Tonkin Gulf Resolution giving him expanded war powers, saw the military finally get his approval for using more air power against North Vietnam.

Dr. Mark Jacobsen from the Naval Historical Center explains the administration's rationale for the major air campaign, designated *Rolling Thunder*, which began in February 1965 and ended in October 1968:

> I want to make one fundamental point at the outset. When the U.S. began bombing North Vietnam in February 1965, it was not trying to smash North Vietnam through air power. Neither was it seeking merely to interdict the movement of supplies through North Vietnam and Laos into South Vietnam. Rather, the purpose of *Rolling Thunder* was to signal North Vietnam that the United States was serious about resisting Hanoi's sponsorship of the Viet Cong in the South. The general belief was that the mere use of American air power would convey this resolution unambiguously.
>
> President Johnson and his advisers also tried to demonstrate American concern not to destroy North Vietnam itself or to endanger the lives of innocent civilians. In addition, the management of the bombing campaign aimed throughout to appeal to the court of world and national opinion. For example, at first, the choice of targets for bombing reflected a determination to strike back tit-for-tat at North Vietnam. The reprisal targets after the mortaring of the Green Beret base at Pleiku in South Vietnam were barracks in southern North Vietnam. The decision a few weeks later to strike at North Vietnamese railroads stemmed not from a determination to destroy the enemy's transportation system but to counter a wave of bombs laid along the Saigon-to-Hue

> railroad. For a time, the American Embassy in Saigon kept a book on all terrorist incidents in the South so that these episodes could be trotted out not only to justify but to select reprisal targets in North Vietnam.
>
> Thereafter, the United States struck targets further north and of greater political sensitivity, including the North Vietnamese oil and fuel storage system in 1966. In 1967, *Rolling Thunder* began to strike selected targets in Hanoi and Haiphong, notably North Vietnam's power plants but also key bridges. The United States also now struck MiG-capable airfields. It's been a temptation for military writers, such as Admiral U.S. Grant Sharp, CINCPAC [Commander-in-Chief, Pacific], in these years, to see in this trend the slow success of their powers of advocacy. The JCS themselves seemed to think that by this gradual approach of their own, by repeating their initial demands often enough, slowly but surely the full weight of American air power was unleashed over the North. Thus, they at last brought the White House to accept the correct approach ... To me, the guiding idea behind *Rolling Thunder* in 1965 and 1966 was a "slow squeeze," a program of steadily increasing pressures that would increasingly bend and finally break the will of North Vietnam to continue its war against South Vietnam.
>
> ...
>
> During this time, American aircraft dropped more than a million tons of ordnance, more than on Nazi Germany and Imperial Japan. The tactical commanders wore uniforms, but the overall commander did not, because he was the Commander in Chief himself, Lyndon B. Johnson. Unlike more recent presidents, who delegated tactical military decisions to the service commanders involved, Lyndon Johnson kept the reins of power firmly in his own grip. You may recall his boast that, "The Air Force couldn't bomb an outhouse in Vietnam without his say so."[1]

Air and land bases in South Vietnam were built to support the expanded military operations and troop build-up. This required more personnel for base security. The vulnerability of land bases was not an issue with the aircraft carriers offshore. North Vietnam, a primitive country, could not mount a real attack against the carriers. Thus, naval air power was a key component in Operation *Rolling Thunder* tasked to project U.S. power in the growing war. The previous chapters illustrated photo-reconnaissance having a major role in the projection of American will in the effort to tamp down communist encroachment into the south. Going into 1965, the augmentation of VMCJ-1 would continue to support VFP-63 meet its commitments (Chapter 1). In this chapter, we focus on VFP-63's missions as the character of the war expanded to North Vietnam, with a resulting loss of pilots and aircraft, told by the pilots who were there.

VFP-63 Photo-reconnaissance in Early 1965

Yankee Team and *Rolling Thunder* placed a higher demand on photo-reconnaissance squadrons. One of the VFP-63 pilots who got that reconnaissance, was Lieutenant Roger Crim. His first WESTPAC [Western Pacific] deployment was with Det. A, CVW-2, on board USS *Midway* (CVA-41), October 1963 to May 1964. That was a period when detachments from both VFP-63 and VMCJ-1 were commencing *Yankee Team* photo-reconnaissance over Laos from Seventh Fleet carriers. He describes how he got his VFP-63 assignment and then his first detachment to a combat zone:

At the time I completed NATTU [Naval Air Technical Training Unit], Navy Photo School Pensacola,[xx] there were a surplus of graduates. Hence, a number of us were sent to VU-7[xxi] at NAS [Naval Air Station] North Island. It was during this first fleet assignment that I became aware of the view that "real" tactical pilots were assigned to VF [fighter] or VA [attack] squadrons. VFP, VU, VR, were a sort of second class. Therefore, when the fighter desk assignment officer visited VU-7, I believed that I had convinced him that I should be assigned to an F-8E fighter squadron. However, VFP-63 lost seven pilots during a six-month period in 1962–63. Therefore, those of us who requested fleet assignments from VU-7, and had attended photo school, were assigned to VFP-63. My first deployment aboard *Midway* was pre-Vietnam.

Aboard *Midway*, VF-21 was assigned as the VFP-63 Det. A fighter escort squadron. They were on their first F-4 Phantom II[xxii] cruise. The pilots were all specially selected, due to prior assignment or reputation. This, in combination with the detachment officer in charge, working closely with the Assistant Air Operations officer, an instructor of mine in Basic Training, gave the photo types a reputational leg up compared to the norm. One other addition to VFP-63 pilots' reputation was that we were now flying night operations off the ship. Since the VFP-63 detachments were the only tactical pilots to have a "real war" mission until February 1965, our standing rose further. It became a desirable assignment to serve as a photo escort.

The *Midway*'s return to CONUS [Continental United States], as we crossed the 180th Meridian for assignment back to 1st Fleet, was punctuated by the news of Lt. Chuck Klusmann's shootdown in Laos (see Chapter 2). It was believed that *Midway* might be turned back to WESTPAC, but that was not to be the case.

The Tonkin Gulf incident started on August 2, 1964. This certainly brought awareness of the potential of conflict during my next deployment with Det. L, CVW-19, aboard *Hancock* [CVA-19], September 1964 to May 1965. Nothing took place on *Hancock* deployment until January 1, 1965. After having our flight suits dyed green during the in-port Christmas liberty in Hong Kong, we readied for the start of photo-reconnaissance over Laos. In my case, the first mission took place on January 1, 1965. The war started in earnest in February, but I had been assigned the duty of ferrying a non-carrier-worthy detachment RF-8A from Cubi Point Philippines to NAS Atsugi, Japan. The aircraft had a spread-keel forward, it could be flown but not landed aboard ship. It had been off-loaded during an in-port period at Cubi Point.

Before flying to Japan, I was given a mission to photograph a highway in Laos. Some 55 years later, trying to recall with complete certainty, I cannot. However, I believe the route was from Phongsaly to Ban Phoukham. I remember that it was basically quite straight and oriented North-South. The altitude was to be somewhere around 10,000 feet. This is the only instance I recall of my being assigned only one fighter escort aircraft.

I was assigned the commanding officer of VA-212, Commander W. B. Muncie, as an escort. VA-212 had new A-4E Skyhawks.[xxiii] Inertial Navigation was new, and no other aircraft aboard *Hancock* had it. Of course, the photo pilots had no such luxury and had been trained to use WAC Chart [World Aeronautical Chart] contours and features, as well as dead reckoning to navigate. My

xx It was common to send photo pilots to the Navy's Photographic School for 11 weeks as part of their training.

xxi VU designates a utility squadron that is assigned noncombat services, e.g., transportation, liaison, etc.

xxii The F-4 Phantom was the Navy's choice to succeed the F-8 Crusader. It had two engines, a pilot and a back-seat Radar Intercept Officer (RIO). It could operate as a fighter or attack aircraft at Mach 2 speed.

xxiii The A-4E was a small attack jet. According to Lieutenant Crim, the trouble with using A-4s for escort was that their 20mm cannon had such long barrels that they were not very accurate.

intentions were to navigate to Vientiane, descend to the required mission altitude, commence the route mapping at the appropriate point, continuing north, to completion, then depart back to the ship. The photo recon pilot was always to be the lead, no matter that I was an O-3 [lieutenant] and my escort an O-5 [commander]. However, Cmdr. W. B. Muncie, so confident of the accuracy of his new inertial navigation system, instructed me that no matter, that I could look right below at the bend in the Mekong, and see the large city of Vientiane; this was not the time for descent. Not wishing to create a confrontation with a senior officer, the route was flown northward, descending much too late. We made a 180 degree turn at the northern terminus, and the mapping was actually accomplished *southbound* [emphasis added].

At some point after returning from the *Midway* Det. L cruise, I believe after we left for CONUS, tactical leadership advised that all photo-reconnaissance, unless special permission was granted, was to be conducted from above 10,000 feet. That lasted no more time than it took for the North Vietnamese to acquire SAMs [surface-to-air missiles]. My view before getting hit, was lower and faster had to be better. Therefore 150–200-foot altitude above ground and as near 600 knots [1 knot equal 1.2 mph thus, 720mph] indicated air speed as possible, was my criteria. I always thought that the reason enemy gunners got so close to me was a landline. Someone saw us and called ahead. My tactic was to be hidden from view, not coming around a hill into the view of the gunners, until quite close in.

The detachment also flew North Vietnam *Rolling Thunder* missions, interspersed with missions over Laos. On March 26, 1965, I was sent to North Vietnam to accomplish recon of five or six bridges, starting at Vinh and proceeding northward. Like most photo-recon missions, I was escorted by two F-8s, normally either F-8Cs from VF-24 or F-8Es from VF-211. In this instance, VF-211 was given the mission assignment. Lieutenant Rich Maughlin was the lead of the escorts. I was the primary lead. The next to last target was "Dragon's Jaw" bridge at Thanh Hoa,[xxiv] with the last target the Dong Phong Thuong bridge just north. However, that day, late in the afternoon, I can recall the high clouds in the sky, sun position fairly low, and no shots fired during our transit of Thanh Hoa. My memory is of how peaceful things were. Little did I know that all hell was about to break loose. We descended and accelerated around a small hill planning that the enemy would not see us coming. I turned toward the coast at a speed approaching 600kts and about 200 feet elevation crossing over the bridge. I saw tracers just to starboard out the windscreen, then felt a hit with a serious vibration immediately thereafter. I pulled up rapidly, attempting to be certain of getting "feet wet" and safety. The escorts never got a shot off. We had received no fire from any of the prior targets.

Then the vibration stopped with things seeming normal. I was advised by the escort that the starboard outer wing panel had been damaged. After reaching Rampage [call sign for *Hancock*], without further incident, I dirtied the aircraft up [lowered the landing gear, tail hook, and raised the wing] to determine how it would handle at approach speed. I could not fly more slowly than 145 knots, which was about 20 knots more than normal, at that fuel weight. If the aircraft were slowed further, it would roll to the right, which I was not able to reverse. The approach and landing were uneventful.

Once aboard ship, Lieutenant Crim saw the heavy damage to his wing. He describes the wing damage:

The RF-8 was built for speed hence the lightest possible materials were used. This seemed to cause no reduction in strength of the airframe. When you look carefully at the damage photo, it appears that the after portion of the starboard outer panel was struck by three 37mm shells. I believe my

xxiv The Thanh Hoa bridge was bombed many times over the years. It was heavily protected and very costly in lives and aircraft of all services. On October 6 1972, a Navy strike brought the bridge down (see Chapter 7).

F-8 Crusaders of Fighter Squadron VF-211 over the carrier USS Hancock *(CVA-19) prior to recovery on board the carrier during operations in the South China Sea in 1963. (National Naval Aviation Museum, Pensacola, FL)*

Battle damage assessment photo of Dong Phong Thuong bridge where Lt. Roger Crim's RF-8A was hit by AAA. (Lt. Roger Crim)

Lt. Roger Crim's RF-8A wing was damaged by 37mm AAA while taking photos of the Dong Phong Thuong bridge. (Lt. Roger Crim)

> altitude was so low that the shells did not arm but simply punctured the outer panel. The significant vibration I experienced was from the section aft of the damage, fluttering until it broke off and calm returned. I was very fortunate, in that the damage was aft of the spar [main structural wing beam] and furthermore, if the shells had struck just a bit more left, at the hinge points, the outer panel would have departed the aircraft with the following loss of roll control.
>
> My understanding of anti-aircraft guns is that the shells do not arm until a safe elevation is reached for the safety of the gun crew. I believe the shell to normally be of the proximity type. There were some that could be set to explode at a pre-set altitude. Antiaircraft crews do not wish shrapnel to injure or kill themselves. Therefore, I don't believe that the shells that struck my wing exploded. If that had been the case, the entire outer panel, at least the spar, would have been badly damaged. In June of 1965, another VFP-63 pilot, Lt. Cmdr. Frederick Crosby was lost at that same bridge [see his memorial this chapter]. The way his trajectory is described, it sounds as though his aircraft lost an outer panel.

The Aircraft Maintainers: The Vital Enlisted Team of Naval Aviation

When one looks at Roger Crim's battle-damaged RF-8A, the question needing an answer is, "How does that get fixed?" A group of hard-working enlisted technicians—graduates of Navy technical schools—are key players in the effort to keep an aircraft in an "up" status to meet mission commitments. In the case of Crim's aircraft, it most likely had to be sent to the Navy's massive Naval Repair Facility in Atsugi, Japan, or Cubi Point, Philippines. Replacing a major part of a wing is impractical on board a ship. Nevertheless, the carrier supported a substantial spare parts availability for the different aircraft aboard. For instance, spare jet engines were sealed in massive containers and hung from the hangar deck's bulkheads (walls). We photomates brought our spare cameras and test equipment with us, but the ship's supply department stored the massive viewfinder. The hangar bay also stored the ship's liberty boats—stacked to the ceiling—used for transporting the crew and officers to shore during liberty visits to a port that could not accommodate a carrier, requiring it to anchor a distance offshore.

The massive hangar deck is where most substantial repair takes place. Aircraft are lowered to the hangar deck from the flight deck by massive elevators. There, they are tightly parked into an organized jumble of various aircraft by the deft skills of the ship's deck handlers who often have to eke out the remaining available inches by hand-pushing an aircraft into position. It's an amazing choreography—and it has to be reversed to return the aircraft to the flight deck.

Once in position, the aircraft are securely chained to the deck which creates hazards for the night maintenance crew when only dim red lights are used while at sea. In a combat environment, the ship practices a black-out for its security. For the maintainers, navigating around and among aircraft to complete maintenance inevitably involved tripping over the chains and risking serious injury. In addition, running into sharp wing edges that can cut a head is another obstacle that makes working on an aircraft at night that much more dangerous. Heaven forbid you drop a tool, vital washer or screw that delays you further from completion, a shower, and hitting the sack. During night flight

With his engine still turning, this photo-recce pilot is directed into his carrier's hangar bay after completing a mission. (Cmdr. Peter Mersky)

VFP-63 Det. G, USS Oriskany *(CVA-34), 1965, RF-8 afterburner damage from AAA. It took four days, night and day, to repair this damage, with countless trips to the flight deck for testing. (Joe Nagel ADJC)*

VFP-62 crew doing major maintenance on the flight deck of the USS Shangri La *(CVA-38). The RF-8A is on a jack while repairing the front landing gear. Note the camera bays are opened for the photomates. The little window on the nose cone is for the viewfinder. Clearly seen is the Bay 1 forward firing camera window. (Larry Plourde PH2)*

Photomate testing cameras from the cockpit camera control panel. The panel is divided into four sections: his hand is on camera Station 1 (forward firing camera). To the right is Station 3; Stations 2 and 4 are on the bottom. On the instrument panel, top center, is the round lens of the viewfinder, used to see the ground beneath the aircraft. Above his thumb are two lights (left, amber blinking when the camera is taking photos; right, green indicating the camera is standby ready). Beneath the left light is a meter indicating how many feet of film are remaining. To the right is an on/off switch. Stations 3 and 4 have a rotary switch that rotates cameras for oblique photos. (Cmdr. Peter Mersky)

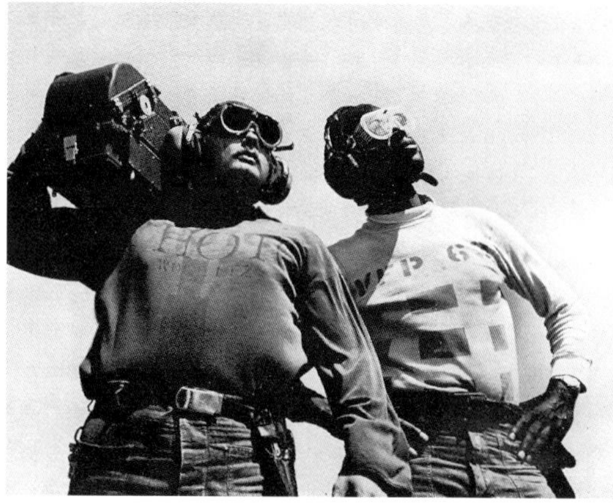

VFP-63 Det. B photomate G. J. Wollitz PH3 and structural mechanic H. E. Dunn AMS2 anxiously await the return of an aircraft from a photo-reconnaissance mission over North Vietnam. Wollitz is holding the large camera film cannister that will replace the removed mission film. (Capt. Len Johnson)

operations, the mess hall remains open all night to ensure everyone gets fed.

The Navy is scrupulous about preventative maintenance of its aircraft. At sea, corrosion control of aluminum-magnesium-titanium metal is a constant battle. In addition, the harsh landings and launches, not to mention the flight maneuvers in a combat environment, mean constant inspections for cracked metal are required. Every 180 flight-hours, the aircraft is partially dismantled for preventative maintenance. For example, the tail section is removed to inspect and replace vital engine parts. On occasion, the engine needs replacement and that process is very tedious. Seeing the giant J-57 engine disrobed is impressive. Once replacement or maintenance is completed, it has to be tested. The aircraft is backed to a special location where the tail can face the ocean and the mechanics go through various tests. Most enjoyed is testing the afterburner. The rest of us have to endure the screaming engine going through its paces.

Less major repairs could be done from the flight deck, which created challenges of its own. A changeout of a camera or electronic black-box is an example of such repair. We photomates rarely had to do repairs on the hangar deck. (The exception was replacing the massive viewfinder.) Our equipment was modular and could be swapped with a spare. Getting electric power to service the jet on the flight deck was a common problem. Finding a 3-inch diameter power cable, that worked and close to the area of the RF-8 was the first hurdle. It was heavy, often greasy, and in high demand by other maintenance crews. Sometimes the aircraft had to be moved (a large effort) to connect it to power. Nothing was convenient working there.

One dangerous flight deck repair was when a component, such as a large and heavy radio, required replacement, necessitating the technician to climb on the wing and fuselage to access it. The danger of walking on a slippery surface could result in sliding overboard—a scary thought that sobers the mind.

The pilots recognize the work done by their maintenance crew and it creates a special bond between officers and enlisted, seldom experienced by other branches of the Navy. Interactions aren't as formal, but military customs and military courtesies to rank are practiced. I have rarely seen it abused. Likewise, it would be rare to see a pilot be unprofessional to an enlisted man. We all looked upon ourselves as a special band of brothers, knowing that a pilot's life depended on us doing our jobs properly. Senior petty officers are key to making it all work successfully.

Lieutenant Commander Scott Ruby supports my assessment:

> I had complete faith in guys keeping the aircraft flying. In one case, I was strapped in and saw that I was leaking hydraulic fluid out of the starboard wing fold area. I got Chief Electronics Technician Ed Murray's attention, and there was a short discussion. He turned to me and gave me a thumbs-up; I prepared to go flying. Taxiing down the flight deck, someone was walking along holding a rag up against the wing fold area to keep hydraulic fluid from leaking onto the flight deck. The Air Boss, Commander Joe Muka, an ex-OinC in VFP-63, called and asked what was going on. I told him it is only a one-rag leak. 'OK—go flying,' he said. He fully understood what was going on. It turned out the hydraulic line was depressurized once airborne.

VFP-63's Detachments On Board 27C Carriers

VFP-63 provided detachments to some of the Navy's 27C (small deck) carriers. These included Midway-class and Essex-class straight-deck World War II carriers that had been retrofitted with catapults and angled decks for jets. Some had wooden flight decks and all had spartan living conditions for the crew. My first detachment was on board USS *Shangri La* (CVA-38), the "Shang" as we called it, and had no air conditioning for the living quarters. Ventilation air was supplied by ducts placed throughout the compartment. We had three vertically stacked bunks (racks)—each bunk had stretched canvas laced by rope to aluminum supporting frames. A thin, but comfortable mattress was placed on top, enclosed within a "fart sack," colorfully named by generations of sailors. All this topped off by a wool blanket and pillow. What else was needed?

Well, for one thing, especially in the tropics, cool air. Once on a Caribbean training cruise, the *Shangri La*'s water evaporators failed and fresh water was rationed, necessitating "Water Hours." On a carrier, the catapults get top priority, next the mess hall, sickbay, and the photo lab. Human consumption is way down the list. Navy showers were required: quickly rinse with salt water; soap down; very quickly rinse with fresh water. If you missed water hours due to required work, you had to go to bed dirty; and by the way, don't get caught violating the procedure by the ship's Sergeant-at-Arms. *Shangri La*'s captain permitted sleeping on the flight deck while in the Caribbean. Oily smelling tarps were issued and you had to make do, fox-hole style (mattress and fart sack not

Frank Bodden AZ3, from VFP-63 Det. 14 on board USS Ticonderoga *(CVA-14), circa 1968, in the enlisted men's berthing compartment. Note the sleeping racks typical of the accommodations of the 27C carriers. A third rack is under these two. Only air ducts (no air conditioning) provided ventilation. The quarters are tight and without much privacy. The Navy demanded cleanliness. Each man has a laundry bag, seen hanging from the top rack. (Frank Bodden)*

permitted). Sleeping under the stars on a hard flight deck, fully dressed, made for a long night—but it was cooler and the stars were beautiful. I did that for one night.

On board the *Oriskany* (CVA-34) in 1965, Aviation Machinist Mate 2nd Class, Joe Nagel, had to "hot bunk" with a VMCJ-1 enlisted man who used the bunk 7am to 7pm. This was more common on board older carriers, but the extra photo detachment made it necessary for a while. Hours had to be coordinated around shift schedules. On some deployments, cots were placed on the hangar deck for VMCJ-1 to use.

Living conditions for officers was a little better. Junior officers had a roommate in a small stateroom but still no air conditioning. Captain Len Johnson relives his experience on *Hancock*:

> My first impression of *Hancock* was the heat. I had never experienced sleeping in an oven. Only a few spaces on the ship had air-conditioning. My stateroom was four decks down and had a big steam pipe running through it up to the flight deck to power the catapults. No surprise that there was an empty bunk in that steam bath. That first night I lay there naked and completely soaked the sheet with my sweat.

The few air-conditioned spaces, where enlisted sailors worked or used, were sickbay, photo lab, intel compartment, chow hall, library, Gedunk[xxv] and a few other places. We aviation photomates became friends with our ship's company photo-lab counterparts to find respite from the heat.

VFP-63 Faces Lethal Danger from SAMs and MiGs as Rolling Thunder *Commences*

VFP-63's tactics initially followed the pattern of its East Coast sister squadron VFP-62's successful low-level reconnaissance during the Cuban Missile Crisis. There, the pilots flew in low and fast to avoid surface-to-air missile radar. While they did encounter

xxv A recreation area where you could purchase sodas, snacks, ice cream, and items from toiletries to expensive cameras and stereo equipment from a "ship's store." It also had a television that broadcast music (even a ship's disc-jockey) and news (ship and U.S.) from the ship's own audio-visual station. A popular place to say the least.

2CF VMCJ-1 Det. B, VFP-63 Dets. A, D and G, and VF-111 on board USS Coral Sea *(CVA-43), April–May 1965. An unusual concentration of marine and navy RF-8A recon detachments; they gathered for a secret mission that never materialized. (USN photo via Joe Nagel)*

Jerry Nolan, VFP-63 ISC, remarks on this North Vietnamese SA-2 SAM missile crew, "The SAM crew gets points for arts and crafts but that foliage isn't fooling anybody. The SA-2 is a big missile and when a site was occupied, the launchers showed up pretty clear on tactical recce photography." (National Naval Aviation Museum, Pensacola, FL)

anti-aircraft ground fire (AAA), the Cuban gunners were not effective in hitting the fast-moving jets. Not so in Vietnam. The North Vietnamese had excellent radar-guided Soviet weapons, both AAA and SAMs.

Another difference in Cuba, each VFP-62 mission was comprised of a senior lead pilot to navigate to the target and a VFP-62 wingman. That configuration allowed the team to maximize the coverage captured by the cameras. In Vietnam, mission requirements were different and that flight configuration would have increased casualties. There, however, escort fighters flew wing to the photo pilot and were required, especially if the target area might have a MiG threat. More on this later.

Even with the history of Soviet SAMs in Cuba, the Americans were shaken when photography from VFP-63 Det. D, flying from the USS *Coral Sea* (CVA-43), revealed the first Soviet SA-2 SAM site near Hanoi on April 5 1965. Now pilots had a new threat to deal with. The lethality of the SA-2 missile will also be discussed later.

The unusual group photo above is curious because of the number of recon detachments gathered on the *Coral Sea*. In researching this occasion, I was not able to find written information on the purpose of the gathering, but personal recollections of a few participants helped to piece together the following possible explanation: The *Coral Sea* was the flag ship for the Commander Task Force 77. Due to the photo evidence of the newly discovered SAM site, a secret operation was planned that required massive photo-reconnaissance to respond to the threat. The detachments were moved aboard at sea during the period May 3–27 1965. The crew moved by COD (Carrier On-board Delivery) and the equipment by helicopters. It never executed according to some enlisted sailors I've contacted. They did not know the purpose of the mission.

Lieutenant Commander Scott Ruby made four VFP-63 combat deployments, one on the USS *Ranger* (CVA-61) and three on the *Midway*. He says, "My one claim to fame is that I have more Crusader landings on the *Midway* than anyone else in the Navy." He describes his *Midway* Det. A's (March 6 to November 23 1965) chaotic experimentation of flight tactics over targets, as well as the dangers of *Rolling Thunder* missions they flew:

> It was not unusual for us to go in as low and as fast as possible, often below 100 feet, and above 600 knots. Depending on the airplane, we could get 625–650 knots [750–780 mph] out of it. We did have one escort fighter get hit while trying to keep up with us, an F-4 Phantom II flown by Jerry Sawatsky. He was in trail, took a 37mm through the wing, broke the main spar, but it stayed on. We all got back to the boat OK.
>
> There was a lot of sorting going on in 1965–66. VFP-63 was losing a lot of pilots [and aircraft] in the early stages of the war, mostly due to stupidity of the Rules of Engagement on how we should be used. We lost two of our three aircraft on our first line [carrier-combat position] period in 1965. I have the distinction of being the only guy that never got hit. Just goes to show that superior skill and cunning never beats black magic and pure dumb luck.
>
> On this deployment, our initial low-altitude restriction was 2,000 feet—they told us we couldn't get hit from 2,000 feet. There were no real guidelines provided, so we made them up ourselves. We were going after some stupid bridge and the Intel people wanted to know what type of construction

it was made of. They told us to go lower, i.e., below 100 feet. Stupid idiot! The type of bridges we were going after were those two-bit wooden bridges that a 500 pounder could easily take out—if they hit the bridge.

Flying at low altitude and high speed was an art in itself. When you are below 100 feet and at the speed of heat you DO NOT put your head in the cockpit. Set the radar altimeter to 100 feet and keep the red [warning] light on, otherwise the "cumulus granitus" will get you every time. I remember putting a row of trees and a rather large sand dune between me and a six pack of 37mm [guns] on one flight. I watched the bursts going off overhead until I was clear of them—that really got your attention. It turned out going low and fast was not the best way to go—and they were right—it lost some good people that way.

In 1971 on my final RF-8G deployment aboard *Midway*, the minimum flight altitude was 3,500 feet—no more losses to small arms fire. On all flights where there was a reasonable expectancy to run into AAA, particularly during *Blue Tree* missions, we always had the escort about one mile abeam, and a little stepped up, looking through us towards where any AAA was anticipated. Generally, it kept them out of the line of fire that might be aimed at us.

On one of our earlier strikes in 1965, the air wing went after some bridge up north, a precursor to the Alpha strikes.[xxvi] Willie (Bill Wilson), one of the other pilots in the detachment, provided BDA [Bomb Damage Assessment]. After the strike pulled off, Willie went in as fast as the RF-8G would go. It did not take the North Vietnamese long to figure out that if something got bombed, a photo pilot would soon follow. Stupid, but we had not learned our lesson yet.

He popped up over the target, took the pictures, and dropped down to the deck—running like hell. He left the cameras running—too busy to turn them off. Looking at the film afterwards, there were these two big bomb craters in a rice paddy a couple of miles down track from the strike. From the size, they were 2,000 pounders. The only aircraft carrying 2,000-pound bombs were the Spads [A-1H Skyraider]. We went to the VA-25 squadron and said, "OK, which one of you missed the target that far?" Nope, nobody raised their hand. After a stare-down, we said, "OK, it looks like we will have to go see CAG [Commander, Air Group] and show him the results." At that, one of the JOs [junior officers] admitted he did it. Seems the Spads were using 85-degree dive angles—literally hanging in their straps—better accuracy it seems. When it came time to release, he kept pickling and the bombs didn't come off. He finally realized he was LOW and did a high-G pullout, still pickling. The bombs finally came off during the pullout and he tossed them down the valley. We deleted those pictures for CAG.

Starting in Laos in 1964, a major air power role was to interdict the movement of North Vietnamese men and material into the South through "armed reconnaissance" missions. Armed reconnaissance means fighter or attack sorties flown not against designated targets but against targets of opportunity, along a particular stretch of enemy highway, railroad, river, or coast within a given area. If any were found, they had the guns and bombs to take them out. *Rolling Thunder* continued armed reconnaissance in a big way with unarmed photo-reconnaissance being part of it. Scott Ruby illustrates this with a mission photographing enemy boats on waterways:

On another occasion, involving VA-25 and PT Boats [Patrol Torpedo Boats], I was looking for a ferry that was supposedly in an inlet, a little north of Dong Hoi, again below 100 feet and as fast as I

xxvi Alpha strikes were used when it was needed to put a very heavy weight of effort on a single target complex in a very short period of time, either for the shock effect or because of the necessity to penetrate very heavy defenses, such as in the case of attacks in the vicinity of Haiphong and Hanoi.

A North Vietnamese supply dump burns after a strike by USS Midway *(CVA-41) attack aircraft, May 28, 1965. (Naval History and Heritage Command)*

An A-1 Skyraider of VA-25 "Fist of the Fleet" unleashes bombs on a target in South Vietnam during a combat mission from USS Midway *(CVA-41) in 1965. (Naval Aviation Museum Pensacola, FL)*

A VA-25 A-1 Skyraider "Spad" on board USS Midway *(CVA-41), circa 1965. The A-1 had 15 hard points to carry 8,000 pounds of ordnance. (National Naval Aviation Museum, Pensacola, FL)*

The danger of the A-1 Skyraider's four rotating propeller blades is apparent, as this one gets lined up on the catapult. Note the bomb on the right wing and the centerline fuel tank. (National Naval Aviation Museum, Pensacola, FL)

could go. I was taking fire from various sites and happened to notice, for some reason, that this "rock" was leaving a wake—also firing at me. Ah Ha! PT boat! I found a couple of attack aircraft, and they managed to kill a few fish. PT boats were instant targets. I went back to the ship and CAG put together a full strike that goes back up there and starts trolling.

A VFP-63 Det. A RF-8, from USS Midway *(CVA-41) in 1965, photographs its shadow as it passes a burning enemy PT boat. During the BDA sortie, the RF-8 was hit in the wing by a 23mm projectile but made it to Da Nang with major damage. (Lt. Cmdr. Scott Ruby)*

As near as we could tell, at least seven "rocks" got underway. They would just sit there in the middle of the inlet, wait for the A-4s to release, and then move one way or the other. With 15–20 bombers dropping bombs, they managed to only slow them down—also increased the food supply with all the fish killed. When they returned to the boat, CAG was really pissed. So, he sent four Spads late in the day loaded with napalm. One Spad would draw fire, and another Spad would make his run. They soaked down three PT boats and left them burning hulks in the water.

Willie was doing BDA on that one—again, below 100 feet. We got a picture with the burning hulk of a PT boat and the shadow of an RF-8 right next to it. What we didn't show was a few frames later with the same shadow, fuel streaming from the left wing. A 23mm round from another PT boat that was firing at him, went in parallel to the wing, and blew the top and bottom of the wing off—but it managed to stay together long enough for him to get to Da Nang. Willie was a three-fifths black ace that deployment.

Willie had to land wing down[xxvii] at Da Nang. At the time, Da Nang only had a single 8,000-foot runway. He also had to do a high-dive approach for the deck and land as best he could. He said he was being shot at while he was trying to land, increasing his problems; he also lost emergency air but was able to land. He told our officer in charge, Ray Dunkin, that the bird was flyable and I got sent to Da Nang to bring it back to the boat. I was Maintenance Officer at the time and I took my senior structural guy with me. At Da Nang we agreed to meet the next morning at the bird. I got bit on my knee by an unknown critter that night as I was sleeping on a borrowed cot in an Air Force tent, covered by netting. I woke up the next morning with pain in the knee and it started to swell.

When I met the structural gent that morning, the first thing he said was, "Mr. Ruby, I don't think the bird is flyable." [In the Navy, it is proper to address an officer below the rank of commander as "Mister."] Sure enough, it wasn't. A 23mm projectile had entered parallel to the wing about 6 feet out from the fuselage. The first thing it hit was the leading-edge spar which was shattered vertically, about a two-inch separation, and split from the fuselage to the wing tip. It also took out the emergency air lines, and fortunately Willie could <u>not</u> blow the wing up. My opinion was that the wing would have disintegrated had he done that. I still do not understand why the wing stayed on. Finally, the projectile exploded and blew the top and bottom of the wing off.

---

xxvii The Crusader had a variable incidence wing: raised for takeoff or landing and lowered for normal flight.

> I found the tip of the slug in the wing and gave it to Willie as a memento. By that time, my leg was swollen to twice its normal size, and I could not bend it. I found a Marine Corps field hospital and saw the doctor. His basic comment was, "Yep, you got bitten by something." I was given a series of anti-venom shots and by late afternoon the swelling had gone down. I released myself from the hospital.
>
> I managed to get the bird on an LST [Landing Ship, Tank] that was headed to Japan. It was sent to NIPPI [naval repair yard in Japan], where it was rebuilt and eventually put back into service.

Night Photography Over Vietnam

As Ruby wrote previously, "There was a lot of sorting out in 1965–66." One of the items on the Intel group's wish list was getting intelligence on enemy activity at night by aerial photography. They knew the North Vietnamese were getting supplies, military and domestic, through its main harbor, Haiphong, at night and moving it about. A little army of men and women was actively hauling supplies down the Ho Chi Minh trail under the cover of darkness. Thus, logically, it was thought the RF-8A should be used for the night-time interdiction effort. That was true in Laos and Vietnam.

The RF-8A did have a night photo capability. It used two types of flares[xxviii] for illumination: the M-123A-1 cartridge, rated at an intensity of 260 million candlepower, and the M-112 with 110 million candlepower. The smaller flares were seldom, if ever, used. The flares were installed in a compartment aft of the cockpit on top of the fuselage. Panels were removed and cartridges were installed in banks by an ordnanceman experienced in handling explosive materials. Scott Ruby provides more detail:

> Airspeed during a night photo run was limited to 400 knots. Apparently, there were times when the explosive charge kicking the "flashbulb" charge out had either deteriorated or was insufficient to clear the aircraft. There were indications that if the speed was more than 400 knots, there were times when the cartridge would bounce down the fuselage and punch holes in the skin of the aircraft. The RF-8 could carry 40 of the larger flares, mounted in two packs in the area behind the cockpit. The ship's captain did not like to launch night photo missions because it required the ship to go to strict EMCON conditions [restrictions on electromagnetic emissions to safeguard setting flares off] while the flares were being loaded. Loading the flares required the crew to use a ladder leaning against the bird while it was on the cat immediately prior to launch; not an easy thing to do and dangerous for the personnel. To my knowledge, the smaller flares were never used in combat, mostly because they were felt to be unreliable.
>
> On a prior deployment, I flew a practice mission into Korea. The Air Force said we could photograph the runway at Osan AFB [Air Force Base]. We sent a message to the Air Force, telling them the parameters, and what they could expect. Back came a message saying to stay 500 feet north of the runway. They said everyone would be wearing steel helmets. A lot of good that would do. When a cartridge is fired, a white-hot ingot comes out of the casing. When the charge goes off, the magnesium filaments ignite and fall to the ground. After the run, during which I fired all

---

xxviii "Flares" used here should not be confused with battlefield illumination flares that float down and illuminate an area for a period of time. These explode into a bright flash and then dissipate quickly (similar to a flash bulb).

> 40 cartridges, there was dead silence when we departed the area. About two weeks later we got this rather large package from the Air Force containing all the stuff that came out of the bird. It seems all the crud and corruption drifted onto the runway and fouled it. The sweeper could not pick it up, and they had to use personnel to walk the runway and pick all the stuff up by hand. We were told never to come back again.

The problem with the RF-8A/G night capability was it had no navigation system to assist pilots find their targets. The mission flight plan plotted a track on maps to the designated latitude and longitude of the point of interest. Prominent landmarks, such as roads, bridges, railroads, and factories, showed up on standard aerial charts. It was basic piloting to use a compass and second hand to time each leg of the flight plan. At night, the problem of navigation compounds the difficulties. Ruby describes the pilot-training challenges:

> Back at home base, the night navigation training syllabus the squadron used was pretty effective getting you used to finding targets at night. There were two basic options: there was enough moonlight to see the ground, or it was too dark to see the ground. When I was first in VFP-63 from 1961–65, there was a night navigation series of flights where you were given a series of coordinates on the ground where you had to go and identify what was there. It got you used to flying around at low level and navigating at night. I got pretty good at it after a while.
>
> These points could be intersections of roads, trails, power stations, or anything that could be properly identified. Except, on about the fifth flight, I went to a set of coordinates and it was in the middle of nowhere. I must have spent 20–30 minutes trying to find something I could identify. I finally gave up and told the photo brief guy, I could not find anything except the side of a hill. It finally dawned on me sometime later, there wasn't anything there, and the photo brief guy was testing me to see if I really knew what I was doing.
>
> If it was too dark to see the ground, you had to use a pathfinder. In the early days, that meant an RA-3B.[xxix] It did not have a particularly good navigation system. If we had been tasked during my 1971 deployment, I would have used an A-6 Intruder. This also meant no lights on and flying in formation. No use telling anyone where you were. Flying at night with no lights can be a little hairy. If it was really dark, I had the pathfinder put a flashlight up on his console where I could see it. If there was any kind of break required because of being shot at, the pathfinder would break left and I would go right, and we would rejoin somewhere upon mutual agreement. When it came time to fire the flares there were two basic methods to keep from going blind when the flares went off. One was called the blink method where you would close one eye when you felt the flares was [sic] expended. It never worked too well since you usually got out of synch. The most common method was to close one eye during the release of flares. Also, I squeezed off a half a percent of power, so I slowly drifted aft of the pathfinder so the danger of hitting him was significantly reduced, because you lose depth perception with only the use of one eye. Of course, the cockpit mirrors were turned inward to reduce the effect of the flash going off. Lots of fun.

Lieutenant Commander Ruby continues describing night photography in combat:

---

xxix RA-3B was a large, two engine photo jet equipped with a suite of cameras. The squadrons were designated as Heavy Photographic squadrons, e.g., VAP-61, and were well suited for mapping photography, but they were slower than the fighters and more vulnerable to enemy fire. This aircraft will be discussed further in Chapter 8.

An RF-8A Crusader and flares during a night photo training mission. The flares are shot out from a compartment behind the cockpit. Note the RF-8A is captured in the photo illustrating how the trail of explosions makes it easy for ground defenses to locate the jet. (Art Scarborough PHC)

> We were tasked with some night photography on the 1965 deployment. As long as I could see the ground, I could find the target. I was sent out a time or two when it was pitch black—could not see the ground. The idea was that the attack weenies would blow something up and I would photograph it. I remember watching the radar altimeter go up and down—never did I see the ground. The attack guys couldn't find anything either so we all went home. I had to salvo the flares over the ocean before landing on the ship.

Photography was accomplished by light passing through the camera's lens and blocked from hitting a light sensitive film by a device called a "shutter," which opened and closed at set speeds. When the photographer pressed a button to record something, the shutter opened the passage of reflected light to the film, the image was recorded, and the shutter closed until the next photo was taken. The cameras on the RF-8A used the same principle.

When a night photo mission was scheduled, the photomates mounted a light detector under the fuselage of the RF-8A. In flight, the light detector would detect the flares' light, send a signal to the camera's electronic controls to open the shutter to record the scene beneath the aircraft. The process would repeat automatically for the trip across the target. The RF-8A's electronic camera system would sequence the interval of firing the flares based on the altitude and speed of the aircraft. Air Force exchange pilot, Colonel Jim Morgan adds some insight on the RF-8A's night-photo capability:

> Night missions in the RF-8, for the most part, were a no-go, as navigation by moonlight was virtually impossible, especially if you had to take any kind of evasive action or were operating in an area of questionable chart accuracy, as we were in Vietnam. Also, in the RF-8 you had to remove the Radar Homing and Warning gear [SAM ECM] to install the photoflash cartridges that were used at night. That would not have been a good thing in an intensive threat environment like North Vietnam.

Of course, when pilots fly night missions, they first have to do a night launch from a carrier. All the dangers detailed in the Introduction exist with the addition of the darkness at sea. The red flight deck lights and maintainer flashlights help to navigate around obstacles and prepare the aircraft for flight. Everyone's adrenaline peaks, while maintaining a conscious awareness of the movements of aircraft lining up on the cats. The ground maintenance crew still has to perform their last-minute checks. Pilots freely admit that night operations raise the "pucker factor." I had one opportunity to stand between the two bow cats at night—my most frightening experience in the Navy. You were close to the jets on both cats, their engines at 100 percent power, and in afterburner, vibrated your organs as they whizzed by—you knew it was a very dangerous place and the experience never leaves you. Having done that, it makes you respect the courage of the enlisted flight deck crew, responsible for directing and connecting aircraft to the catapult cables. They work in close proximity to the aircraft with many opportunities to get hurt or killed. Without them, the aircraft wouldn't fly.

A VFP-62 RF-8G, on board Roosevelt, *being positioned next to A-4s in preparation for night operations over North Vietnam. (Jim Macino ATR2)*

A side note to this topic is that during peacetime, when VIPs were aboard, an airshow was frequently provided. The photo-Crusaders were loaded with flares and made their flybys with flares popping off behind them, simulating flak during combat. They were always a hit with the visitors.

As the war progressed, RF-8A night photography diminished and was supplemented by other recon assets. That part of the story is picked up in Chapter 8.

Political Leaders Start to Question the War's Strategy

According to Secretary of Defense Robert McNamara's memoir, *In Retrospect*, by the end of 1965 he was starting to question the war's strategic merits. The Commander-in-Chief, President Lyndon B. Johnson's forte was in the Senate where he was a master at legislating domestic policy and had little experience in foreign policy. Nevertheless, he was encouraged by an August Gallop poll reflecting "57 percent of the public approved versus 25 percent disapproved of the administration's handling of the situation in Vietnam."[6] According to McNamara, "In Congress, approximately ten senators and seventy representatives could be counted severe critics … but on the whole, the legislative branch remained supportive."[7] Antiwar protests were insignificant. However, Secretary McNamara remembers one protest that wasn't: "Then came the afternoon of November 2, 1965. At twilight that day, a young Quaker named Norman R. Morrison, father of three and an officer of the Stoney Run Friends Meeting in Baltimore, burned himself to death within forty feet of my Pentagon window. He doused himself with fuel from a gallon jug. When he set himself on fire, he was holding his one-year-old daughter in his arms. Bystanders screamed, 'Save the child!' and he flung her out of his arms. She survived without injury."[8]

With that and McNamara's urging, a reluctant President Johnson announced a temporary halt in the air war starting on Christmas Eve. Later, that deadline for the standdown was extended to the end of January 1966—the first of many stop-and-go pauses in the air war.

During 1965, VFP-63 provided detachments to eight carriers in Vietnam combat. Seven VFP-63 RF-8As and two VMCJ-1 RF-8As were shot down (one flown by VFP-63's Lt. (j. g.) Robert Rudolph), four VFP-63 pilots were rescued and four killed. The stories of the tremendous loss and sacrifice for naval aviators, their families, and country increased as *Rolling Thunder* accelerated in the following year.

By December, the U.S. force level in Vietnam was 184,300 troops, a 100,000 increase from July. Another increasing statistic: 1,594 were killed in action.[9]

1965 Non-fatal Combat Losses

On May 8 1965 a *Midway* VFP-63 RF-8A (Bu. No. 145620) was hit by AAA fire over North Vietnam, the pilot, Lieutenant W. B. Wilson ejected and was rescued. Lieutenant Commander. Scott Ruby provides additional information on this incident:

> On the morning of the 8th of May, *Midway* made the first ever strike on the Vinh airfield. The boss and I did the BDA on the morning strike. I was the decoy to get their attention, and Lieutenant Commander Ray Dunkin did the actual BDA. The attack weenies managed to get five bombs somewhere near the runway. CAG was pissed and ordered a re-strike in the afternoon.
>
> On our mission, the skipper, Commander James D. La Haye, of VF-111 was hit doing flak suppression, a poor choice for the use of F-8 assets. He ejected into the water off the coast. The remaining F-8s formed an overhead coverage mission at the crash site. There were a bunch of those little "putt-putt" fishing boats around and they all started heading for the crash site. The first F-8 rolled in and put a row of 20mm shells across the bow of one. He kept on coming. The second F-8 rolled in and put another row of 20mm across his bow. He kept on coming. The third F-8 rolled in and obliterated the fishing boat with a really big burst of 20mm. The rest of them turned away. Commander La Haye was not recovered.
>
> On the re-strike, we were down to one up-aircraft [ready to go], and it was Willie's turn in the barrel. We told him to not fly down the runway, use the panoramic camera [at a distance]. The runway was lined with trenches, plus numerous 37/57mm gun emplacements. Willie ignored us, and flew down the runway—at 500 feet, straight and level. They hit him with everything but the kitchen sink, probably because they could not get it high enough. His voice went up a few octaves I was told and he beats feet out over the water. He had holes all over the bird. I talked to his escort later on, and he told me he could see through the engine section. Not likely, but at least the engine was running.
>
> When asked what his fuel state was, he said zero—fuel system shot up probably. He managed to get his refueling probe out before he lost his utility system. The engine was running pretty rough, but at least it was running. He found a tanker and plugged in. They ran 2,500 pounds into him, or I should say, through him. He still said his fuel state was zero. Of course, most of it came out through all the holes in the bird. The bird was flying in a JP [jet fuel] fog around it. Finally, the bird decided it had enough, there was a huge explosion, and the engine finally quit—must have hit a live wire somewhere. "Texaco" [tanker] was not a happy camper, since he was still plugged in. Willie's RF-8 was on fire from the cockpit aft. He finally ejected, picked up and returned to the boat. That was the second time he got shot up in ten days. Did not listen too well. At least he got the first bird to Da Nang where it was given an honorable burial. That's also the one that got shot up by a PT boat.

★ ★ ★

On June 1 1965, another *Midway* VFP-63 RF-8A (Bu. No. 146881) was hit by AAA fire over North Vietnam; the pilot, Marvin R. Fields, ejected and was rescued.

Scott Ruby describes how a design vulnerability contributed to this loss:

> The RF-8A had some strange design features. There were places where PC1 and PC2 (pneumatic control systems) were actually tied together. In this case, Marv took a single, small arms round that hit exactly where the two lines were tied together. When he ran out of hydraulic fluid, the nose pitched down and he ejected over water. An inch or two either way and he would have been alright—the so-called golden bullet got him. This problem was removed when they went to the RF-8G version.

★ ★ ★

On August 13 1965, a *Coral Sea* RF-8A (Bu. No. 146849) was hit by AAA over North Vietnam and the VMCJ-1 pilot, Major P. A. Manning, ejected and was rescued. From Chapter 1, we read that Manning had several other serious hits to his aircraft on previous missions. He managed to safely land on those occasions.

Scott Ruby provides more details:

> In the early days, some detachments were augmented with [VMCJ-1] Marine pilots out of Iwakuni, Japan. Major P. A. Manning was one of them. He's up in Indian country, and got hit in the wing. The flaperon [control surface on edge of wing] on one side was shot off, and he only had control with his flaperon on the other side. He did not lose both PCs [pneumatic control]. He was flying the bird with full stick deflection, opposite to the lost flaperon.
>
> Major Manning managed to maintain a wings level flight path. He decided low-speed flight was not an option, and decided to do a controlled ejection. He got in touch with a small boy [helicopter], and they set up a procedure where as soon as the small boy got their gig in the water and they had mutual contact, he would eject over the gig. It came time, and he ejected. One hand on the stick, and one hand pulled the curtain. Ejection occurred and the seat pulled his hand off the stick, and the bird snap rolled before he cleared the rail. He felt a terrific pain in his back. The chute opened, and he was drifting down towards the water. He tried to raise his arms, but for some reason, he couldn't move them. He tried to say something and found he couldn't talk. He was paralyzed. Apparently, he broke his back. He landed in the water, unable to get out of his chute. The gig pulled up along-side, and apparently the boatswain asked, "Sir, are you all-right?" Of course, he couldn't talk and had a few unkind words to himself. The boat crew cut him out of his chute, and got him back aboard the small boy. He eventually recovered.

★ ★ ★

On October 8 1965, another *Coral Sea* VFP-63 RF-8A (Bu. No. 145617) was lost due to control system failure; the pilot, Lieutenant M. E. Dunne, ejected and was rescued.

In Memoriam

Lieutenant Commander Frederick Peter Crosby
June 15, 1933–June 1 1965
Lockport, New York

On June 1 1965, the RF-8A (Bu. No. 146852) flown by VFP-63 Det. E pilot Lieutenant Commander Frederick Peter Crosby, from USS *Bon Homme Richard* (CVA-31) was hit by enemy fire and crashed. The incident occurred five miles from Thanh Hoa Province, North Vietnam.

In 2017, *The San Diego Union-Tribune* reported:

> Two U.S. Navy planes came in fast over a bridge in Dong Phong Thuong, North Vietnam. Cloud cover forced them to descend extremely low. The enemy was waiting. Heavy ground fire erupted and the plane was on fire as it plummeted toward a fish pond. The RF-8A reconnaissance aircraft rolled before it crashed, spraying up water and mud.
>
> Lt. Cmdr. Frederick Crosby, a 31-year-old father of four, was listed as killed in action, though his body remained missing. It left his wife to grieve, pick up the pieces and provide a life for their children. Deborah Crosby—6 years old when her dad died, the family's only daughter—always felt a void in her chest, especially on each Memorial Day, when people mourn at the graves of the fallen.
>
> Deborah didn't start inquiring about her father's remains until the 1990s. The family left the topic alone before then, in part because of high anti-war sentiment in the nation. In 1973, nearly 600 American prisoners of war returned from Vietnam in airlifts called Operation *Homecoming*. Deborah remembers looking at the list of names. Her father's name wasn't on it.
>
> Eventually, her father's mother urged her to launch the search. She said, 'Frederick Crosby should be brought home and buried.'
>
> Crosby learned that the Pentagon's recovery branch, now consolidated as the Defense POW/MIA Accounting Agency, had conducted investigations and interviews as early as 1993 in search of Lt. Cmdr. Frederick Crosby's remains.
>
> There were two sites: One, where the Navy thought the RF-8A went down. Another, where Vietnam villagers said the aircraft crashed. In the end, they found an 89-year-old resident who

witnessed the plane going down. The man was close enough to be splashed with mud upon impact. He even kept a piece of the RF-8A's broken glass in his home. The bulk of the wreckage was hauled away by North Vietnamese authorities.

Deborah Crosby also learned that she needed to get mitochondrial DNA from her aunt, her father's sister, as it is best for identification of remains.

With that to go on, a Defense Department team excavated the fish pond between October and December 2015. They used buckets to empty the pond and then sifted through the mud. The pilot's wedding ring and clothes along with his bones were found in the pond.

In May 2017 Frederick Crosby's remains finally came home to San Diego—thanks to the tenacity of his daughter, the long memory of the U.S. Defense Department and the will of the taxpayers to keep searching for troops missing in action. The flag-draped coffin arrived at Lindbergh Field just after noon. Six sailors in dress whites met the plane on the tarmac.

Crosby's four children—now adults with salt-and-pepper hair and grown kids of their own—gathered to touch his casket as it emerged. They wept. 'It's nice to let out the tears and have relief in our hearts,' Deborah Crosby said afterward.

The decorated pilot was buried at Fort Rosecrans National Cemetery, virtually within eyeshot of the Point Loma house where his children grew up.

His headstone read, 'He is home.' She never remarried and died in 2002. Her side bore the inscription, 'Wherst thou goest, so go I.' It's from a pendant that Mary Crosby wore around her neck, made from aviator's wings.[10]

VFP-63 veteran Frank Bodden AZ3 was there and provided photos of the ceremony for this book. He wrote:

His ceremony was very moving and touching. There was the motorcycle self-appointed color guard in attendance, as well as, one elderly Medal of Honor recipient, and California State House of Representative Jackie Speier spoke at his services. Ed Velasquez [another VFP-63 veteran], who really was responsible for us going to the funeral, and I went up and introduced ourselves to his daughter, telling her that while we got to VFP-63 a year after her dad was shot down, we were in the same squadron. She was very appreciative to hear what little we had to offer.

Commendations

- ★ Distinguished Flying Cross (DFC)
- ★ Air Medal
- ★ Purple Heart
- ★ Combat Action Ribbon
- ★ Navy Expeditionary Medal
- ★ National Defense Service Medal
- ★ Vietnam Campaign Medal
- ★ Vietnam Service Medal
- ★ Navy Presidential Unit Citation
- ★ Vietnam Gallantry Cross
- ★ Naval Aviator Wings

Details of the DFC:

On June 1, 1965. Lieutenant Commander Crosby was leader of a two-plane flight launched from the carrier to conduct bomb damage assessment photography against a heavily-defended bridge site at Dong Phong Thuong, North Vietnam. Lieutenant Commander Crosby, because of cloud coverage at the target area, executed his run at an extremely low altitude in the face of heavy enemy ground fire. After completing the run, his aircraft was hit by hostile fire and crashed. His courageous and selfless devotion to duty throughout the run were in keeping with the highest traditions of the United States Naval Service.

Frederick is honored on the Vietnam Veterans Memorial in Washington, D.C. His name is inscribed at Wall, Panel 01e, Line 129.

Lt. Cmdr. Crosby funeral ceremony. (Frank Bodden AZ3)

Lt. Cmdr. Crosby procession to grave. (Frank Bodden AZ3)

In Memoriam

Lieutenant (junior grade) Charles Bernard Goodwin
August 2, 1940–September 8 1965
Haskell, Texas

Lieutenant (junior grade) Charles B. Goodwin from VFP-63 Det. C was the pilot of a RF-8A (Bu. No. 146826) on a combat mission in Quang Binh Province, North Vietnam, on September 8 1965. As a young 25-year-old man, he flew his aircraft off *Coral Sea* for his photo mission over Vietnam. Prior to launch, he was scheduled to have a fighter escort, but he elected to go single, stating that he thought the escort would draw more attention to him. Fifteen minutes into his flight, he reported he was caught in a severe thunderstorm prior to arriving at the target area and that was the last transmission heard from him. He was about five miles east of the city of Quang Khe.

Search efforts in the area were unable to spot any wreckage. It is possible a thorough land search was not necessary because of his bad weather transmission offshore. It was felt there was no evidence of death and a chance that Goodwin survived. Therefore, he was declared Missing in Action for the succeeding years.

In February 1988, a Vietnamese refugee provided information regarding the location of possible human remains and material evidence, including a military identification card for Goodwin. Between April 1993 and December 2016, multiple attempts were made by the Vietnamese Office for Seeking Missing Persons and Joint U.S./Socialist Republic of Vietnam teams to locate the crash site and remains of the pilot, without success. In December 2016, a Joint Forensic Review team received possible human remains that had been in the possession of a Vietnamese national. The remains were sent to the DPAA (Defense POW/MIA Accounting Agency) laboratory for analysis. Those remains were later identified as those of now-Lieutenant Commander Goodwin and his status was changed to Killed in Action.

The remains of Charles Goodwin[xxx] arrived at Dallas/Fort Worth Airport and were met by the Patriot Guard Riders (PGR), who escorted him to just west of Weatherford, Texas, where members of the West Texas PGR escorted him to Abilene, honoring this true American hero and welcoming him home after 53 years. He was laid to rest with full military honors (including a U.S. naval aircraft fly-over) during the service at the Texas Veterans Cemetery in Abilene.

He is honored on the Vietnam Veterans Memorial in Washington, D.C.: Wall, Panel 2E Line 78.

Commendations

- ★ Purple Heart
- ★ Naval Aviator Wings
- ★ Vietnam Campaign Medal
- ★ Navy Presidential Unit Citation
- ★ Navy Expeditionary Medal
- ★ Combat Action Ribbon
- ★ National Defense Service Medal
- ★ Vietnam Service Medal
- ★ Vietnam Gallantry Cross

xxx Rank was advanced to what his expected promotion would have been.

In Memoriam

Lieutenant Henry Sterling McWhorter
November 19, 1934–August 29 1965
Savannah, Georgia

On August 29 1965, VFP-63, Detachment G pilot Lieutenant Henry Sterling McWhorter launched from *Oriskany* towards his combat reconnaissance mission to Nghe An Province, North Vietnam. As he was about 25 miles northwest of the city of Vinh, his RF-8A (Bu. No. 146828) was hit by enemy fire and crashed. It was thought Lieutenant McWhorter may have safely ejected, but no parachute was seen and no emergency radio beeper signals heard.

He was given a slim hope of survival and was declared Killed, Body Not Recovered. McWhorter was listed among the missing because his remains were never located to return home. In February 1987, the Vietnamese discovered remains they identified as Henry S. McWhorter and returned them to American control. The U.S. confirmed this identification and returned the remains to McWhorter's family for burial in Hillcrest Memorial Park on March 6, 1987.

Commendations

- ★ Distinguished Flying Cross
- ★ Vietnam Service Medal
- ★ Vietnam Campaign Medal
- ★ Air Medal with Multiple Oak Leaf Clusters
- ★ Navy Aviator Wings
- ★ Purple Heart Medal
- ★ National Defense Service Medal

He is honored on the Vietnam Veterans Memorial in Washington, D.C.: Wall, Panel 2E Line 68.

Tributes and Memories

Lieutenant Commander Scott Ruby remembers Lieutenant McWhorter:

> Hank and I were in the squadron at the same time, a good guy and a friend. He wanted to be a Landing Signal Officer (LSO). He was on the LSO platform behind several other officers one night while *Oriskany* was doing Carrier qualifications (CARQUALs) with F-8s. He was in the back of the crowd observing. It looked like an F-8 was going to hit the ramp [rounded edge of the aft flight deck], and everyone jumped into the net. The F-8 successfully trapped [landed]. Hank, being low man on the totem pole, ended up on the bottom of the pile and had his leg broken—a simple fracture. While he was waiting for the corpsmen to come and get him, a later F-8 actually hit the ramp and everyone jumped in the net and landed on top of him again. Now he had a compound fracture.
>
> After healing, he fought tooth and nail to get an "up" [from the flight surgeon] to go on the next cruise. Finally, about a week or so before deployment, he got an "up" and away he went.

Fighter escort pilot Lieutenant John P. Humbert of VF-162:

> Hank briefed me on the mission he was assigned that day. We called it a milk run since it would be at 20,000 feet, would begin at the DMZ [Demilitarized Zone], when we would fly North up the coast line of North Vietnam to Thanh Hoa, taking pictures of all the coastal cities for intelligence. Our maximum bombing line, up to that time, was Thanh Hoa. As Hank briefed, if we picked up any flak which we both thought unlikely, we would "break right" out over the ocean. We also briefed what other possibilities we might encounter that were very long shots like MiG reports in our area, rescue options, etc. A typical brief for most flights over North Vietnam.
>
> It was a beautiful day that day, unlimited visibility all up and down the coast of North Vietnam. I flew slightly in trail of Hank's plane weaving left and right, from a little below and then above Hank's aircraft. We started our run North from the DMZ and as we flew over the city of Vinh I spotted some flak coming up to our altitude, most likely 50mm, self-detonating a little below and above our altitude but not very close, mostly ahead of us. I immediately called for a "break right" to Hank which I did. When looking back at Hank's aircraft, he didn't break right but kept heading Northward. My initial thought was that Hank had more, putting it politely, internal guts than I did. When I joined back up with Hank's aircraft it was straight and level, no doubt on auto-pilot for taking the pictures, but Hank's canopy was missing, the ejection seat tube extended into the jet stream, pieces of parachute on the back of the extended tube, and on his plane's elevator and vertical fin. When I flew under the plane there was a hole directly under where his ejection seat would have been, that I estimated to be about 6–8 inches round. No other damage to the aircraft at all except for the hole, missing canopy, and parachute pieces hanging on. After reporting what had happened to our controller and Search and Rescue notified, I took pictures of the entire aircraft top and bottom which air intelligence took from me for evidence.
>
> What I estimated to be about 10–15 minutes after the flak first appeared Hank's plane began a slight right wing low and drift down. After I told my controller what happened to Hank and that his plane was functional and flying, I was switched over to Search and Rescue. Before I left my controller's frequency, I asked what I should do about a pilotless airplane still basically functional. He said that the plane presented no hazard to anyone and they had it on radar if it became a problem.

I descended to sea level searching for any signs or pieces of anything but to no avail. I assumed Hank's plane eventually crashed into the ocean on its own. The initial report put out by the Navy reported Hank "missing in action," but to me and the people who I briefed, no doubt Hank was hit by what we called the one unlucky shot which actually didn't explode on contact with Hank's plane but just blew Hank out of the aircraft. I firmly believe Hank never knew what hit him before he was killed.

This is the first time I have written this story down to anyone. I only have told my wife and one of my sons what happened that day since my younger son became an Air Force F-16 pilot who was over in Iraq and Afghanistan. I thought he would like to know what can happen in war.

Viet Cong search wreckage identified as Lt. Henry McWhorter's VFP-63 RF-8A. This was the 500th U.S. aircraft downed by August 29, 1965 over North Vietnam. Official U.S. Navy photo dated August 30, 1965. Some retouching was done to highlight details. (Robert L. Lawson Collection, National Naval Aviation Museum, Pensacola, FL)

In Memoriam

Lieutenant (Junior Grade) Robert David Rudolph
February 26, 1942–September 8 1965
Encino, California

Oriskany lost its second photo-reconnaissance Crusader of the cruise when VFP-63's RF-8G (Bu. No. 146825) was hit by AAA while looking for SAM sites near Thanh Hoa. Soon after crossing the coast, Rudolph and his wingman, VMCJ-1's First Lieutenant K. J. Sienicki, were targeted as they flew BDA for an *Iron Hand* mission. Their flight was called into an area on Highway 1 about 25 miles north of Thanh Hoa to photograph some trucks that had been attacked by the A-4 strike group. As the two RF-8As entered the area at 1,000 feet and 600kts, they encountered extremely heavy light-automatic and 37mm fire. Robert Rudolph's aircraft was hit and his wingman watched him roll inverted and the canopy fall away, but lost sight due to his own evasive maneuvering. He was unable to see if Rudolph ejected prior to the aircraft impacting 15 miles northeast of Thanh Hoa. Though SAR efforts were launched, they were unsuccessful. Rudolph was reported missing and ultimately declared dead on September 8 1965. His body was not recovered. His remains were recovered on December 15, 1988 and identified on March 13, 1989. He was laid to rest at National Memorial Cemetery of the Pacific in Hawaii.

He is honored on the Vietnam Veterans Memorial in Washington, D.C.: Wall, Panel 2E, Line 78.

Three VFP-63 Det. A RF-8As from USS Midway *(CVA-41) pass over Mount Fuji, Japan. The top RF-8 (#916, Bu. No. 146825) was lost to AAA on September 8, 1965. Lt. (j. g.) R. D. Rudolph from VFP-63 Det. G, USS* Oriskany *(CVA-34), was killed. (Robert L. Lawson Collection, National Naval Aviation Museum, Pensacola, FL)*

Tributes and Memories

Aviation Machinist's Mate First Class Joe Nagel recalls:

> He wanted to go into combat. He would volunteer to stand Ready Cat with one of the F-8 fighter squadrons. He was one of the best officers I have ever served with. R.I.P. May God be at your side always.

Commendations

★ Air Medal
★ Vietnam Campaign Medal
★ Purple Heart
★ Combat Action Ribbon
★ Naval Aviator Wings
★ Vietnam Service Medal
★ Navy Presidential Unit Citation
★ Vietnam Gallantry Cross
★ Navy Expeditionary Medal
★ National Defense Service Medal

CHAPTER 4

1966: Operation *Rolling Thunder* Intensifies

In early 1966, the Johnson administration reassessed its Vietnam strategy. One year of *Rolling Thunder* failed to get the North Vietnam leader, Ho Chi Minh, to bend to American bombing pressure.

Naval aviators have been frustrated with their government's pursuit of the air war down through the years. Dr. Mark Jacobsen from the Naval Historical Center explains the complicated chain of command for target selection:

> In company with a handful of civilian advisers and cabinet members who lunched together almost every Tuesday and talked over national security affairs, Johnson determined not only which targets would be struck but the weight of effort of the total air war. Over this meal in the family quarters of the White House, he and his official family hashed over the issues and came up with a consensus on how the air war should be managed.
>
> …McNamara or Chairman of the Joint chiefs, Army General Earl G. Wheeler, conveyed the decisions of the Tuesday lunches to the Joint Staff, which passed the execute orders to the Commander in Chief, Pacific (CINCPAC) at Pearl Harbor. In turn, CINCPAC, a joint commander, distributed the execute orders to the Commander in Chief, Pacific Fleet and the Commander in Chief, Pacific Air Force. In turn, these service commands informed the relevant tactical commanders, the Seventh Fleet and the 2nd Air Division (later 7th Air Force). And down it went to the airmen.[1]
>
> The process by which the military made known its wishes operated in reverse, with CINCPAC coordinating requests for targets, sending a recommended list of targets and sorties required to the JCS [Joint Chiefs of Staff], who in turn proposed this to Secretary McNamara, who in turn sought the approval of the Tuesday Lunch Group. We have the testimony of Admiral David McDonald, Chief of Naval Operations for the period, that the Joint Chiefs frequently scaled down CINCPAC's requests to minimize friction with the administration. In practice, the lengthy chain of command did not work well. A 1975 Navy study of *Intelligence Lessons Learned in Vietnam*, now declassified, observed: Target lists issued by CINCPAC and JCS did not include those targets for which targeting materials had been produced [by tactical commanders]. Other [approved] targets were included that had been rejected on the scene. The lists [of approved targets] also included targets unknown to the strike forces that had been developed in Washington from photography and other sources not available to fleet intelligence.[2]

What could those "sources" have been? Most probably, U-2 high-altitude spy planes or satellite imagery. The above discussion regarding air war planning suggests tactical intelligence gathered by fleet recon assets, such as VFP-63's RF-8 Crusaders, had a poor chance of arriving at the desks of the Washington decision makers. This implies that RF-8 and other reconnaissance assets in Vietnam served mostly a tactical need for accomplishing and assessing tactical bombing efforts. In other words, bomb damage assessment, which was the "bread and butter" of VFP-63—reconnaissance obtained at great cost in lives and aircraft—was unlikely to be part of the intelligence briefings to Washington decision-makers. A good example is the repeated bombing of the Thanh Hoa bridge.

The air war continued to evolve by fits and starts. The beginning of another war year "was regarded by responsible Americans with a mixture of hope and concern—hope that the lull in the bombing of North Vietnam that had started on Christmas Eve 1965 would evoke some reciprocal action on the part of Hanoi to end the war, and concern for what might happen otherwise."[3] In fact, the North Vietnamese took advantage of the pauses and improved their defenses.

In his State of the Union message, President Johnson said:

> We seek neither territory nor bases, economic domination or military alliance, but fight only for the principle of self-determination—that the people of South Vietnam should be able to choose their own course, choose it in free elections without violence, without terror, and without fear. We will meet at any conference table; we will discuss any proposals—four points or 14 or 40—and we will consider the views of any group. Let me be absolutely clear: the days may become months, and the months may become years, but we will stay as long as aggression commands us to do battle.[4]

Reaction at home and abroad was generally favorable. Nevertheless, there was nothing in the peace message nor the holiday cease-fire to slow the thrust of the build-up of forces in South Vietnam. By January's end there were 200,000 Army, Navy, Marine, Air Force, and Coast Guard personnel in the country and more to come. Of these, the Navy had over 9,000 ashore and the Marines more than 38,000, which together exceeded one fifth of the total. Another 50,000 sailors and Marines were offshore in 100 Seventh Fleet ships.[5]

The political situation in the Republic of (South) Vietnam remained tense and continued into June and"

> …erupted in the sacking and burning of the American Consulate and Consul's residence in Hue by 500 to 800 Buddhist youths on June 1. On June 10 the government sent two companies of Saigon combat police and an Airborne Battalion to Hue to establish order. By the 18th, the Government regained control and had arrested the leaders of the 'Struggle Forces' or forced them to flee. Throughout the remainder of the month, Buddhist-led riots and demonstrations continued in Saigon but were effectively contained.
>
> Somewhat of a political landmark was reached on the 19th as the Nguyen Cao Ky Government completed its first year in office, the first of the successor governments to do so since the overthrow of Diem in November 1963.[6]

In February, the standdown of air operations in North Vietnam (NVN) terminated. By the first week of June:

> ...the tempo of operations started at a furious pace with more than 650 sorties over NVN. Attacks were directed against various lines of communications, supply areas and railway targets. One pilot reported box cars exploding 'like a string of firecrackers.' Waterborne targets were fewer, however, apparently due to the pressure against them during April and May. The rest of the month was punctuated with MiG engagements, as well as attacks on POL [petroleum, oil, lubricants] sites around Haiphong that caused severe destruction of oil reserves and concomitantly increased the pressure against Hanoi.[7]

The reader will note that with the previous VFP-63 shootdown tabulations, it is clear there were a large number of VFP-63 pilot ejections. Ejecting from an aircraft is always a hazardous event. The ejection seat is powered by an explosive device that gives the pilot a "kick in the butt." This is necessary to propel him quickly so he does not get hit by the vertical tail on his way out. The normal sequence is for the canopy to separate first, but if it does not, the pilot gets ejected through it, still attached to his seat. With a normal ejection, the pilot would separate from his seat automatically at a predetermined altitude.

When ejecting over water, new dangers face the pilot. Separation from the 'chute is critical so he does not get entangled in the lines. Many pilots facing this harrowing event were drowned when the parachute sank, dragging its passenger with it, or, if in front of the carrier, having the aircraft and pilot sucked under the ship into the gigantic propellers.

Should the pilot survive ejection and land safely in the water, he faced the prospects of getting rapidly rescued, especially in hostile waters. A number of pilots became guests of the Hanoi Hilton by being captured during this vulnerable time. With ejections increasing, the pilots relied on the SAR (Search and Rescue) squadrons comprised of skilled and brave men.

On the last four-fighter mission of an 11-month deployment, from USS Coral Sea *(CVA-43) in 1965, VF-154's Lt. (j. g.) Jack Terhune's F-8 Crusader was hit by AAA. His wingman, Lt. Jim Ginn, is seen tucked-in very close to check his crippled aircraft for damage. Note the tail hook and speed brake (under fuselage) are down to slow the jet for ejection. (Lt. (j. g.) Al Zink via Lt. Terry Stent)*

Ejection sequence begins: wingman has moved out; canopy is seen floating (above and to right of wingman). The pilot is ejected. (Lt. (j. g.) Al Zink via Lt. Terry Stent)

Lt. (j. g.) Terhune is still in his seat and his wingman maintains his distance as two other Crusaders are now out of sight but watching the ejection. (Lt. (j. g.) Al Zink via Lt. Terry Stent)

Lt. (j. g.) Terhune is still in his seat and his parachute has opened. The seat will automatically detach at a lower altitude. VFP-63's Lt. (j. g.) Al Zink had been listening to the earlier conversation while at a lower altitude. He decided to join the group to take oblique photos of the ejection. (Lt. (j. g.) Al Zink via Lt. Terry Stent)

For January through June 1966, naval air operations over Vietnam lost a total of 170 aircraft and 133 airmen. Eighty-five of those were rescued. The first loss for VFP-63 was on April 19 when Lieutenant Ron Ball's RF-8A (Bu. No. 146843), from USS *Ticonderoga* (CVA-14) Det. B was hit by AAA (anti-aircraft artillery). Detailed accounts by fighter pilot Lieutenant Hal Loney from VF-53, followed by those from a SAR helicopter pilot, provide for us the danger and excitement of getting hit, ejecting over water and being rescued. Lieutenant Loney:

> Again, I was assigned to fly escort on a photo mission to determine what type of AAA had been moved into the karst ridge area from which an aircraft was shot down during egress from a raid on Hanoi the day before. Since we had flown together many times, and taking the actual photos over land was to take less than three minutes, VFP-63 pilot, Lt. Ron Ball, still exuded confidence, even during the rather short briefing. I was to lead [the photo pilot usually was the lead], ostensibly due to having a radar with which to pinpoint coast-in location, pop up to 500 feet then pass lead, so Ron could take forward-looking photos crossing the beach, breaking 90 degrees, take lateral photos, then 90 degrees again descending back down to wave tops and egress.
>
> But on this day, neither of the two carrier air wings' joint three-or-four-mission raids into the North, with many different types of aircraft per mission, nor rooster tail flat-hatting [flying fast and low over the waves] for some 30 minutes, diverted attention from our two Crusaders—for when we passed some fishing boats and popped up—the AAA lit up. Ron crossed the beach, with tracers going in several directions, then he broke 90 degrees. While he was belly up

> to me, a tracer crossed my nose entering the center of his aircraft hitting the main fuel cell, and immediately catching fire. I broke radio silence with a couple of "Ron?" pause, "Ron?" Then he finally and calmly responded, "I think I have been hit." Which I confirmed by telling him he was on fire and to "go gate" [max power]. Ron smoothly pulled around and down toward the water to get under the AAA and out to sea. Quickly passing the fishing boats and out of range of shore guns, he started a smooth climb while I was calling for support and RESCAP [rescue carrier air patrol].
>
> At approximately three or so thousand feet I told him that I could see through the holes in his aircraft, both main gear and hook [landing gear and tail hook] were hanging out, burning, and to think about getting out. He said, "Temp is going through 1,000 degrees. I'll see you back at the ship." The canopy came off, seat came out, aircraft exploded within a fraction of a second and then, the separation and beautiful chute. The rescue went well and as someone has said: "the rest is history." [Captain Ron Ball passed away in July 2013.]

This following, wonderfully narrated account from the anonymous HS-4[xxxi] rescue helicopter pilot describes how the rescue was accomplished:

> I [rescue pilot] brought the helicopter into a hover over the pilot who was still in his raft. That always caused a problem because the rotor wash pushed the raft across the water, at times with surprising speed.
>
> "Pilot, after station, the survivor is still in his raft," my crewmen said.
>
> "Roger, after station. I'll keep it in a high hover."
>
> That meant I would hover at sixty-feet to limit rotor wash, but shortly after that, the after station called to say that we were too high. Not watching my instruments, I had inadvertently climbed to a ninety-foot-high hover. Was there a little adrenaline running through my body or what? Regardless, my mistake took valuable time, and time was the enemy. Fortunately for everyone, as I lowered the helicopter to the proper altitude, the pilot exited his raft. Shortly thereafter, we had him aboard.
>
> By now the Seventh Fleet photographer was shooting away with his camera and, in the process, he got the first actual photos of a combat rescue in North Vietnam. The picture that was on virtually every major newspaper across the country, showed Lieutenant Ron Ball looking up as he was being hoisted aboard Big Mother–six eight [helicopter's identification]. I told the lieutenant that we had just made him famous, but he had no idea what I was talking about.
>
> Lieutenant Ball had been flying an RF-8G, photo-reconnaissance aircraft, from VFP-63 off *Ticonderoga* when he was shot down. He was on his last flight of the cruise and told me that as he sat on the catapult that day, he knew he was going to get "bagged." I don't know if it was last-flight jitters or if he had a real premonition, but for whatever reason, he was right. As he made his photo run across Haiphong, he was hit and had to eject. In his chute he saw his aircraft explode shortly after he exited.
>
> We hoisted him into the helicopter within about twenty minutes of the shootdown, and I told the crew to sink his raft with the M-60 before we departed the area. I didn't want someone to see it and have us called back into that area to search for what we had already picked-up.
>
> With that last chore taken care of, we headed to the relative safety of the open ocean. At that point, however, we got the call I did not ever want to hear.

---

xxxi HS-4 was an anti-submarine squadron flying the Sikorsky SH-3A helicopter. During the 1966 cruise, the pilots and crew rescued 24 downed airmen under hostile fire, a record for a single deployment.

Lt. Ron Ball of Det Bravo was shot down on April 19, 1966 during a photo mission. After ejecting from his RF-8A (Bu. No. 146843), he was rescued by an SH-3A of HS-4 from USS Yorktown *(CVS-10). Ball has inflated his personal flotation bags, and his survival radio dangles below the left bag. (Cmdr. Peter Mersky)*

Navy destroyer: "Big Mother this is 'Steel Hawser'. Bandit bearing two-eight-five at sixty-five miles, tracking one, zero, five degrees."

...

By all appearances, we had a MiG coming after us, and there was nothing we could do about it except run. We headed back out to sea skimming off the top of the waves and going as fast as the helicopter could possibly go. The red line on our airspeed indicator was there for decoration only. We continued to get the bandit calls, but in the end, the contact came to the beach and turned around, with us never seeing him or him seeing us. That was just fine with me. Because of the considerable missile capability of the destroyer USS *Coontz* (DLG-9), he did not want to come out over the water. Had he ventured just a little farther, the hunter would have become the hunted. That did little to settle my nerves until he turned back inland, however. I hate to think of myself as bait.

We returned to North SAR station, USS *Yorktown* (CVS-10), with our wet but otherwise fine RF-8 pilot ... That guy had no idea just how lucky he had been, first to have just been present when we made a pick-up and secondly, that this had been a relatively easy pick up with little opposition, and he didn't get shot in the process ... It was late in the afternoon, just before dark, when we retrieved Lieutenant Ball for the flight back to his carrier. He had been treated to some dry clothes and pretty much wined and dined all afternoon. Now it was back to the real world of carrier aviation. *Ticonderoga* was a little more than an hour south of us, and they were waiting for the return of their pilot so they could depart Yankee Station. They were finally headed home after a tough deployment. When I reported in with them on the radio, I got exactly what I expected: "Big Mother, this is Panther [carrier tower control], expect a Charlie on arrival."

That meant I could expect to be cleared for an immediate landing just as soon as I got there, but I was ready for them, and it was my game now.

"Negative Panther. We don't intend to return your pilot without a suitable ransom."

"Roger Big Mother, what would you consider a suitable ransom?"

"Tower, we would consider a gallon of ice cream and five spoons just about right," I replied.

When I set the SH-3 down on Tico's deck, people welcoming Lieutenant Ball home surrounded us. As he exited the helicopter to a hero's welcome, a huge cake was shoved in the after station along with a five-gallon drum of ice cream. We launched into the inky night for the short flight over to *Yorktown*. We ate cake and ice cream, but by the time we finally landed, we had melted ice cream all over everything. Five gallons was just too much.

An SH-3A Sea King of HS-8 refuels from the destroyer USS Carpenter *(DD-825) during operations in the Tonkin Gulf in October 1967. This is called a Helo In-Flight Refueling or HIFR. Most of the "Tin Cans" in Vietnam did not have a helo landing capability, but most could do a HIFR which allowed the helos to continue their mission. (National Naval Aviation Museum, Pensacola, FL)*

Many of the VFP-63 pilots on war detachments were very young men. These so-called "nuggets" were inexperienced pilots and had to learn on the job, while taking their share of new-guy harassment in the ready rooms. They had much to prove but showed the same naïve youthful spirit that previous generations of aviators had, looking forward to the excitement and challenges ahead—and the urgent need to prove themselves. One such nugget, (then) Lieutenant (junior grade) Len Johnson, shares his entry into this exclusive club:

In the spring of 1963 Lt. Wright showed up on the Bowdoin College campus recruiting seniors for Naval Flight Training. This seemed like a good idea at the time, considering that I didn't have any other ideas for what to do with myself. It was great fun for two years learning to fly Navy aircraft, but three years later, getting shot at over North Vietnam, I realized that I had again made a bad decision.

I reported to my first fleet squadron (VFP-63) at NAS [Naval Air Station] Miramar in September 1965. The Naval Aviator "Wings of Gold" on my blouse were bright and new.

Without giving it much thought, or consulting with my wife, I walked into the Skipper's office and volunteered for duty flying over North Vietnam. I had not completed my training, had very little flying time, and, of course, no combat experience. I was a disaster waiting to happen. The commanding officer (CO) didn't give it much thought either. He accepted my offer on the spot! Obviously, I had solved a problem for him. It was a really dumb thing for me to do. I wasn't at all ready for what awaited me.

The following two weeks was a whirlwind of activity. I had to relocate my wife and month-old son to another state. And, I needed to complete night carrier qualifications. A few priority messages [wartime urgent] were sent, and one night I got exclusive use of an aircraft carrier deck. I think it was *Ticonderoga*. It was kind of lonely flying out there by myself, but turned out to be pretty routine.

Lt. (j. g.) Len Johnson, "Rocky the flying squirrel", VFP-63 Det. L, USS Hancock *(CVA-19), 1966. (Capt. Len Johnson)*

VFP-63 Det. L, USS Hancock *(CVA-19), 1966 enlisted: (L–R) (Kneeling): J. W. Dannelly AN; W. H. Gilbertson AE3; M. R. Brands AT3; F. B. Bodden AN; R. M. Stow AE3; E. M. Jordan ADJ2; W. C. Moody PH3; and E. J. Lujan, Jr. YNSN; (Standing): R. E. Bennett PT3; K. L. Channel AME1; R. R. Silver ADJ3; W. J. Williams AMH2 J. G. Simmons AT1; R. R. VanCourt AMS1; J. M. Sullivan AO3; B. M. Anderson PH1; J. R. Re AK2; and T. G. Rose, AN. (Capt. Len Johnson)*

VFP-63 Det. L RF-8G making a flyover of the USS Hancock *(CVA-19) 1966. (Capt. Len Johnson)*

My mind was already looking ahead to events awaiting me on the other side of the Pacific. This was just another box that had to be checked on my way there.

The RF-8 is not an easy aircraft to bring aboard a 27C [small deck] carrier at night. Completing night carrier qualifications in a Crusader was a source of pride, but no tie-cutting at the Officer's Club followed this one. I drove home and went to bed.

The time interval between walking into the Skipper's office and landing on *Hancock* [CVA-19] two weeks later was a blur. I had boarded an express train to my destiny. My fate was no longer mine to influence. It certainly was not going to be my skill that would get me home.

Assignment to RF-8 flying during wartime, although dangerous, was a great opportunity for a new pilot. Instead of flying on a senior pilot's wing for a year, the nugget RF-8 pilot was completely on his own. I planned and led 100 flights into North Vietnam. I flew very fast and very low. What young kid doesn't dream about that?

The basic rules of survival were: don't fly below 3,000 feet (anyone with a pea shooter can hit you down there), go very fast (600 knots plus), and keep the airplane constantly moving around the sky.

Unfortunately, to take photos it was often necessary to fly straight and level at 3,000 feet over a fixed point. This greatly simplified the shooting geometry for the guys on the ground. Often the gunners didn't bother with geometry. They could see the patch of sky we intended to penetrate. Their gunnery solution consisted of merely filling that patch with lead and letting the "recce" [recon bird] fly through it.

Four weeks after I reported aboard Detachment L, Lieutenant John Heilig, our operations officer, was shot down. He was taken prisoner and thank goodness he survived the war. Lieutenant Len Eastman, his replacement, was with us for only two weeks before he met the same fate. He, too, was taken prisoner and eventually returned home. The squadron did not send us any more replacements.

Detachment L for most of the cruise had only three pilots instead of the allotted four. In all, nine naval aviators were assigned to Detachment L during *Hancock's* 1965–66 WESTPAC [Western Pacific] cruise. Three refused to go. Three were brought down by enemy fire. Only three of us went and came back at the end of the cruise. Unfortunately, one died.

The Rescue Attempt of a Downed VFP-63 Pilot Leads to a MiG Dogfight

On June 21 1966, three *Hancock* F-8E pilots from VF-211, after providing TARCAP [target combat air patrol] for a strike on a highway bridge near Haiphong, joined the search for a downed VFP-63 Det. L RF-8A. The pilot, Lieutenant Len Corbett Eastman, had ejected and reported over his survival radio where he was located and that he was about to be captured. His VF-211 F-8E escort pilot, then-Lieutenant Richard "Snuffy" Smith describes how this shootdown occurred and the dogfight with MiGs that happened afterwards:

I was the escort pilot for Lt. Len Eastman. He was taking photos of the rail-line, I think it came out of China and ran to Hanoi. We were several miles north of Hanoi heading south towards Hanoi. I had backed off a few hundred feet so I could look for ground fire and also maybe spot MiGs, as there were two enemy airfields just to the west. As an escort, you were unable at times to give any warnings and you always felt that you might have missed something, such as ack-ack, all the time checking for MiGs. I did not see any antiaircraft fire until after I saw his aircraft streaming fire from his tailpipe. They must have hit him with the first shot. As briefed, he immediately broke left toward the high mountain range to our west. He ejected well before reaching the range.

I sent a mayday and tried to keep him in sight, but was under heavy fire myself. I made two passes over where I thought he went down, drawing heavy fire both times. As I came over the ridge the second time, I saw Lieutenant Commander Cole Black's flight of three F-8s. Cole was senior officer so he took over the flight. One of his wingmen, Lieutenant, Junior Grade Phil Vampatella, joined on me. I made one more pass to point out where I thought he probably was. On this pass Phil took a hit and Cole thinking we were low on fuel instructed us to go out and tank [refuel].

An ordnanceman on board USS Hancock *(CVA-19) pushes a load of AIM-9 air-to-air Sidewinder missiles, circa April 1967. (National Naval Aviation Museum, Pensacola, FL)*

We were at low altitude heading for the coast when we heard Cole call, "MiGs!" I checked my fuel and made a one-eighty heading back. Phil, his aircraft having a pretty good hole in his UHT [universal horizontal tail] was unable to make the tight turn and fell behind. I saw two MiGs and headed for the nearest one even though I was out of position, as we were almost head on and I was climbing and the MiG was diving towards me. Even though it was a high angle, I got off a quick burst [20mm cannon]. As I went right over the top of him, I heard Phil call out, "F-8 you have a MiG on your tail!" Thinking it was probably the other MiG that I saw on my six, I dived for the deck to get some higher airspeed, all the time checking my six. Actually, it was Cole that Phil saw and then he saw Cole take a hit.

Lieutenant Gene Chancey engaged the second MiG section with a burst of 20mm cannon fire, after which fuel was observed streaming from one of the MiGs. He then fired a Sidewinder, but it failed to guide.

About that time, Lieutenant Vampatella saw some tracers come by his cockpit, so he hit the burner and was trying to outrun the MiG, which he did. Even though his jet was low on fuel and had problems turning due to its battle damage, he decided to engage the MiG. He made a 180, got a good tone on a Sidewinder,[xxxii] which guided perfectly and exploded at the tail of its quarry. When last seen, the MiG was trailing black smoke and spiraling off in a steep turn. In view of this, the action was evaluated as a confirmed kill. With his damaged F-8E, down to 200 pounds of fuel, Vampatella fortunately made a successful rendezvous with an A-4E tanker, low on fuel itself. However, he was just able to make it back to his carrier with no fuel to spare for a second go-round. On inspection, he discovered that his Crusader had been hit in the tail by a 37mm flak round and was peppered with small shrapnel holes. Lieutenant Vampatella received the Navy Cross for the action.

After getting my airspeed up I went vertical and saw a MiG way off as he headed west. Being extremely low on fuel I headed out for a tanker. All three of us were really split up and found the tanker and recovered on the *Hancock*. I never did see Cole's other wingmen until back on the carrier.

This complex combat event, of four VF-211 F-8Es, (three strike escorts and Lt. Eastman's escort, Lt. Richard Smith), illustrates the selfless code of bravery of protecting a downed aviator. They continued to circle Lieutenant Eastman's position while taking fire themselves. That bravery led to Lieutenant Commander Cole Black being shot

xxxii The AIM-9 Sidewinder was the standard short-range, supersonic, heat-seeking, air-to-air, missile carried by the U.S. Navy on its F-4 Phantom and F-8 Crusader fighters. The pilot would get a high-pitched tone in his headset when the missile locked on to its target.

down by a MiG while he engaged the first MiG section and Lieutenant (junior grade) Phil Vampatella getting hit by AAA.

Captain Cole Black describes his shootdown

In the late-fifties, Cole Black flew F9F-8P Cougars and RF-8As for VFP-62. On June 21, however, he was a fighter pilot in the middle of the MiGs vs. Crusaders gaggle detailed above. He was one of three Crusader pilots known to be shot down by MiGs during the war. He described how it unfolded during a speaking tour:

> On June 21, 1966, I was flying escort for a flight of bombers targeting a bridge near Haiphong, deep in North Vietnam near the China border. Everything went well—not a MiG showed up and the bombers hit the bridge without any trouble—until a reconnaissance plane [VFP-63's Len Eastman] was shot down. The pilot of the downed RF-8A was a good friend of mine, and Lt. R. 'Snuffy' Smith who was escorting the recce [recon] plane was low on fuel.
>
> I went up there, saw the airplane burning on the ground and made a turn, being very careful to duck the flak site that was shooting at us. Just as I was coming around, I saw the orange smoke flare from the downed pilot. I reported it to the air wing commander, who said to make one more turn and see if he'll come up on his survival radio and tell us if he's okay.
>
> I came back around, and just as I was going to turn left, I heard my wingman say, "There they are fellows!" I looked up and there's four MiGs coming at us, a little bit above us, but they hadn't even seen us yet. I knew I had to engage them because we didn't want them jumping on the bombers. So, I bent that airplane around to the right as hard as I could pull it. I was going to pull inside of the flak site. About halfway through the turn my wingman said, "You took a hit, Nickel [squadron call sign], you've got smoke trailing."
>
> I didn't really care and continued my turn and then tried to roll out but the controls were really sluggish. I booted the rudder and got the plane level, but then had another problem. I looked in the rearview mirror and there's another MiG coming in at about 5 o'clock. He was already shooting at me, so I pulled back on the stick and got the nose up maybe ten degrees, and that took all the rest of the hydraulic fluid in that airplane. When the Crusader loses all its hydraulic fluid, it goes into a violent nose-over pitch, and of course that throws the pilot up against the canopy. I'm stuck up there, and I know I've lost it then. My last transmission on the radio was, "This is Nickel One. I'm getting out." and then I went for that curtain [ejection seat handle].
>
> The canopy came off the airplane, but the damn seat didn't go. Now I'm sitting in the seat, still doing 500 knots and headed toward the ground. The face curtain blew out so I could see the ground, and I was very highly motivated. I got that face curtain and yanked on it once more with all of my strength, and the next thing I heard was a bang. I came out of the airplane, the chute opened and made one swing before I was on the ground. That's why I say those classmates back in school who taught me that physical fitness was probably a good thing, helped save my life that day.[8]

Unfortunately, the attempt to protect the downed Crusader pilots failed. The SAR helicopter got lost and never showed, and both Black and Eastman became prisoners of war (POWs). They spent nearly seven years as POWs in North Vietnam. It's ironic, Len Eastman was the replacement for VFP-63's Lieutenant John Heilig, who was shot down and taken prisoner on May 5. They were repatriated on February 12, 1973 during

Operation *Homecoming* with 566 other military POWs. Cole Black retired in July 1986 as a captain after 36 years active-duty service. He died November 20, 2007 as a passenger in a Piper Aerostar 602P.

A Forgiving Engine Saves a Pilot's Life

On the 1965–66 *Hancock* detachment, Lieutenant Len Johnson learned to love the Crusader's Pratt & Whitney J-57 engine:

> I was over the Gulf, headed for Haiphong, NVN's main harbor where all the Russian-made SAMs [surface-to-air missiles] were off loaded. Ten minutes out, my wingman told me he saw what looked like a film of fluid on the lower fuselage of my Crusader. I checked my gauges and saw nothing amiss. "It was probably some excess hydraulic fluid that had pooled in the engine bay and was now leaking out," I thought. F-8s are well known for bleeding hydraulic fluid. I continued on.
>
> Skimming along at 500 knots, just above the wave tops, in Haiphong Harbor, weaving around ships and islands of karst, about to pop up for a photo run, the red engine warning light illuminated brightly. This was not good. My gaze dropped quickly to the small oil pressure gage. The needle was as far left as it could go—zero! Now I knew what that fluid was. It was the lifeblood of my Pratt & Whitney J-57 turbojet engine.
>
> I pulled the throttle back to 86 percent where, according to the F-8 manual, the engine might, if you were lucky, continue to run for up to 15 minutes before the bearings seized. I set my course for the nearest airfield, which was *Hancock*. It was 30 minutes flying time away.
>
> There was no way I could make it back to the ship, so I prepared for ejection, stowing my gear, lowering the seat, checking my equipment and mentally went through the procedures I had practiced months before back in San Diego. But the engine, defying the laws of physics, kept running.
>
> The flight deck of *Hancock* was crowded with aircraft. The [ship's] captain decided to take me aboard and ordered an emergency pull-forward to clear the landing area. The huge ship turned into the wind. The green lights on the glide slope lens signaled a ready deck upon my arrival two miles aft and three thousand feet above her wake. The ship was ready for me. Unfortunately, I was not prepared to come aboard.
>
> I had not considered the possibility that I would be in a position to come aboard. The engine couldn't run that long without oil! As events quickly unfolded, I had to shift gears in my thinking. I realized that I was above maximum landing weight. Dump fuel! Quick! Where is that switch?
>
> Unable to move the throttle to IDLE for fear the engine would seize and overweight with unused fuel, I "called the ball" high and fast in the "groove."
>
> The LSO [Landing Signal Officer] acknowledged my call with what was painfully obvious, "You are high and fast, keep it coming!" Ordinarily, he would have waved me off immediately, but we both knew that this might be my only shot. He let me continue the approach.
>
> I hit the landing area but did not catch a wire, and continued off the angle into the air again. My nose attitude was wrong due to the excess airspeed. The tail hook had bounced over the steel cables lying across the deck waiting to grab my tail hook. The hoped-for jolt of that quick, violent stop did not happen. Now what? I had blown it!
>
> Now came the moment of truth. I had to climb back to 600 feet, turn downwind and try it again. This meant that I would have to *move the throttle*, which almost certainly would cause

the engine bearings to seize. Then I would have to eject and plunge into the ocean. That J-57 had already run 20 minutes longer than I dared hope it would. I hesitated to move the throttle. The aircraft almost stalled due to low airspeed and my low-power setting. I had no choice. Fearing the worse, I shoved the throttle forward. The engine kept running.

There was another factor in coming aboard with a crippled aircraft. If the engine failed on final, due to the low altitude and sink rate, the ejection seat would work but the chute would not open before I hit the water.

A young Lt. Len "Rocky" Johnson in the cockpit of his RF-8G. Note the ejection seat handle behind his helmet. (Capt. Len Johnson)

Turning downwind for another try, I saw myself at the "long green table" trying to explain to the mishap board why I hadn't gotten aboard the first time. I had a greater fear of losing the aircraft, when I was so close, than I did of dying. So instead of doing the smart thing and ejecting when I had the opportunity to safely do so, I again opted to continue.

I turned the corner and for the second time called "Crusader ball." This time I was on speed and on glide slope. The LSOs like to say that a good start results in a good finish. And sure enough, it did.

Once I was safely aboard the air boss said, "Shut it down" as I came to a stop. They were in a hurry to get me out of the way and get on with launching the other aircraft.

The engine froze in that moment. It had run for 40 minutes without oil, 25 minutes longer than P&W said it might. A miracle? Depends on your world view.

Facing Anti-Aircraft Fire for the First Time

The training of a fighter pilot cannot prepare for the eventual time when he/she has to face mortal danger to accomplish the mission. In the summer of 1966, Lieutenant Andre Coltrin was making his first VFP-63 combat detachment on board USS *Oriskany* (CVA-34). He describes his first encounter with AAA:

The RF-8 was a great airplane. It was fast, maneuverable, and had long legs. Most who flew her, loved her. I was one of them. However, during the war I was a little disappointed that it took so long for the Pentagon to make some much-needed upgrades. The radar and missile alert system for one [in the RF-8A]. Another they never made, was a salt-water-activated life vest for all pilots and air crew.

As with most, I wondered how I would react during my baptism under fire. It concerned me a little because I personally knew pilots, whom I had great respect for and were very talented, give up their much-coveted "Wings of gold" to avoid flying in combat. I was eased into it which may have helped. Our first ten days in Vietnam were spent on Dixie station, flying against targets in South Vietnam with no worry about enemy fighters, AAA, or SAMs. When I did observe my first AAA tracking me it did not frighten me that much. I did always jink though. I got to the point that I welcomed the opportunity when I could see the muzzle blasts. I knew the gun was aimed right at me, but I also knew that by the time the shell got there I would be long gone. What did raise more concern for me, however, was heavy concentrated AAA fire that would fill a box of air with shells

The Oriskany *Det pilots in 1966 wearing a pre-deployment orange flight suit. Lt. Andre Coltrin is seen second from left, while the Det. OinC, Lt. Cmdr. Tom Tucker, is standing second from right. The four pilots flank the non-aviator PI officer, seen in his dress blues. (Cmdr. Peter Mersky)*

> exploding at multiple altitudes and I did not have a chance to get around or above it. I did take hits a few times. As I would say, I did get shot up but never shot down.
>
> With this in mind, one mission I recall which I refer to it as my jack rabbit mission. Not so sure who thought it up but it was briefed as follows: There was a very active NVN AAA training school in the central part of NVN. It had a large number of AAA sites—some were manned and active and some were not. Not to waste ordnance on unmanned sites, we needed to determine which were active. It was decided that I would fly directly over the school to see which site reacted, while the main strike force was faking an attack on a near-by target. Once the sites became active, they were engaged by our bombers. I think that day all the instructors were manning the guns. I could not get away from them. I do not know how many sites got taken out, but I did take a couple of hits. One took a chunk out of my canopy directly over my head. I would have had to be in a 90-degree jink turn at that time. I also had damage to my trim pot which gave me heavy nose down trim. The latter added difficulty to getting back aboard ship.

Fire! Fire! General Quarters! This is not a Drill! The USS Oriskany *Fire*

As opposed to World War II Pacific battles, the Vietnam carrier task force never saw carrier versus carrier battles or enemy air attacks. Nor did they have to fear submarine danger. Had China or the Soviet Union entered the war, that would have been different. However, that doesn't mean carriers were immune from mortal threats. The one danger all Navy ships feared most was fire; the Vietnam War had three carrier fires that caused a heavy loss of life. The July 29, 1967 USS *Forrestal* (CV-59) flight deck fire was discussed in the Introduction. The first disaster, the *Oriskany* fire on October 26, 1966, is told here in graphic detail by (now) Commander Andre Coltrin:

Smoke envelopes Oriskany. *The captain turned the ship so the wind could divert smoke away from the fire fighters battling the fire. (Official U.S. Navy Photograph # USN 1121718 via http://www.navsource.org/)*

> In the early morning hours of October 26, 1966, the pre-dawn launch had been scrubbed and the ordnance men were downloading flares from the A-4s and preparing the aircraft for daylight operations. It was determined later after a thorough investigation that the lanyard of one the flares caught on something, igniting the flare. The edge of the ship was not far away, but in his panic, one of the airmen threw the burning flare into the flare locker instead of overboard. It was also believed at that time, that once the flare was ignited it could not be extinguished. At my next duty station, NAF [Naval Air Facility] China Lake, we found that by putting a fire hose into the burning end of the flare it could easily be extinguished. Once the lit flare was in the flare locker, the reaction was almost instantaneous. Before one of the sailors could shut and dog the locker door the first explosions started. Lucky for the sailor, he had his elbow locked while trying to dog the door. The first blast ripped the door open with such force that the dogs were torn out of the edge of the door like large bites. The sailor, because of the locked elbow was thrown well clear of the door as it smashed the metal ladder behind it, as if it were made of paper. Fire balls soon emerged. Every few seconds fire ball after fire ball, shot out like a huge roman candle. These fire balls with temperatures in the thousands of degrees shot out of the locker and raced up and down the passageways of the ship. Oxygen and any burnable material fed the fireballs as they went.
>
> I was asleep in my state room one deck below the flight deck, which I shared with three other officers, two pilots and a photo officer. The 1MC [ship's announcement system] was blaring and the message that I thought I was hearing was "THIS IS A DRILL. THIS IS A DRILL. FIRE, FIRE, FIRE. THERE IS A FIRE IN THE HANGAR DECK!" I did not think or get too excited about it because we had had many fire drills, at various hours so far on the cruise, during combat operations or not. As an air wing officer, we had no assigned duties other than report to our fire station which was the squadron ready room, but few adhered to this if it meant giving up much needed sleep time for a drill. I stayed in my rack.
>
> Two of my roommates had left long before; one, a pilot had an early daylight launch scheduled and the other, our photo officer, was a briefing officer for those getting ready to launch. My third roommate, Vince, another pilot, got up and said, "I heard something that sounded like an explosion," and left the room. Still not too excited, I rolled over to go back to sleep. A short time later I heard the door again open and someone enter the room and heard a strange voice say, "Is anyone here?" I asked, "Who are you?" and he replied, "Seaman so-n-so." (I cannot remember his name.) I replied back, "Seaman, this is Lieutenant Coltrin. What are you doing in my stateroom?" He replied, "Well, sir, the ship is on fire and we are trapped." It was time to get out of bed! I went

to the door and pulled it open and was met by a solid wall of thick smoke. I reached into the smoke and could feel a solid wall of human flesh—people trying to go down the passageway to escape. The human wall was too solid to get in. I shut the door.

When my roommates and I first occupied the room, we mounted an air conditioner by cutting a hole in the wall that separated us from the head [bathroom and shower] to dump the hot exhaust air. To make the air conditioner as efficient as possible, we were very meticulous in sealing any air leaks into the room. Because of this, the smoke from the fire had, up to this point, been kept at bay. The only smoke we had, was when I had first opened the door for a very short time. I took this time and put on my Nomex flight pants and shirt. Seaman X got on the phone and called the ships damage-control team for a rescue effort. Short reply, FAT CHANCE. We were very low on a very long priority list. I tried the door another time with the same results we had experienced earlier. By now the room was starting to get hot. The tile on the floor was starting to buckle, the room is starting to fill with smoke. I put on my flight boots. It was time to move one way or another. We had a sink in the room. I grabbed two towels turned on the sink to soak them thoroughly and threw one to Seaman X to wrap around his head and act as a shield from the flames and filter from smoke. I wrapped the other, a black one (which I kept for years as a good luck piece) around my head and opened the door. Seaman X charged out the door turned left and disappeared unbelievably fast. I knew that direction was a dead end, the only way out was to the right. I yelled out that information and headed out. The passageway was now clear of people.

Shortly beyond the head was a passageway that went across the ship. I knew I was there when I ran into the knee-knocker [part of steel-hatch door opening]. I remembered from the fire announcement that the fire was stated to be on the starboard [right] side of the ship, so I did not want to go that way. Straight ahead of me facing aft was Admiral Country. The shortest way out I figured was to the right. As I was making the turn I ran into a locker of some type and hurt my hand. How did that get there? I knew that shortly ahead of me, on the left side of the passageway, was a ladder that led down into the hangar bay. That was going to be my escape route.

As I was heading in that direction, the smoke was filled with red flashes, both on my right and left, and I became disoriented. The next thing I knew I was at a hatch [door] that led to the catwalk [flight deck passageway] outside the ship. The only problem was that condition Zebra had been set and the door was dogged down with about six dogs [manual locks]. Scared, disoriented, and finding it very hard to breath, I tried to undo the hatch. I thought I had undone all the dogs but the hatch would not open. I heard screams—I did not know whose, maybe mine. Frustrated and thinking I was going to die I angrily kicked the hatch. To my great surprise, it opened. I stumbled out onto the catwalk and laid there a few seconds breathing the fresh air. I did not lay there long. As I got up, I could see across the flight deck to the island. There was a smoke-free zone from the deck up about 12 inches. I could see many legs and feet of people gathered at the island and decided to crawl over there. As I was about half way there, someone was crawling towards me from the right side. It was the CO of VF-111. As he approached, he said, "Andre, do you have a cigarette? I am dying for a smoke." "A what!" I responded, and told him to just raise his head two inches and he could get all the smoke he would ever want. He said, "No, No, I really need a cigarette," and crawled off.

When I made it to the island the skipper had turned the ship so the wind crossed the deck in a way to keep the island clear of smoke so he could navigate and help the crew fight the fire. I found a mustering officer and checked in. Shortly after I located Vince. He was fairly easy to spot because he was wearing his red and white striped night shirt. I asked him about his exit experience. He stated that after he left the room and got to the cross-ship passage, he went straight ahead into Admiral Country and somehow ended up in a room with the admiral and his staff. Being the admiral, he had fresh air pumped into his spaces. His staff, therefore, pulled the end caps off the venting system and everyone gathered in a circle with their heads close to the open vent to breath.

An Oriskany *fire team throw flammable equipment, including bombs seen here, overboard. In the background, a fire team hoses fire from the sponson. (National Naval Aviation Museum, Pensacola, FL)*

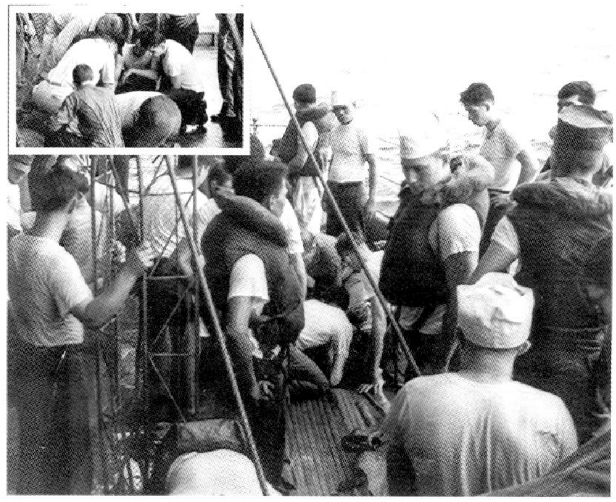

The inset photo shows CPR being administered to a sailor overcome by smoke. The men with white hats are cooks. Every sailor has a battle station during a crisis. (USN photo via http://www.navsource.org/)

As I mentioned before, about Seaman X's call to damage control, the admiral was on the opposite end of the priority list than I was, so Vince was rescued fairly early in the game. Also, I did run into Seaman X again. He explained a couple of mysteries to me. First, why did he turn left out of my room? It turns out he had a couple of buddies that worked in a secret compartment at the dead end of the passage. That is, the work they were doing was highly classified not that the compartment was classified. As it turned out they had all left before he got there. It very much impressed me that he would face such danger to check on his buddies. The next question was, how did he disappear so fast? He explained that as he turned, he tripped over a body in the passageway. It was an officer that lived in the stateroom directly across the passage from me. Seaman X determined he was dead and could not be helped at that point in time.

I found out later that the locker I had run into and hurt my hand was an OBA locker. OBA stands for Oxygen Breathing Apparatus. Just what I needed at that time, but I had not been trained and did not know how to use it. One of the major faults found by the fire investigation: almost none of the aircrew had any fire training what-so-ever. That was soon changed. I also found the disorientation I experienced with the red flashing in the smoke was caused by two things: the port cat had caught on fire and caused flashes on my right. And in the hangar bay a helicopter, parked just below the ladder I was trying to find to use as my escape route, caught on fire causing flashing on my left side. There was another officer, a friend of mine, who had used that ladder in his escape route and was on it when the helicopter lit off. He was roasted on the spot. Earlier in the cruise, this officer, when climbing up a short ladder from a sponson to the flight deck had his head very close to a A-4's tail pipe when the pilot started his engine. He received serious burns to his head and face. They were just about healed when he died. My guardian angel was very busy that day as he had been that whole cruise.

While standing around the island I noticed a lot of activity going on in the sponson just one deck below the flight deck. Men were pushing bombs and other explosives overboard. Then I noticed men bring them out to the sponson. Men with OBAs were entering smoked-filled compartments to retrieve those explosives. One of them was a young pilot I knew from one of the fighter squadrons that escorted us on missions. His name was Jim "Flaps" (he had big ears) Andrews. The vest that he was wearing had a cable attached to the back. Flap's job was to enter an ammunition locker directly above the fire on the hangar deck level just below, remove the ordnance, bring it out so others could throw it overboard. The cable attached to him was used to pull him out of the compartment in the event he was injured or passed out while inside the ammo locker. More than once while I was standing there one of these brave men had to be dragged out of the compartment by his safety wire because he had been overcome by smoke. I always had respect for young Flaps, but it jumped 1,000 percent that day. I was lucky to serve with Flaps again at my next shore duty station, NAF China Lake.

I also noticed that a small class was going on near me on how to use an OBA. I knew there were several search teams going back into the ship to hunt for survivors and dead. So, I grabbed an OBA from a pile on the deck and attended the next demonstration. As soon as it was over, I joined up with a Marine and two sailors to form a team and we headed into the ship. We were assigned the task to go to a stateroom of an officer that had not been accounted for. We picked up the basket we would put the remains in if we found him. The basket, as I recall it, is what you see slung below helicopters as they rescue injured in remote areas. They're made of a metal mesh and reasonably light weight. In this team I was tail-end Charlie, I picked up the far end of the basket.

Just as we were to enter the ship, I put on the OBA for the first time. Big mistake. The reason there was a big pile of these on the deck is that they were the rejects. The mask would produce oxygen, but the eyepieces were so scratched I could barely see through it in good lighting conditions. Inside the dark ship it was worthless. I continued with the team. I just let the guy in front pull me along. Inside the ship the water was above our knees and the temperature felt like 200 degrees. It felt like being in an oven, very hot, muggy and difficult to breath.

To make matters worse there were live electrical wires sparking all over the place and here we are carrying this metal basket in knee-deep water. I was told that if you do not go between the two hot wires you will be OK. It must have been true because we never got zapped, but I was not too confident.

When we found the assigned stateroom of the missing officer, we thought no one was there, but looking more closely, we found a lump of what we thought at first was a pile of clothes or laundry in one corner. Getting closer, we realized it had been a man. The room had gotten so hot he had just melted. They could not even use his teeth for identification. It was determined that since everyone else had been identified, this melted mass had to be him.

Later, I helped carry a man whom I did not think I knew. It turned out to be a good friend I had flown with many times. The fire had charred his skin and singed his hair. Only when we rolled him over and I saw his unburned side did I know who it was. This same pilot had survived two ejections earlier in the cruise.

There were two cases that involved portholes. In the first case I always think of it as rich man, poor man. In this case the officer from one of the fighter squadrons was able to select a stateroom that had a porthole that opened over a sponson. During the fire when he tried to get out the door the fire was raging so bad that that exit strategy was impossible. He decided the porthole was his only option. Before attempting his exit, he went to his safe and removed a large roll of bills he had accumulated on the cruise. Since he had just woken up, the only clothing he had on was his shorts. The porthole was so small that as he squeezed his way through, it stripped his shorts right off of him. So, there he was, on the flight deck with a huge wad of bills in his hand, nude as a Jay bird. Rich man, poor man. It did not take too long before a uniform was located for him. But for a while it was a funny sight.

The other port hole case involved an officer that had a porthole that opened over the open sea with about a fifty-foot drop to the water. In this case the officer, an A-4 pilot, also tried to exit the door and was unable because of the flames. While at the porthole, he was able to signal the helicopter circling the ship. The helicopter contacted the ship and informed them of his location so a fire hose could be lowered from the flight deck to him. He brought the fire hose in and let the water run down his back with his head out the port hole while his room burned around him. I understand the worst injuries he had was to his knees because he kept banging them against the bulkhead trying to get away from the heat.

In one of the fighter ready rooms the SDO [squadron duty officer] received a call from some shipmates who were trapped in their stateroom on the third deck. He told them that all the rescue teams were very busy and they would have to find their own way out. Shortly thereafter there was a loud horrible noise that sounded like uncontrollable screaming over the phone, then it suddenly went dead. We did not know if it was the sound of the men being burned to death or a strange sound made by the phone lines as the wires melted. It made the hair on the back of every man's neck in the ready room stand on end. One man out of the eight did escape from that room.

As a couple of the men succumbed, an LDO [limited duty officer, a former enlisted man who had been commissioned in his area of specialty] from VF-111 decided he was not going to die this way and busted out of the room. He raced to the ladder that took him to the second deck. As he was running blindly across the deck, he passed out from the smoke, falling to the deck. He regained consciousness, bathed in the smoke-free air close to the deck. Getting to his feet he again started running across the deck to the port side of the ship. Passing out again, he fell down a ladder to the third deck. At the bottom of the ladder, he was knocked unconscious when he slammed into the stateroom door of one of his shipmates from the other fighter squadron, who had been able to sleep through all the previous commotion. The loud bang against his door woke him up. As he opened the door, he became aware of the dangerous situation they were in. Throwing his unconscious shipmate over his shoulder, he carried him to the safety of the flight deck. They had saved each other's lives.

Another terrifying experience was a man trapped in a compartment when the water used to fight the fire flooded his space. The lights were out and it was pitch black. As the water rose, the man shimmied up a pipe in the corner of the room to escape the rising water to breath. He stayed in this dark, torturous situation for hours before rescue. He suffered psychological trauma, but later recovered.

Shortly before the fire, *Oriskany* was involved with the rescue of the Chinese crew of a British merchant ship. The *August Moon* had been driven aground on the Pratas Reef during the Elsie Typhoon. The Helicopter crew from *Oriskany* did a heroic task in the rescue of the 44-man crew from the *August Moon*. In fact, the weather and bad seas during the rescue caused one of the rescue helicopters to be lost during the rescue operation. The Chinese crew showed their "gratitude" by demanding they be put ashore immediately, when they found out they had been rescued by an American war ship. Many a man on *Oriskany* was very willing to throw them overboard then and there. The story of the *August Moon* rescue can be found at the U.S. Naval Institute: *Angels of Oriskany—August Moon Rescue.*

It seemed like a very long time before the fire was under control and finally put out. Much help and assistance were received and appreciated from other ships on the line at the time. We left the line and headed to the Philippines, and then home. En route to Cubi Point, we had a burial at sea ceremony for killed shipmates [Some bodies were transported to the United States; 156 others were injured.] That was tough. Almost 55 years later I still feel the emotion and I am happy that I finally got the stench of death and burning flesh out of my nostrils.

The *Oriskany* set course to Cubi Point to offload some dead crewmen for transport to the United States for burial. The ship then proceeded to San Diego, California, for repairs. The *Oriskany* returned to Vietnam in July 1967.

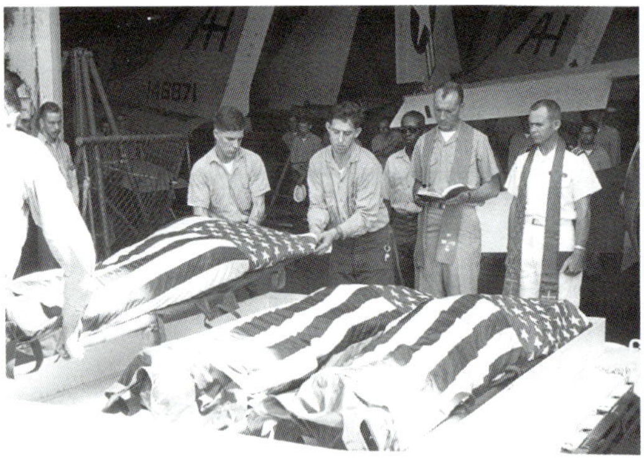

The tragic fire on USS Oriskany *(CVA-34), October 26, 1966, killed 34 crew members. This photo, on the hangar deck, shows the body preparation of men who had previously requested to be returned to the U.S. for burial. The VFP-63 RF-8G (Bu. No. 146871) in the left background was lost in an operational accident on December 2 1976. This jet was used by Capt. William B. Ecker during the Cuban Missile Crisis. (National Naval Aviation Museum Pensacola, FL)*

Bodies of men who lost their lives in the fire on board USS Oriskany *(CVA-34) on October 26, 1966 are off loaded at Cubi Point, Republic of the Philippines. (National Archives and Records Administration photo, # 428-K-34318)*

USS Oriskany *survivor, Capt. Richard Schaffert, recalls, "My roommate Norm Levy, Wingy Bill McWilliams, and Sundowner Cody Balesterie were among those who were flown by C-130 from the pier at Subic Bay to the mortuary at Clark AFB. By special request of his parents, Norm was then placed on our Flying Tigers 707 and traveled home with the surviving Air Wing." (Capt. Richard Schaffert)*

Lt. Cmdr. Omar R. Ford, one of the 34 fatalities of the fire, is buried at sea during funeral ceremonies held on USS Oriskany*'s flight and hangar decks. (National Archives and Records Administration photo, catalog # USN 1121689)*

The third disastrous carrier fire was the USS *Enterprise* (CVAN-65) on January 14 1969, off the coast of Pearl Harbor, Hawaii. A Zuni rocket exploded under an aircraft's wing starting an inferno. Twenty-eight were killed and 314 injured.

During 1966, VFP-63 lost five aircraft: two pilots were rescued, one killed in action, and two were captured and became POWs.

As the year drew to a close, President Johnson continued to throttle back Air Force and Navy aircraft from hitting key rail lines and port facilities in the Hanoi-Haiphong area in fear that China would enter the war. We will see that would change in 1967 as air raids would expand, facing more AAA, SAMs, and MiGs over more intensely defended targets.

1966 Non-fatal Combat Losses

On April 19 1966, an RF-8A (Bu. No. 146843) from *Ticonderoga* was lost to AAA. VFP-63 Detachment B pilot Lieutenant Ron Ball (see above story) ejected and was rescued.

★ ★ ★

On May 5 1966, an RF-8A (Bu. No. 146831) from *Hancock* was shot down by AAA. The pilot, Lieutenant John Heilig ejected, was captured and became the first VFP-63 North Vietnamese POW (earlier Lieutenant Chuck Klusmann was a Laotian POW but escaped). He was released on February 12, 1973.

★ ★ ★

VFP-63 Det. B RF-8A (Bu. No. 146843) from USS Ticonderoga *(CVA-14) was hit by AAA on April 19, 1966. Lt. Ron Ball ejected and was rescued by SAR helicopter. (Robert L. Lawson Collection, National Naval Aviation Museum, Pensacola, FL)*

VFP-63 RF-8As near San Diego, CA, August 10, 1965. The peeling-off RF-8A (Bu. No. 146831) was shot down on May 5, 1966. Lt. John Heilig ejected, was captured and became a POW until February 12 1973. (Robert L. Lawson Collection, National Naval Aviation Museum, Pensacola, FL)

A VFP-63 Det. A RF-8G (Bu. No. 146899) and an A-1E on the forward catapults of USS Coral Sea *(CVA-43), 1966. Note jet blast deflector up behind the RF-8. This RF-8 was later lost to AAA on October 8, 1966. The pilot, Lt. (j. g.) F. D. Litvin, ejected and was rescued. (Robert L. Lawson Collection, National Naval Aviation Museum, Pensacola, FL)*

On June 21 1966, a second RF-8A (Bu. No. 146830) from *Hancock* was shot down by AAA. The pilot, Lieutenant Len Corbett Eastman, ejected, was captured, and became the second VFP-63 POW of North Vietnam (see above story). Ironically, Eastman was Heilig's replacement. He was released on February 12, 1973.

★ ★ ★

On October 8 1966, another RF-8A (Bu. No. 146899) was lost to AAA. USS *Coral Sea* (CVA-43) pilot, Lieutenant (junior grade) Fred D. Litvin, ejected and was rescued.

In Memoriam

Lieutenant (junior grade) Thomas Gavin Walster
February 7,1941–April 9 1966
Salt Lake City, Utah

On April 9 1966, Thomas Walster's RF-8A (Bu. No. 144611) was hit by AAA fire. He was from VFP-63 Detachment L, on board *Hancock*. He ejected offshore South Vietnam but drowned before SAR forces arrived.

Memories and Tributes

Captain Len Johnson, remembers his shipmate:

> Detachment Lima on *Hancock* lost its first pilot when Tom Walster was hit over Vinh. The damage sustained precluded a safe landing, so it was decided that he would make a controlled ejection off the coast of South Vietnam.
>
> For some reason Tom's flotation gear did not inflate and he was dragged below the surface by the parachute. The rescue diver jumped into the water, grabbed a piece of Tom's chute, and hung on to it as long as he could. Finally, he had to let go as he too was being dragged below the surface. The weight of Tom's equipment and the sinking chute ended his life.
>
> I remembered Tom Walster at the previous departure party when *Hancock* left Vietnam for home. He was a young father and a loving husband with a sweet wife. He too should have lived. But he gave it all up in the Tonkin Gulf because of that stupid war.

Lieutenant Commander Scott Ruby provides additional information on the loss:

> His aircraft got hit in the area aft of the cockpit, the bottom of the engine area. I ended up talking to his escort and he told me the whole bottom of the burner section was sort of open to the air stream—just hanging out in the air. He got hit at low altitude but managed to get the bird up to about 1,500 feet and about 300 knots. The Crusader was apparently vibrating, running rough, and

> just not doing well, but it was still flying. A sea plane was launched out of Da Nang to pick him up after he ejected. For whatever reason, he ejected before the rescue bird got there. By the time the rescue bird landed in the water and got a rescue swimmer in the water, he was at least 20 feet down.

Thomas is honored on the Vietnam Veterans Memorial in Washington, D.C.: Wall, Panel 06E, Line 94.

Commendations

- ★ Purple Heart
- ★ National Defense Service Medal
- ★ Vietnam Service Medal
- ★ Navy Expeditionary Medal
- ★ Naval Aviation Wings
- ★ Combat Action Ribbon
- ★ Vietnam Campaign Medal
- ★ Navy Presidential Unit Citation
- ★ Vietnam Gallantry Cross

CHAPTER 5

1966–67: VFP-62 Enters the Vietnam War

Light Photographic Squadron 62 (VFP-62) was the Atlantic Fleet sister squadron of VFP-63, which was shouldering all of the Navy's small-deck carrier photo-reconnaissance and needed some relief. VFP-62 sent a detachment to Vietnam on board USS *Franklin D. Roosevelt* (CVA-42). On June 21 1966, the *Roosevelt*, fully loaded with its carrier air wing, departed Mayport, Florida, headed towards the Puerto Rico operations area and conducted operational training before heading to Saint Thomas in the Virgin Islands. After one day in port, it headed back to sea towards Rio de Janeiro for crew's liberty, while conducting training operations along the way. On July 1, it started its transit to WESTPAC (Western Pacific) and then on to Subic Bay in the Philippines for six days of replenishing provisions and more liberty for the crew. Finally, it made the three-day trip to Yankee Station off Vietnam and commenced a month of combat operations on August 12 1966.

The last time VFP-62 had been in a combat environment was in its starring role during the Cuban Missile Crisis. On October 23 1962, the squadron flew the first low-level photo missions over the Soviet medium-range-ballistic missile sites being secretly constructed in Cuba. The operation was designated *Blue Moon* and VFP-62 was charged with obtaining detailed low-level intelligence to assist President Kennedy determine the operational status of the nuclear missiles.

VFP-62 took the reconnaissance lead and the photos were shown to the president and his executive committee the next day. The president was restraining his more hawkish advisors advocating air attacks against the missile sites. Until that point, only Air Force and CIA U-2 high-altitude photography had been used to locate the launchers of the four medium-range offensive missile and 21 defensive surface-to-air missile (SAM) sites. Marine squadron VMCJ-2 (East Coast sister squadron of VMCJ-1) augmented VFP-62 and the Air Force flew RF-101 Voodoos on alternate schedules.

Pilot's eye view of landing aboard USS Franklin D. Roosevelt *(CVA-42). LSO station on left-hand corner. (Cmdr. Norm Green)*

VFP-62's tactics involved flying three missions, each with two RF-8As in section formation to cover the missile sites. The pilots departed from NAS (Naval Air Station) Boca Chica at Key West, Florida, flew low-level over the Straits of Florida, sometimes getting salt spray on their underside. They entered Cuba (going feet dry) and proceeded to their targets at high speed and low altitude to avoid SAM radar. They frequently caught the Cubans off guard, but often encountered anti-aircraft fire as the missions continued. None of the speedy RF-8As was ever hit, but a U-2 piloted by Air Force Major Rudolph Anderson was shot down by a SAM. He was the only fatality during the overflights.

Over Cuba, the RF-8As were unescorted by fighters, who were restricted to remain offshore by President Kennedy. The Soviets had shipped a number of MiGs to Cuba, including the delta-wing supersonic MiG-21. On one occasion, a section of RF-8As was chased by two MiG-21s. The VFP-62 pilots evaded them by hitting the deck at supersonic speed and outracing them to the safety of American fighter protection offshore. For its performance during the crisis, President Kennedy personally presented the Navy Unit Commendation, the first time the award was presented by a president, to the squadron and the Distinguished Flying Cross to the pilots. In a letter to the commanding officer, Captain William B. Ecker, President Kennedy wrote, "As I said at our meeting in Boca Chica, the reconnaissance flights which enabled us to determine with precision the offensive build-up in Cuba contributed directly to the security of the United States in the most important and significant way."

Unlike Cuba, targets in North Vietnam included urban areas heavily defended by SAMs and AAA (anti-aircraft artillery) batteries controlled by radar; both were deadly accurate. During its Vietnam combat tour, VFP-62 pilots encountered these, and MiG, threats.

Flying a successful reconnaissance mission demands cool skill, rather than the frenetic aerial maneuvering associated with fighter versus fighter combat, because the pilot must keep his photo-airplane perfectly level and precisely on course over foreign territory that is often prickling with SAMs and AAA. VFP-63 pilot Captain Len Johnson flew 100 missions over North Vietnam, and describes his survival tactics:

> The best defense against flak was to keep constantly moving (called jinking) around the sky—changing altitude and speed. Never descend below 3,000 feet (the limit of most AAA).

> I didn't line up on my targets. Never fly in straight lines! I would fly in a zigzag path to my target and turn at the last minute to pass over it going as fast as possible, which would be speeds in excess of 600 knots. My favorite approach, again weather permitting, was to descend from high altitude, say 20,000 feet, to pass over the target at supersonic speeds. Unfortunately, I still had to fly over the target at between 3,000 and 4,000 feet, which the North Vietnamese gunners knew. They simply filled the sky with lead, and I had to fly through it.

A North Vietnamese SA-2 SAM site. Seen here are many bomb craters in the area, revetment walls, guidance radar, control stations, and multiple SAM firing positions. (Lt. Phil Sherman)

In Vietnam, VFP-62 was flying the RF-8G, which had Electronic Counter Measures Detection (ECM) gear to detect a SAM's searching and guidance radar. The Cuban Missile Crisis caused the Navy to start thinking about the technology. One of the *Blue Moon* pilots, Lieutenant Commander Tad Riley, was given a primitive ECM device that was plugged into his radio. He was told that if he heard a "whoop, whoop" that was the indication that a Soviet radar was searching. If it was followed by a higher-frequency rapid "beep, beep, beep," that meant it had "locked on" and he should dive for the deck. Riley says he heard the "whoop, whoop" once but not the "beep, beep, beep." When I left the Navy in July 1963, we were starting to see RF-8As show up at NAS Cecil Field with mysterious tubular devices mounted on the fuselage and, later, under the wings. We guessed they were experimental ECM gear and were warned not to discuss the devices with anyone. Fortunately, in 1965, the photo-Crusader was remanufactured as an RF-8G with ECM gear as standard equipment.

The Soviet SA-2 *Guideline* (NATO designation) was a Mach 3+ two-stage SAM. It was about 34 feet long, carried a 430-pound fragmentation warhead and had a blast radius of about 300 yards. It had about a 21-mile range and could reach over 70,000 feet. Before Vietnam it was responsible for shooting down a number of American spy aircraft, including the secret high-altitude CIA U-2, flown by Gary Powers, near Moscow in May 1960, presenting President Eisenhower with a huge diplomatic crisis. Powers miraculously survived the shootdown and became a prisoner. Another high-profile shootdown was Lieutenant Commander John McCain's (later senator) A-4 over Hanoi in 1967. During that time, his father, Admiral John S. McCain Jr., was Commander-in-Chief Pacific Command in the Pacific theater during much of the Vietnam War.

If detected soon enough and utilizing evasive quick-turn maneuvers, pilots had a reasonable chance of avoiding being shot down. The encounter became a deadly ballet matching the skills of a pilot with a supersonic, lethal, determined, flying robot with one goal: destroy its target. Many American pilots ended up prisoners of war, or worse,

An SA-2 SAM detonation after Lt. Norm Green and his VFP-62 wingman, Ens. Ed Andrews, evaded it. (Cmdr. Norm Green)

due to SAMs. VFP-62 pilot (now) Commander Norm Green, describes his encounter with several SAMs at one time:

> I and my wingman, Ensign Ed Andrews, were running along a karst ridge northwest of Thanh Hoa, when the ECM lights up and about 15 miles at our 9:00 o'clock a SA-2 SAM lifts, climbs to 5,000 feet, tilts over and tracks us. We push the power up and turn into the SAM. Waiting for the appropriate time to make our break, Ed transmits, "Uh lead, check our 3 o'clock"; another SA-2 also has us bore-sighted. Afterburner now, hard right break, go for the deck, we successfully evade both.
>
> In the excitement, Ed loses me and is gripping the power lever so hard that for the next 30-40 seconds the only thing that can be heard over the radio is his deep, raspy breathing [he jammed the transmit button]; it sounds like he has been hit. But all is well—we were just glad to be still flying and we made it back to mother Rosie [*Roosevelt*].

The photo jets were also involved with the fighter and attack jets as they made strikes against the SAMs, as Norm Green again describes so well:

> On November 1, 1966, I flew an early morning recce to the northeast of Haiphong and my escort was one of our F-4B Phantoms. East of Haiphong we were targeted by several SA-2 missiles from a SAM site. The photo bird had no armament and the F-4B had no air-to-ground weapons—only air-to-air missiles to protect us from MiG aircraft. However, we did dive over the site, took pictures of the launchers (several now minus missiles) and marked the position on our maps.

We returned to the *Roosevelt*, debriefed the Admiral's staff and headed to the ready room. Soon the phone rang and I was summoned back to the staff office. SAMs were relatively new to the battle in 1966 but they were "hot tickets." The staff wanted to suspend our daily flight schedule, assemble a large strike package and go after the SAM site. Though mobile, they can't move the radars and launchers that quickly. They asked, "Can I find the site again and am I willing to lead the strike group to the location?" I wisely answered, "Yes" to both questions.

About two hours later we were off, armed to the gills with a large strike group. As we made our ingress into Indian country, we were fired upon by *another* SAM site—not the one we were targeting. Great headwork by a couple of the element leaders and we expended part of our ordnance on the new site, putting it out of action. We regrouped and continued to the original target, destroying it as intended. Needless to say, the Admiral and his staff were ecstatic over the results. There were medals and decorations all around—Air Medals, Distinguished Flying Crosses, and Silver Stars. Overblown praise? Yes, I think somewhat, but I also recognize that the awards also helped to maintain the spirit of the troops on the carrier, who had worked and sweated so tirelessly to pull off such an evolution.

Naval aviation is a stressful profession for officers and enlisted. To break that tension and stress the crew finds "creative" ways to demonstrate their technical prowess. Such an instance was when the VFP-62 technicians "borrowed" a Sidewinder and mounted it to the RF-8G's wing. The electricians were sure they could wire it up but were stopped at the better discretion of the officers. Squadrons differentiated themselves by colorful paint schemes on their aircraft or innovative nicknames. Some favorites are: VF-191's "Satan's Kittens," World War II's VF-10 (later VF-101) known as "The Grim Reapers," and VFP-62's "Fightin' Photo." Even the F-8 Crusader was dubbed, "The Last of the Gun Fighters."

Entertainment for the ship's crew also came in the form of USO (United Service Organizations, Inc.) entertainment on the hangar deck. Comedian Bob Hope made many

Bombs used in a day's work by Roosevelt*'s aviators are stored for ready use in Hangar Bay 4. (John Glenn)*

An F-4 Phantom II of the Fighter Squadron VF-41 "Black Aces" launches from the waist catapult of USS Independence *(CVA-62) while A-4 Skyhawks of Attack Squadrons VA-86 and 72 await launch from the bow cats during Operation* Rolling Thunder *operations in 1965. (National Naval Aviation Museum, Pensacola, FL)*

A Sidewinder missile on an RF-8G; a Det. 42 "tongue-in-cheek" demonstration that the new wing-attach point on the "G" model could hold a missile and wiring could make it work. It never flew in this configuration. (Cmdr. Norm Green)

Lt. Phil Sherman, while on a USS Coral Sea *(CVA-43) catapult, pulls a joke on the Air Boss by sitting backwards in the cockpit. The optical device on the canopy rail above his head is used to aim cameras for air-to-air photography. (Lt. Phil Sherman)*

Lt. Cmdr. Scott Ruby, officer in charge, with VFP-63 Det. 3 on board the USS Midway *(CVA-41), enjoys a prank by the maintenance crew hanging from the air-to-air refueling probe. The 35 stars represent 35 straight days in "Up" status. (Col. Jim Morgan USAF)*

tours to military units all over the world. He visited the *Roosevelt* at the end of the cruise, bringing along several scantily clad female stars, such as movie star Marilyn Monroe in earlier years. Hope would taunt the female-deprived audience with risqué jokes and everyone would go nuts.

Other pranks usually get a free pass from senior officers such as the one pulled by Lieutenant Phil Sherman on one of USS *Coral Sea*'s (CVA-43) catapults prior to launch (see photo). A VFP-62 pilot, known for his difficulty catching a wire on recovery was shocked to find his maintenance crew had tied a grappling hook to his RF-8 when he arrived to man his aircraft. He wasn't amused, but let it pass.

Defenses against the threats of Soviet supplied, but North Vietnamese flown, MiGs, especially near the Hanoi-Haiphong area, included radar detection by electronic warfare aircraft and ships offshore. The North Vietnamese MiG pilots preferred to ambush, either from behind, below or above their quarries. MiG versus fighter encounters are thrilling stories of the Vietnam War. Commander Green tells how Navy radar picked up several MiG-21s stalking him and his escort:

> In the Fall of 1966, while leading a recce flight a few miles south of Haiphong, my fighter escort was an F-4B Phantom, but I don't remember if it was VF-14 or VF-32. We were headed generally

> westward at 4,000 feet and about 480 knots. Red Crown [northern-most U.S. guard cruiser] called and warned of two high-speed bogies, 15 miles north and closing fast.
>
> Our air group's Phantom pilots were very frustrated, no one had shot a MiG, not sure if anyone had even seen one. For a brief instant I wanted to turn into the oncoming threat, but then good sense took hold. I'd be putting my escort into a one-vs-two situation and all I'd be able to do is cheer for him. Also, I was not sure such a move would meet with the approval of the "big boys." So, I called, "Hang on." We turned hard port [left], stuffed the nose down, and lit the burners.
>
> As we accelerated, they continued to close—Red Crown advised us, "seven miles, six miles, five miles." We got to about 690 knots at 1,500 feet, they held at five miles briefly and then we started to open the range. I think we were well in excess of the speed limits on the F-4's 600-gallon centerline [fuel] tank, but no one's complaining. We ran straight south for 30 miles gradually opening to seven miles, at which time the bogies broke away and turned north. Due to their speed, we presumed they were MiG-21s. I do remember being briefed that the MiG-21s don't like very high airspeeds in a high Q [aircraft stress] environment—I guess that's a fact.
>
> Due to the "extensive" navigation gear in the photo-Crusader, I now had no idea where in the hell we were. This is somewhat tongue-in-cheek. Better wording would be "less than extensive"; most tactical jets of that era had crappy navigation capabilities with the exception of the A-6A Intruder and later the A-7E Corsair. I also knew that the escort would shortly be screaming for fuel, so we called it a day and headed for the tanker to get him some JP [jet fuel]. Escorting photo-Crusaders was not the strong suit of the F-4B. [As mentioned previously, the Crusader had a large fuel capacity.]

On another mission, Commander Green had another close call over North Vietnam when his RF-8G was hit by North Vietnamese AAA during a reconnaissance run. The shell destroyed the aft edges of the left wing. With expert flying skill, he brought the jet back to the ship and received a commendation. The photos of the damage are a testament to the ruggedness of the RF-8G Crusader. With typical pilot humor he says, "They show the result of attempting to occupy the same space as a well-aimed 57mm round."

Landing a Crusader aboard ship is difficult under the best of circumstances. Controlling speed and angle of attack is critical for a safe landing. Norm Green continues with a description of the events that led up to his most difficult carrier landing:

> I don't remember the admiral embarked as the carrier division commander on the Rosy, but he really liked photo-reconnaissance. All of the photo detachment pilots had a standing invitation to visit his staff at any time we had any info that we thought the staff would be interested in. As the detachment operations officer, I frequently visited the staff each evening to see if they had any specific recce requirements for the next day. On the evening of September 5, they had a couple of requests, which would require missions pretty far to the north. I talked with our boss, Lieutenant Commander John Baals, to see if he had any guidance regarding the next day's flight schedule. He said to use my own judgment, so I scheduled myself for the first launch headed for the port of Haiphong. Lieutenant, Junior Grade Norm Bundy was on the second launch going a little bit farther south.
>
> The next day after the normal briefing, I headed for the flight deck with my escort crew. It was absolutely still, not a breath of wind—the Gulf of Tonkin was like a lake, not a ripple. The weatherman had been right on. The *Roosevelt* had two C-11 catapults, the shortest and least capable of any catapults in use at that time, so we knew that my escort would be launched about

3,000 pounds [a gallon of fuel is six pounds] light on fuel; our first task would be to find the tanker and fill the escort up. While holding just behind catapult No. 1, I heard a banging on the side of my aircraft, it was the catapult officer. After getting my attention, he walked out about 15 feet to the side of my plane and using a large piece of chalk he scribbled the number six on the deck. The Cat officer's rules dictated that each aircraft would be launched with a minimum of six knots above stall speed. He had indicated to me that he could only give me six knots above stall, the ball was in my court. If the breakfast sausage hadn't settled too well, I could shake my head "no," then I would be parked next to the island, shut down and the mission would be scrubbed. After some consideration and my usual adherence to the oriental proverb "better to die than look bad," I gave him a thumbs up. I had ultimate faith in the Crusader, six knots it would be. Someone once asked me what was the minimum catapult end speed that I would accept? The least that I ever launched at was five knots over stall. Would I have gone at three or four knots excess? I don't really know, no one ever asked me to launch at those speeds. After launch we filled up my escort and headed north for Haiphong.

On missions to the southern end of North Vietnam we were allowed to fly our own escort missions, since there was little chance that we would run into enemy MiG aircraft. Above 20 degrees north latitude (Thanh Hoa) we were required to drag along an F-4B armed escort. I mean no disrespect to our F-4 pilots nor their trusty steed. In its environment the F-4 was a fine airplane and it served both the Navy and Air Force very well in Vietnam. However, 3,000ft at 500kts is not the Phantom's strong suit. The photo-Crusader was slick [no weapons, bomb racks, pylons, or drop tanks]—absolutely clean! The F-4B had to drag all of the above accoutrements and had two very smokey versions of the J79 engine. To keep up with the photo bird and to kill the smoke, the F-4B spent lots of time in minimum afterburner.[xxxiii] The F-4B would win no miles-per-gallon awards, they would frequently require airborne refueling twice during a mission and on a few occasions, three refuels.

The reason for the mission was to get an up-to-date reading on the munitions being off-loaded in Haiphong. Unfortunately, we were not allowed to touch those weapons while off-loading at the piers. The munitions disappeared into the jungles of the North, only reappearing when they were used to attack and kill American forces both on the ground and in the air. On behalf of the families of the troops who died as a result of these stupidities I would like to thank leaders like Lyndon Johnson, Robert McNamara and various other politicians in Washington; let's make sure the enemy has all the ammo he needs before we engage him. The shame is that nothing was learned from the politician's mistakes in Vietnam. American lives continue to be squandered on the altar of political and diplomatic aspirations. Sorry, I can get carried away, but I feel better now.

Back to the tale at hand. I had planned an ingress into Vietnam about 30 miles to the east of Haiphong to take advantage of some radar cover from the hundreds of karst islands which lie to the east along the coast. Once over those islands we turned west and headed directly at Haiphong. Just before Haiphong we made a hard turn to the south staying over the east bank of the river. I turned on the cameras just before we turned south and left them on until we cleared land. Anti-aircraft fire was light to medium as we traversed the harbor area, mostly 37mm and 57mm and not particularly accurate. No SAMs were fired. So far, so good. Just to the southeast of Haiphong is a highway which goes about 25 miles ending at a small peninsula known as the Do Son peninsula jutting slightly into the Gulf of Tonkin. Along that highway were three or four targets, which were on our

xxxiii Unlike the one stage—on or off—RF-8 afterburner (AB), the Phantom had four stages of afterburner on each engine that would increase the thrust from 10,900 pounds at military power to 17,000 pounds at full AB—a major increase in thrust of about 56 percent. Unfortunately, that corresponded with an increase in fuel flow from about two to eight times that of the basic engine in military power.

monthly tasking list from the Pentagon. At this point they were in sort of a "nice to have" priority, however, sooner or later they would probably go to a "We want them NOW!" priority. Anticipating that we would be sent to photograph them, I reasoned that sooner might obviate another walk in the park later on.

We headed on down the highway and we would only be over the North for another three minutes before going feet wet. Anti-aircraft fire tracked us towards the Gulf but was still not catching us, we had it made. Well maybe, but not quite! I felt a bit of a jolt, similar to what we might expect when flying through another aircraft's turbulence. Only problem being that there were no aircraft ahead of us to cause turbulence. I checked all the cockpit instruments, everything appeared normal. We continued the run to the coast. Clearing the coast, the escort closed up the formation to check for any obvious damage. He called, "903, you've got a bit of the left wing missing." I answered, "Are you sure? It feels OK." "Oh, I'm quite sure," he replied. "There's also some damage back by the afterburner." We climbed to a medium-altitude, he would still have to get some gas before recovery.

Due to the cockpit location on the RF-8, the pilot can only see the leading edge of the wing, all of the damage was out of my view. I considered the possibility of diverting to a shore base, probably Da Nang in South Vietnam, but was really not all that enthused about spending time on the ground with the Marines—besides they shoot at you with mortars down there. If at all possible, I wanted back to the warm arms of mother *Roosevelt*.

After more fuel for the escort, we got down to serious business. The order of the day was to see what would happen at slower approach speeds. The first effects were felt at about 260 knots; the left wing got heavy and I had to start rolling in trim to the right. We slowed to 210 knots and lowered the landing gear. Additional right-wing trim was needed. About 190 knots I raised the wing and added more right-wing trim. Somewhere around 175 knots I had used all the lateral trim available. I now had to start holding in some right wing down with the primary flight controls. I slowed to about 165 knots and did some gentle turns. Would it go slower? I don't really know, but with full trim rolled in and holding some pressure to the right I'm not sure I wanted to try. Unfortunately, there are no procedures in the pilot's pocket checklist for partial wing landings. I'd like to tell you that I knew exactly what I was doing and had everything under total control, but that would be pure B.S..

I had reasoned that the angle-of-attack indicator, our primary speed indicator while landing, would be useless since it is calibrated for a complete wing. The airspeed indicator, while functioning and accurate, was the only thing I had. Unfortunately, I had no idea what the appropriate airspeed would be with some of the wing missing. I was basically flying by that old aviator's instrument, the seat of the pants and what felt right. There was no way I would make a normal pattern entry—left hand break, left hand pattern—so a straight-in approach was decided.

About 10 miles aft of the carrier I descended to 500ft and drove it straight in at 165kts expecting to pick up the "meatball" (visual glideslope aid) at about two miles. I was aware that with the carrier making all its own wind I would be flying with a right crosswind on final approach. A right crosswind would mean that the area of turbulence from the ship's structure, known to carrier pilots as the "burble" would occur just as the aircraft was on close final. I sure as hell didn't want any roll to the left as I approached the back end of the ship. Now the good news: old RF-8G Bureau Number 144615 was a thoroughbred. She cut right through the turbulence, slammed into the deck and snatched the two-wire. Though I was never an LSO (landing signal officer) I can still remember his debrief for the pass: "(OK) (HS) (FAW) (DNAR) (TWO)." The layman's translation reads: (OK)–fair pass–not the best, but acceptable; (HS)–little high start (I wasn't used to straight-in approaches); (FAW)–(underlined in the LSO's notes) – very fast all the way (hell yes, I was fast); (DNAR)–a little drop nose at the ramp (this was on purpose—there was no way I wanted to miss the wires and go around for another try); (TWO)–two wire (anything from the 1-wire to the 4-wire was quite alright with me).

I busied myself with raising the tail hook, adding power to get out of the landing area, engaging the nosewheel steering with my right hand and unlocking and folding the wing as I taxied forward. I got only the briefest glance in the mirrors at the left wing as I taxied forward. The wide-eyed open mouths of the flight deck crew told me a lot as they stared at the wing. I didn't spend a lot of time on the flight deck after I climbed out of the cockpit—I headed below to debrief and get something to drink. I was really thirsty.

Below decks I debriefed the admiral's staff and our photo interpreters so that they would know what they were looking at as soon as the film was processed. I found a place to relax and catch my breath. While discussing the flight with the officer in charge, John Baals, we got a heads-up from Air Ops that Lt. (j.g.) Norm Bundy had disappeared as he was heading into Indian country. About 45 minutes later Norm's escort pilot landed and told us that he had apparently hit the water as they were preparing to cross the beach. A rescue helicopter was launched and apparently found the crash site. They brought back the aircraft nosewheel and Norm's helmet, the only objects floating.

In my mind there were four possible causes of the crash, some more probable than others. Enemy action—there were always fishing junks just off the coast. However, it would take an extremely lucky shot from small arms to hit a jet aircraft and disable it. Engine failure—not likely, at the speed he was flying he would have enough kinetic energy to zoom climb to 1,500–2,000 feet for an ejection. Flight-control failure—a possibility—at a couple of hundred feet of altitude there would be almost no time to comprehend and react to a failure. Pilot error—despite the macho attitude of the Crusader pilot, the simple fact is that we are all human and we all make mistakes. The sea was very flat, hardly a ripple—the horizon was very hazy at low altitude and it was almost like flying in a milk bottle—not good conditions for low-altitude high-speed flight. It's possible that he lost his perspective relative to the surface of the water. We will never know for sure—the answers are lying in thousands of pieces on the floor of the Gulf of Tonkin.

I guess you could say it had been a hell of a day, full of a range of emotions. There was the anticipation of a combat flight; the ever-present thrill of a cat shot in a supersonic aircraft; the gnawing in the pit of your stomach as you went inland and the flak started; the uncertainty about whether you would make it home in one piece; the thrill of beating the odds and making it back; and then the crushing desolation of the loss of a squadron mate, a wingman, a buddy, your roommate.

I think that the flight surgeon dispensed a generous supply of medicinal brandy that evening. I would imagine that we even dipped into personal supplies—we needed it. I exempted myself from the flight schedule the next day to perform one of the more difficult tasks of my flying career: inventorying and packing Norm's gear to be shipped to his parents. Packing his gear was tough, but nowhere near as hard as a weekend stay with his parents some five months later.

Norm Green's addendum to his damaged RF-8G:

On the 14th of September, we arrived in Yokosuka, Japan for some R&R. As we were docking in Yokosuka, I happened to wander up to the flight deck and saw the outer wing panel of my damaged RF-8G, Bureau Number 144615, strapped to a pallet waiting to be offloaded.

Surrounding the pallet were four Japanese engineers, notebooks in hand, making copious notes... I was told that Vought Aircraft had shipped a complete set of engineering drawings for the outer wing panel while we were en route. I don't know whether they rebuilt the existing panel or built one from scratch, but I flew 144615 again on the 29th of October.

Prelaunch flight deck activity on board USS Franklin D. Roosevelt *(CVA-42), 1966–67. The plane captain is leaning into the cockpit preparing it for the VFP-62 pilot following his pre-flight inspection. To the left is a VF-32 "Swordsmen" F-4B Phantom and, on the right, an A-4 Skyhawk. (Jim Horgan)*

VFP-62 crew surveying the flak-damaged wing of Lt. Norm Green's RF-8G in the hangar bay. (Jim Macino ATR2)

Lt. Norm Green's VFP-62 RF-8G in USS Franklin D. Roosevelt*'s hangar bay showing another view of AAA damage. (Jim Macino ATR2)*

VFP-62 Vietnam Det. Officers: (L–R) Lt. (j. g.) Norm Bundy, Ens. Art Erz (PI), Lt. (j. g.) Ed Andrews, Lt. Norm Green, Lt. Cmdr. John Baals (OinC), Lt. Walt Pass (LDO Maintenance Officer), and Lt. (j. g.) Jim Ernst (PI). (Cmdr. Norm Green)

VFP-62 Det. 42 Vietnam detachment on board USS Franklin D. Roosevelt *(CVA-42). (Cmdr. Norm Green)*

VFP-62's final detachment to the Mediterranean was on board the USS Shangri La *(CVA-38) after VFP-62's disestablishment. Due to a mid-air collision, an RF-8G and pilot were lost and VFP-63's Lt. Len Johnson was assigned as replacement. He flew cross-country and arrived aboard in January 1968. Two RF-8s on the "Shang" were still in VFP-62's paint scheme. (Capt. Len Johnson)*

On January 18 1967, *Roosevelt* departed Southeast Asia for its Mayport, Florida, base. Norm Green transitioned to A-7 Corsairs in August 1967. After that, he spent three years as a VA-174 instructor, two years as flight deck officer on the USS *Saratoga* (CVA-60), and then joined VA-37 in 1972, flying A-7 combat missions over Vietnam. His last combat mission in the A-7 was on January 8, 1973 before the long voyage back to Mayport. With his wry sense of humor, he says, "Two VA-37 pilots who were shot down in 1972 and became POWs actually beat us home back to Jacksonville."

On January 5, 1968, VFP-62 was dis-established and VFP-63 assumed responsibility for East Coast carrier RF-8 photo-reconnaissance.

In Memoriam

Lieutenant, Junior Grade Norman Lee Bundy
January 26, 1941–September 6 1966
Miami, Florida

On September 6, 1966, Norman Bundy was the pilot of a VFP-62 RF-8G (Bu. No. 144624) launched from *Roosevelt* and, with his escort pilot, headed towards North Vietnam. Bundy's aircraft crashed before reaching the shore, about 20 miles east of Thanh Hoa Province, North Vietnam. He was on a combat mission, although his loss is classified as noncombat. It was felt that there was little or no hope he survived and Bundy was declared Killed/Body Not Recovered.

He is honored on the Vietnam Veterans Memorial in Washington, D.C.: Wall, Panel 10E Line 72.

VFP-62 Vietnam Det. 42 on board USS Franklin D. Roosevelt *(CVA-42), 1966–67. Note the 25 combat mission symbols on the fuselage. Lt. (j. g.) Norm Bundy was killed in this RF-8G on September 6, 1966. (Jim Macino ATR2)*

Tributes and Memories

Commander Norm Green:

Norm Bundy and I spent the summer of 1965 cruising the waters of the Mediterranean but we had never met. As so often happens in large squadrons which do not deploy as a unit, but sends detachments in various directions, we were in the same body of water, in the same squadron, and our paths never crossed. I had left Jacksonville in early February aboard *Shangri La* [CVA-38] and Norm must have arrived in the squadron just after I left. After some appropriate indoctrination, Norm was dispatched to the Mediterranean in June aboard *Franklin D. Roosevelt*. It would be half a year before we would meet. Norm became my "little brother," a year younger than I was. Norm and I were like two peas in a pod and our attitudes were in sync on almost all subjects.

A couple of months later word leaked out that *Roosevelt* would depart in early summer, destination the Gulf of Tonkin and Vietnam. This would be the squadron's only combat deployment to Southeast Asia. All of the participants from the squadron's Cuban crisis flying had departed the squadron and we would all be rookies at the combat game. Though we didn't know it at the time, we would be flying the "friendly" skies of North Vietnam before year's end. I was initially assigned as one of the four pilots in the detachment and when one of the other pilots dropped off the roster, Norm was the replacement. In mid-June we flew our aircraft to Naval Air Station Mayport and our Crusaders were hoisted aboard the Rosy, the beginning of the trek to southeast Asia.

On the evening of September. 5, 1966, I made my evening visit with the admiral's ops staff; they had two requests for recce of targets quite far north, both would require armed escorts. Exercising schedules officer's prerogative, I put my name next to the first mission. I asked Norm if he wanted the other mission and he answered in the affirmative.

I believe the ship was currently on the noon to midnight schedule, so my mission to Haiphong was scheduled for the first launch at noon with Norm's mission, a bit farther south on the 1:30 pm launch. It was a hot, windless day in the Gulf of Tonkin. The FDR was cranking on every knot she could produce and the C-11 catapults were taxed to the limit.

The first half of the Norm [Green] and Norm [Bundy] "show" was successful in that I got photography of the Haiphong harbor with freighters offloading cargo; the price, a bit high, was a shattered port outer wing panel [see above]. The price for the later performance was unacceptably high as documented in history, and Norm Bundy paid the price. He was very well liked, not only within our detachment, but across the entire air wing. He had made the previous Mediterranean cruise with many of those pilots, so it was a somber night on the Rosy boat.

I have been asked, many times, what my opinion was of the cause of the crash. Of course, we could never know for sure, but here is my guess. As I mentioned earlier, there was no wind, and that translated into a perfectly flat sea. There was no texture to the sea surface, it was like a smooth lake. Couple the sea conditions to a typical Gulf of Tonkin summer haze—a very indistinct horizon, then add in very low-altitude and high-speed flight and you have a perfect recipe for disaster. I suspect something distracted Norm for a fraction of a second and under those conditions, he didn't have a fraction of a second to spare.

The next day, my name did not appear on the flight schedule. The boss had told me to take the day off. In retrospect, I would rather have flown. Instead, I spent the entire day packing Norm's personal effects for shipment to his parents. This was a task I was totally unprepared for. I had no formal guidance, but common sense dictated a very careful inventory of his belongings to prevent shipment of any object which might cause further grief for his family. This even required a careful reading of all of his correspondence, especially letters from his girlfriend, Sherri. I think there were a couple of those that did not make it to the boxes along with the June issue of *Playboy* magazine.

If you have never had to perform such a function, I can assure you it was no fun. Another somber event was a memorial service on the flight deck, probably a week later, as we headed for the Philippines. I remember little except the boss, John Baals, casting the wreath to the waters, and the playing of taps.

I knew that the ship's CO had written a letter of condolence to Norm's parents [see below]. I imagined that our CO back at Cecil Field would have sent a similar letter, but I cannot recall ever seeing it. I wasn't sure what Navy policy was, if any, concerning individual shipmates corresponding with the family, and so after waiting a respectful time for official correspondence to be delivered, I sent a brief letter to his parents and promised to contact them after returning home. Then it occurred to me that there was another communication that should be made and it would definitely not be accomplished through government agencies, there was his girlfriend, Sherri. She had no official or legal relationship to Norm—there were few of us in the squadron who were aware of her existence, and yet I felt she should somehow be included. I got off a short note to her. I knew that I would see her in person after I returned.

In an unusual coincidence two months later, I was heading towards North Vietnam one afternoon. I had just checked in with Red Crown, the Navy cruiser that controlled all air traffic both going into and coming out of North Vietnam. Suddenly, there was a familiar voice on the radio. It was Bill Worley, a roommate with Norm and me. He had transferred to VF-191 and was flying from *Ticonderoga* [CVA-14]. We had just the briefest of conversations. I wondered if he had heard of Norm's death. The frequency was monitored by North Vietnam, so I could say nothing about Norm. In a strange twist of fate, Bill would die a year and a half later when his Blue Angel F-11F crashed into the desert while training near El Centro, Ca[lifornia]. Flying low and fast can be very dangerous.

We returned to Jacksonville on January 19, 1967, and I moved in with another pilot from *Roosevelt*. He had known Norm through the last two deployments and we frequently spoke of his accident. Early in the year I touched base with Norm's parents and they invited me to visit them if ever in Miami. I promised that I would visit, and in March I drove to Miami and spent a weekend with them. When you mention Miami, many people think of the beach, the glitzy mega hotels, the money and swankiness of South Beach, etc. This was not the Miami of Wayne and Gladys Bundy. They lived a quiet life in a middle-class working neighborhood of North Miami. I was a bit apprehensive, how would this work out? Wayne, Norm's dad, was rather introspective and quiet, but then what would you expect of a gentleman who six months ago had lost his only child. Gladys, Norm's mom, was the sweetest lady you could hope to meet. She hugged me and held on as though she was afraid that I would disappear. She could not have been more gracious. They were thoroughly nice people and I thanked myself for having so thoroughly sanitized Norm's belongings to be shipped home. Over the next couple of years, we exchanged greetings and occasional notes. A year and a half later they made the drive from Miami to Jacksonville and were in attendance at my wedding.

One other possible tragedy may have resulted from Norm's death; a couple of years later his girlfriend committed suicide. Who knows what motivations influence people who have experienced intense sorrow and trauma?

In the big picture I had known Norm for an extremely short part of my life, less than nine months, but it was a friendship rooted in our similarities and our respect for each other's qualities. I continue to my best to uphold the reputation of the "terrible trio." R.I.P. little brother.

Former Navy Lieutenant Hank Miller was a VA-152 Skyraider driver on *Oriskany,* 1966–68:

Norm Bundy was my roommate at Auburn University and a great guy. I still miss him.

Captain Bob Kiem USN (ret.):

> Norm was a good friend through the training command and as we were both doing our thing in respective RAGs [Replacement Air Groups] at NAS Cecil Field, he in VF-174, me in VA-44. I was in VA-12 on the *FDR*, he of course, was in the VFP-62 det. A real heart breaker of a day when we lost him. I am not the type who cries easily, but must admit that I shed more than a few tears during his memorial service.

COMMANDING OFFICER
USS FRANKLIN D. ROOSEVELT (CVA-42)
FPO NEW YORK 09501

7 September 1966

Mr. & Mrs. W. W. Bundy
42 N.W. 92nd Street
Miami, Florida

Dear Mr. & Mrs. Bundy:

By now you have been informed of the tragic loss of your son, Norman. I realize no amount of words said or written can change the fact that he is gone or make you feel the loss any less acutely. However, being ~~the father of a boy almost Norman's age, I know that in your place, I~~ would want the best explanation possible, and from the most senior officer available as to what happened and why.

I only assumed command of ROOSEVELT recently, and I had not become personally acquainted with your son. The work which he and his detachment were accomplishing was quite well known to all of us aboard, however, who have a hand in directing the Navy's combat efforts here off Vietnam. This work is vital to the entire task force, and Norman was a valuable member of this important team.

He was launched at 2:30 PM on a photo reconnaissance mission from our position close to a hundred miles off the coast of Vietnam. He was accompanied by an escort F4H piloted by LT P. G. Tremmel of squadron VF-14. The two pilots effected a rendezvous and headed for the coast. A few miles prior to penetration, Norman began letting down in a high speed turn in preparation for coastal entry. He was below and slightly ahead of the chase plane. As he reached a low altitude at a speed of about 500 knots, instead of leveling out, he flew into the water while still a few miles short of the coast. The

approx. 625 ~~miles~~ per hr,

exact position was 19° - 48'N, 106° - 05'E. LT Tremmel, the chase pilot, saw the crash. He immediately informed rescue elements in their vicinity and a rescue helicopter was promptly launched for the scene. LT Tremmel remained on station over the crash site until the helicopter arrived, and a thorough search was conducted.

There was no sign of survival, and from a crash at that speed there could have been none. The helicopter was able to retrieve Norman's helmet and his life vest (flotation), but that was all.

The cause of this crash is, of course, undetermined. It is highly unlikely that it was caused by enemy fire because they were still a few miles off the coast. I can only offer an opinion based on my own experience in this and similiar type aircraft. It is very likely that Norman was concentrating on setting up his cameras for his photo run which would commence momentarily, and consequently failed to monitor his altitude at a very critical time, i.e., while descending at high speed, close to the surface. This has happened to many pilots, having their attention diverted at a crucial moment.

It may be of some comfort to you to know that your son was highly respected and esteemed by his fellow officers and men in VFP-62 Detachment 42. He was truly a professional naval aviator in every sense of the word, and he died under the most honorable circumstances in the service of his country. We are all, aboard ROOSEVELT, grieved at his loss, and we will honor his memory with appropriate religious services within the next few days. I will insure that you are informed completely concerning these services aboard ship, although our location and present employment will preclude your attendance.

If there is any service I can render or any further information I can provide you, please feel free to call on me.

Sincerely,

GEORGE C. TALLEY, JR.
Captain, U. S. Navy

2

Major Larry Gibson USMC (Ret.):

Norm and I were in the same pre-flight class that commenced on April 1st, 1963. Our rooms were side-by-side in the old wooden BOQ [Bachelor Officer Quarters] that has probably long been demolished and replaced. Norm was my best friend while going through the training command and I was certainly one of his best. Norm had an advantage going through VT-1 in the T-34B as he already had his private pilot license. I believe he had received it through Naval ROTC [Reserve Officers Training Corps] at Auburn University. Of course, we never flew together in T-34s, but he was chosen as "Student of the Week" once, while in VT-1 and he certainly breezed through the syllabus there.

Norm had another even more permanent influence on my life. He had met a Meridian girl through having his car repaired after someone backed into it. Although he never developed an interest in her, he introduced us and the rest is history, as we married one week after getting my wings.

CHAPTER 6

1967–68: Dangerous Skies Over Hanoi and Haiphong

Dr. Mark Jacobsen from the Naval Historical Center gives us his reflections on the war at this point, "In 1967, *Rolling Thunder* pilots began to strike selected targets in Hanoi and Haiphong, notably North Vietnam's power plants but also key bridges. The United States also now struck MiG-capable airfields."[1]

Rolling Thunder was still causing death and destruction on both sides. At the same time, anti-war protests were still raging in the U.S. In Southeast Asia, naval aviators followed their orders and faced the increasing danger of the formidable air defenses in the heart of North Vietnam. During 1967–68, VFP-63 would lose six RF-8s including three pilots killed in action.

The photo and escort pilots still teamed together to improve the odds. On a photo-reconnaissance mission, the VFP-63 pilot was the lead and a fighter escort pilot assigned as his wingman, even if the fighter pilot was of senior rank. This arrangement generally worked well but there were exceptions. They flew a loose deuce formation—either pilot, depending upon the combat situation, could adopt the role of lead while the other covered as wingman—with the escort flying 50–100 feet aft and at a slightly higher altitude. His responsibility was to watch the photo jet's tail for any anti-aircraft artillery (AAA), surface-to-air missile (SAM), or MiG threats, giving the photo pilot the freedom to navigate to the target and prepare for his photo run. There were good reasons for this unusual arrangement. Commander Andre Coltrin provides the following for our understanding of this dynamic:

> In general, two different policies were followed. The one that was used by the air wing I was in, specified that on a photo mission, the photo pilot was the flight leader, no matter the rank difference between the photo and escort pilots. The photo pilot briefed and led the mission. In almost all cases, the escorts I had assigned to me were outstanding and I felt very comfortable with them flying a very loose wing on me. As long as they kept me in sight, called out "flak" that was starting to track me, while my head was buried in my camera viewfinder, I did not care how loose a wing position they flew.

Most of the escorts were very happy to fly the photo escort role for a couple of reasons. First, the flight altitude was a lot lower than they normally flew on other escort missions and especially CAP [Combat Air Patrol] missions, just burrowing holes in the sky. Secondly, there was a greater sensation of speed and a feeling of being in the middle of the action—and, you were. I can only remember one flight that I did not see any shots fired at me over NVN [North Vietnam], and that flight was over Haiphong harbor during bad weather. Maybe shots were fired, but because of the weather they were just not observed. Because of my propensity of getting fired at, I had a reputation of being a flak magnet.

Different fighter pilots would approach me and inquire when and where my next mission would be and then approach their schedules officer to see if they could be assigned as my escort for that flight. On one flight over Haiphong harbor, the squadron's operations officer reserved that flight for himself. He was very disappointed at the lack of activity.

And then there was a second policy for fighter escorts: On another occasion, I was assigned to Photo Det. 11 aboard USS *Intrepid* (CVA-11). When the officer in charge of the *Coral Sea* [CVA-43] photo detachment, Lieutenant Commander Jim Vescelius, was shot down (see "In Memoriam" this chapter), I was temporarily assigned as officer in charge to replace Jim, until a more senior replacement from the United States could arrive in just a couple of weeks.

On *Coral Sea*, the fighter squadrons flew F-4 Phantoms. When I went to my first flight briefing with my escort, he quickly informed me by lifting his collar to show me his rank that he was senior and was therefore going to lead the flight. Up to that point it had never occurred to me that the flight lead polices between air wings could be different. I had been informed by CAG [Commander, Air Group] when I arrived that if I saw any changes that needed to be made, to contact him. That was now at the top of my list. As it turned out the F-4 driver determined the target was weathered in and we did not even cross the beach.

My rationale for the photo pilot to lead the flight was:

1. He knew the photo requirements.
2. He knew the capabilities of his equipment.
3. He knew what could be achieved in various climatic conditions.
4. Most important, it would not require a lead change at the most critical time of the flight, when the photo pilot had to fully orient himself in relation to the target, adjust his reaction to the threat i.e., AAA, SAMs, weather conditions, and ensure cameras are ground tracking properly.
5. It would increase his skills in navigation when missions had to be flown and a two-seat escort was not available, due to mission overload or just plain maintenance availability. Many photo missions were flown where the photo aircraft was escorted by another photo bird because of lack of fighter availability.

Lt. Andre Coltrin in an RF-8G during a carrier qualification period at NAS Miramar. Note the cloth strap attached to the canopy to the fuselage; this simple device helped to protect the canopy's hinge pins from breaking in wind gusts. The canopy rail has an optical device that can be moved while the pilot looks through it to center a subject for oblique air-to-air photos. (Cmdr. Peter Mersky)

The flight deck officer is giving the signal to launch this VFP-63 Det 43 RF-8G from USS Coral Sea *(CVA-43), October 27, 1967, in the Gulf of Tonkin. Note the "Eyes of the Fleet" logo on the edge of the raised wing. (Robert L. Lawson Collection, National Naval Aviation Museum, Pensacola, FL)*

USS Coral Sea *(CVA-43) sailors take a short rest during a lull in flight operations on Yankee Station off North Vietnam, circa 1966. They are by the steam chest where the proper setting of steam pressure is set for a given aircraft. Notice there is a pressure gauge by the sailor's foot. That is the last thing looked at to ensure the proper setting is in place before the cat is fired. (National Naval Aviation Museum, Pensacola, FL)*

USS Intrepid *(CVA-11) in her attack carrier guise with a deck load of A-4s, A-1s and F-8s spotted aft as she prowls the South China Sea in November 1968. Note the bow elevator is lowered to the hangar deck. (National Naval Aviation Museum, Pensacola, FL)*

6. It also provided a great training and confidence building experience.

I did not push it through CAG. The det had not been operating this way and I was not sure how hard the transition would be. Also, they were going to get a new permanent officer in charge very soon and I did not know his desires.

On January 5, 1967, USS *Hancock* (CVA-19), with VFP-63 Detachment B aboard, returned to Yankee Station, just five months after Det. L departed on August 1, 1966—a quick turnaround. Det. L had one pilot killed in action and two became prisoners of war. Lieutenant (junior grade) Len Johnson (now Captain) was on both detachments and recalls how many young, inexperienced, but eager, recon pilots learned to fly and survive the hostile skies of North Vietnam.

The fighter pilot who was assigned recce escort duty would meet me in Air Intelligence to brief the upcoming flight. I enjoyed watching their reaction when I answered the big question, "Where are we going?" Relief could be seen on their faces if it was a simple road recce mission in a lightly protected area. Concern could be read in their eyes if the mission was a BDA [Bomb Damage Assessment] flight, in the heavily defended Haiphong-Hanoi area. When it was the latter, they would become grave and very interested in my planned route and tactics. Otherwise, for the escort, it would be a joy ride.

VFP-63 Det. B officers on board USS Hancock *(CVA-19) in 1967. Lt. Cmdr. Schulze (kneeling with mascot). Standing (L–R) are Ens. John J. Czekanski (PIO), Lt. Bill D. Stiehman (CVW-5 flight surgeon), Lt. j. g. E. H. Haffey (senior PIO), Lt. Ron Ball, Lt. Colin M. Clark and Lt. (j. g.) L. E. Johnson. (Cmdr. Peter Mersky)*

Another perspective from (then) Lieutenant Dick Smith of fighter squadron VF-211:

> I don't think anyone liked being an escort. The photo pilots had a hard mission as they flew straight and level taking their pictures and several were shot down. As an escort you were unable at times to give them any warnings and you always felt that you might have missed something such as AAA, at the time you're checking for MiGs. I have a huge respect for all the photo pilots.

Lt. (j.g.) Len Johnson Gets Lost Over North Vietnam and Earns a Medal

Flying off *Hancock* in 1966 and 1967 was the most exciting and challenging experience of my career. Although it was exciting, it was not enjoyable because of the strong possibility that I might not come home. There were certainly plenty of thrills and we did have fun, but it was always tempered by the reality of the situation.

My mission was a road recce in the Thanh Hoa area. Dennis Duffy was my escort. Thanh Hoa was known for its bridge that we were never able to completely destroy. The weather was marginal, with low ceilings and rain. As I approached the city my electronic counter measures equipment gave me a missile launch warning. I went into a hard, descending turn and headed back out to sea. The low cloud cover had me concerned and the warning convinced me to abort. I never saw the SAM.

I headed for Nam Dinh hoping for better conditions. I flew across the coast at 500 feet to stay below the clouds. For the first time flying over NVN I saw extensive ground activity—trains and truck convoys moving about. Due to the bad weather, there were no bombing missions being flown, and the North Vietnamese were taking advantage of the situation. I had coasted-in more to the west than I thought. Instead of being south of Nam Dinh, I was north of Thanh Hoa and had picked up Route One, the main artery that runs from Saigon to Hanoi.

I was surprised to see the extensive truck and train activity and proceeded to activate my cameras. The film moves through the cameras like movie film to compensate for the high speed of the aircraft. By looking through a scope in the cockpit and timing the speed of the film to that of the ground passing beneath, each opening of the aperture, in effect, captures a "still" (i.e., the subject is not moving) image.

Maneuvering the aircraft over the trains and trucks and monitoring the camera operation kept me busy. I was lower than normal, which was definitely not a good idea. Each time I was about to quit and head home I would spot another train or truck convoy. AAA was starting to catch up with me. I had been overland longer than usual and I was dangerously low, flying in and out of rain showers. The heavy AAA increased so much that I had to break off my mission.

I thought I was in the vicinity of Nam Dinh, so I turned to the east. This heading would be the shortest route to the Gulf of Tonkin and safety. After about ten minutes with no water in sight, it was clear that my position had been a lot further inland and to the north of Nam Dinh. "I should be out of here by now," I thought. Finally, in about another ten minutes, I was over the coast.

That night at dinner in *Hancock*'s ward room, our two photo interpreters walked in with a large map and laid it on the table where six of us were seated. This was a bit unusual. Al Lipskey, one of the PIs asked me in an accusingly, exasperated tone, "Do you know where you were this afternoon?" It had taken them several hours of looking at film to match the images to points on the chart. My debriefing had not helped them any, for in fact, I did not know where I had been that afternoon. "Somewhere north of Thanh Hoa," I had told them.

The route that I had flown, with the cameras on, was highlighted on the map of NVN. I had flown right up to the outskirts of Hanoi! No wonder the AAA was so heavy. John Allen, sitting to

Lt. (j. g.) Len "Rocky" Johnson receives a commendation for photo recon over North Vietnam. (Capt. Len Johnson.)

Two VFP-63 Det. Bravo RF-8Gs astern of USS Hancock *(CVA-19) during the carrier and its air wing's (CVW-21) Vietnam deployment in 1967. (Robert L. Lawson Collection, National Naval Aviation Museum, Pensacola, FL)*

> my left, commented sarcastically, "Rocky the flying squirrel."[xxxiv] For the next eleven years my name was *Rocky*. I did not mind being identified with the squirrel. We each had our share of adventures, and we were both harmless.
>
> The Navy gave me a medal for that flight. There was probably some debate on whether to give me a medal or a reprimand. The citation stated that the intelligence obtained from my film was valuable to the war effort. A few days later Denny's (my fighter escort) squadronmates gave us a more meaningful remembrance of that day—a flower in a cup, they called it the "Steeped in S--t but Smelling Like a Rose" award. Denny told me recently that he got a chewing out from his CO. Not sure why, he was just following my lead, doing his job.

Johnson remembers another learning instance on his 1965–66 Det. L, while still a nugget, when a very senior officer was assigned as his escort:

> The Skipper of VF-24, Commander Harry Post, was my escort on one of those "easy" road recces in the southern part of NVN. I decided on a backdoor entry—entering NVN airspace from Laos to the west. I naively thought that I would surprise the enemy by coming in that way. Anyway, it was a different challenge and new territory to see.
>
> I navigated by flying from one landmark that I recognized to another that I could pick out in the distance. My course over the ground was a series of misshapen Ss. Straight lines for a timed period on a set course were a no-no.
>
> When we arrived in Laos, over what I calculated, very roughly, to be my letdown point, there was an extensive cloud layer below us. We were over mountainous terrain. The Skipper was rightfully hesitant about descending into that cloud layer, over unknown territory, on the wing of a very junior pilot, known as "Rocky the Squirrel," because he often wandered off course.
>
> I was hesitant too, but I was not going to let him know that. I told him to stay high; I would go down and see if we had enough room under the cloud cover to operate. I descended into the dark clouds, trusting in the terrain elevations on my chart. I would descend no lower than the highest peak in the area. I was confident that I would break out well above the ground, and call the Skipper down, and we would continue the low-level portion of our mission east into NVN.
>
> The cloud cover was thicker and lower to the ground than I had counted on. I broke out of the clouds into a valley with the ground less than 1,000 feet below me. The mountain peaks surrounding that valley rose above me into the clouds. This was not good!
>
> I briefed the Skipper about the conditions. He suggested that I abort the mission. That was fine with me, since he suggested it. When you are twenty-two years old, you know by observation that guys get killed in this profession, but you don't believe it will happen to you. When you reach the mature age of thirty you know very well that it may happen to you and it will be sooner than later, if one isn't very careful. The Skipper had reached that age.

A number of VF-24 pilots accounted for a number of MiG kills: Lieutenant (later Rear Admiral) Commander Bobby C. Lee and Lieutenant Phillip R. Wood became the first VF-24 pilots to shoot down MiG aircraft over North Vietnam on May 19, 1967. The MiGs were downed with AIM-9 Sidewinder air-to-air missiles. Then, on July 21, 1967, Commander Marion H. Issacks (Executive Officer) and Lieutenant Commander Robert L. Kirkwood made the 3rd and 4th MiG kills for their squadron with 20mm guns and Sidewinder missiles.

---

xxxiv "The Adventures of Rocky and Bullwinkle" was a popular TV show during the 1960s.

F-8C Crusaders of Fighter Squadron VF-24 and F-8E Crusaders of VF-211 on the catapults and positioned behind jet blast deflectors during flight operations on board USS Bon Homme Richard *(CVA-31) off the coast of North Vietnam, March 3, 1967. During this cruise, each of these squadrons splashed four North Vietnamese MiG-17 fighters in air-to-air combat. (National Naval Aviation Museum, Pensacola, FL)*

This view of the Vietnam People's Air Force airfield at Kep in 1967 shows revetments housing a few aircraft. (Cmdr. Peter Mersky)

A MiG scare and SAM encounter happened to (then) Lieutenant Andre Coltrin when he was temporary officer in charge of Det. 11 on board *Intrepid* in 1967. Being alert avoided an encounter with a section of MiGs scouting for prey. On a following mission, he had an adrenaline pumping near miss with multiple SAMs. He describes how that happened:

> My second cruise in 1967 to Vietnam was aboard *Intrepid*. The Air Wing was structured a little different. Due to space and size, major changes had to be made. Where other air wings consisted of two fighter squadrons and two attack squadrons, *Intrepid* had two attack squadrons and one four-pilot fighter detachment from VF-111. Because of the small number of fighter pilots, their availability was spread very thin. It was very common for them to launch with the attack squadron to cover them during an attack and then rendezvous with the photo pilot for his mission. These guys were definitely over worked.
>
> On one such day, I was orbiting over the water southeast of Haiphong waiting for my escort who was guarding for an attack near Hanoi, when several bandit calls were issued. From the sound of it there were many MiGs in the area. It was a beautiful bright clear day without a cloud in the sky. Out of the east, a few thousand feet below and forward of me, two MiGs appeared. It would have been a fighter pilot's dream. But, for an unarmed, unescorted photo pilot it was more like a nightmare instead of a dream. The only thing I could do was stay high, try to keep me between them and the sun and keep them in sight. Shortly they disappeared—I think landing at Dang Lam air field just southeast of Haiphong. I appreciated my escorts so much more after that day.
>
> I had another heart thumping flight with one of the fighter detachment's pilots, a very young Lieutenant, Junior Grade Rick Wenzel. Rick joined the fighter detachment while we were in the Philippines just before we set sail for Yankee Station. Soon he was assigned an escort mission with me. It turned out to be one that neither of us will ever forget. The target was heavily defended and the AAA was constant. As we were exiting the immediate target area, the SAM alert warning system, we now had in our planes, went from search mode to lock on and firing mode. SAMs were in the air! A typical description of a SAM is a telephone pole with fire coming out of one end. One came so close to Rick's airplane he felt he could reach out and touch it. It is very common when SAMs are fired, they are fired in multiples. That way when the targeted pilot is concentrating on evading the one, the second or third one sneaks in behind. On that day we had FIVE fired at us—one right after the other. There was no thought of navigation, just evasion. We seemed to be twisting and turning forever. When we finally landed aboard the good ole *Intrepid* and exited our planes, we met on the flight deck and gave each other a big grin followed by a back-slapping hug. It was great to be alive! In an interview, Rick Wenzel remembers, "feeling they were being

In 1967, during an Iron Hand *mission over North Vietnam, Lt. Cmdr. Mike Estocin aggressively attacked three SAM sites, his A-4 Skyhawk suffering such extensive damage that he had to be refueled virtually the entire way back to USS* Ticonderoga *(CVA 14). He displayed extraordinary airmanship recovering aboard, his battle-damaged aircraft pictured here. Seven days later, Estocin was killed in action on another* Iron Hand *mission. He received the Medal of Honor posthumously. (National Naval Aviation Museum, Pensacola, FL)*

> bore sighted by the NVN SAM crew. He watched one SAM flying at Mach 3 heading for him and pulled his F-8 into an 8G turn. He reflexively picked up his feet to protect himself as it exploded beneath his jet. His ECM [Electronic Countermeasures] gear was in a rapid high-pitched warble."

Mission Planning: A Requirement for a Photo Pilot

The detachment photo intel officer provided briefing material to the photo pilot on his mission objectives and any anticipated dangers. The following story by Andre Coltrin illustrates the importance of mission planning:

> On my first flight during my second cruise aboard *Intrepid* in 1967, I was assigned a road recon flight in the lower central part of North Vietnam. For a flight like this, it is to basically fly up the road with the cameras continually running to catch all road traffic. In the RF-8A, this was relatively easy to keep the road centered in the viewfinder by just applying rudder and skidding the aircraft keeping the wings level. Later, in the RF-8G, fins were added near the tail to add stability during high-speed runs. Those fins made it more difficult to skid the aircraft.
>
> In any case, I considered this to be a no sweat, low threat task and did minimal pre-mission planning because I had been there before and was way overconfident. As I continued up the road, it dawned on me that I was concentrating on keeping the road in the viewfinder and that I really did not know how far I had traveled. Suddenly, my escort started calling out heavy flak all around us. I broke out of there and headed for a clear area. In so doing, I was able to get a clear view of where I had stupidly led us directly over—one of the most heavily defended bridges in North Vietnam, the Thanh Hoa Bridge.
>
> The section of road I was assigned ended many miles before the bridge. With luck we were able to escape without damage, especially since I had been flying mostly level without much jinking and altitude changes. We should have been sitting ducks. My escort was all excited about all the fireworks and had a big grin on his face when he debriefed. I never admitted to him my mistake, but I swore to myself I would never lead another flight with such poor pre-mission planning again. It was a real wakeup call for me, as to what overconfidence can do. I would have had a horrible burden to carry if he had been shot down or killed.

Late 1967 Peace Initiatives Fail

Several promising opportunities raised hopes for peace negotiations in July–September 1967. A new player on the diplomatic stage, Henry Kissinger, became involved and the North Vietnamese leaders seemed receptive to discussions. However, a tragic lack of White House communications on these efforts with *Rolling Thunder* commanders collapsed the initiatives when massive bombing attacks around Hanoi and Haiphong enraged the North Vietnamese and they balked. There were several of these clumsy diplomatic attempts.

With the upcoming presidential election in November 1968, President Johnson faced the progress of the war and his accountability for the lack of any. He had withdrawn from the election and the Republican candidate, Richard Nixon, promised a negotiated settlement and withdrawal with honor. President Johnson countered by trying to get negotiations started again and commanded the Navy and Air Force to cease

A railroad and highway bridge in Haiphong receives attention from CVW-15 in 1967. While these strikes could have helped bring the communists to the peace talks much sooner, the incomprehensible bombing halt instituted on November 1, 1968 by President Johnson undid everything the intense campaign had accomplished and kept the war going for at least another four years. (Cmdr. Peter Mersky)

Rolling Thunder missions over North Vietnamese targets after March 31, 1968. Unarmed Navy photo jets would still fly reconnaissance missions to watch North Vietnamese operations. They were still in danger.

MiG Attack—A Fighter Escort Pilot Earns His Pay

Throughout this book, and in particular this chapter, fighter escorts are discussed. The majority of photo pilots welcomed the extra security they offered, but a few thought they were a hindrance and drew more attention to them. The following story demonstrates that where MiGs were a threat, the unarmed photo pilot could only rely on his jet's speed and his fighter escort pilot for a safe return to his ship.

On July 9, 1968, VFP-63's Lieutenant Bill Kocar and his F-8 escort pilot, VF-191's Lieutenant Commander John B. Nichols III, launched from USS *Ticonderoga* (CVA-14) and headed toward their targets along the Song Ca River. Bill Kocar describes how they were attacked by a MiG:

Well, in looking back at the incident of the MiG encounter that I was involved in, it certainly seems like a distant memory. The incident has been written up in several books about the naval air war in Vietnam, but I think the best is told in the book, *On Yankee Station*, co-authored by John Nichols III and Barrett Tillman. Just to add some additional information I have of that particular day, here are several things that I recall that aren't featured in the book.

First, John was not the primary escort pilot for the mission. I can't remember who he was, but whomever it was, his plane went "down" [maintenance problem] before launch. John was the back-up pilot but had not been briefed on the hop. Once airborne, we went to a secure frequency and I outlined what we would be doing over North Vietnam. As we went feet dry, John armed his 'winders [Sidewinder air-to-air missiles] and off we went. To my recollection, I was not flying the mission at 2,000 feet, rather I was at 4,000 feet, basically my minimum when I flew over the North. I was flying at approximately 400 knots, jinking very little as we were flying over an area that was mostly isolated; I was just looking for targets of opportunity that I could photograph. John got my attention when he said "Corktip (my call sign) you have 37s coming at you, then yelled 57s [37mm & 57mm AAA], then all of a sudden said, (I have it on tape!) "You have a f—ing MiG on your tail, break left," which I did pulling about 7Gs in afterburner! I think at first, John was out of position and that is why he was calling the flak rather than seeing the MiG. So, if he were in proper position, he would have been just aft and above me covering my six and clearing the area. In that position he would have seen the MiG as soon as he starting shooting at me.

Anyway, the encounter went as told in the book ["Nichols fired a Sidewinder at the MiG and missed, but scared the pilot into his gun sights, and the North Vietnamese pilot then engaged

A VFP-63 Det 14 RF-8G is towed into position on board USS Ticonderoga *(CVA-14) in preparation for launch operations, circa 1967–68. This aircraft was lost on December 16, 1969 when Lt. Victor Buckley disappeared without a trace. (Frank Bodden)*

afterburner that made him a perfect target for another missile."], Nichols' second Sidewinder scored a direct hit. However, the first 'winder went by my wing about 20 feet. I thought that the MiG had shot it and was somewhat worried that another one would be coming along! I asked John where was the MiG and that is when the MiG rolled wings level and hit burner. The rest being history.

I pulled up and tried to cover John, that's when I saw the debris of the MiG falling earth bound. I did tell John I wanted to take pictures as the MiG fell to earth. At that point, we heard CAG say, "Get the hell out of there, there are more MiGs in the area." [Apparently the carrier air wing commander received radar or electronic intelligence to that effect.] So, we headed for feet wet. [Then the two jets headed to an overhead tanker]

I do remember John was so excited it took him about six or eight times to get the basket connected so he could take on some fuel. I hooked in first try! We requested a carrier fly-by, *Top Gun* style and flew deck level past the carrier, then we both broke skyward and did several rotations—fun stuff.

After we did our flyby and landed, it was just like the movie *Top Gun*, all the Brass were waiting on the flight deck to congratulate us, John more than me because I was just the decoy! It was the first MiG kill for our air wing, so it was a real big thing.

The next day when I was assigned a mission, I showed up at the ready room to brief my escort and lo and behold there were six fighter pilots that had been assigned to escort my mission! They all wanted a MiG! That lasted several days, then the flights got back to normal.

A VF-191 F-8E Crusader over Mount Fuji, Japan, circa 1968. (Lt. Bill Kocur)

Ordnancemen loading a Sidewinder missile onto an F-8 Crusader of VF-194 on board USS Ticonderoga *(CVA-14), Gulf of Tonkin, 1965. (National Naval Aviation Museum, Pensacola, FL)*

Aircraft Maintenance Administration Third Class Frank Bodden was in the Ready Room when Bill Kocar came back from that hop. He remembers, "Lieutenant Kocar was the most excited and shaken up pilot you've ever seen." In March of the following year, Kocar started his flying career with Continental Airlines.

A Fighter Escort Gets Hit by AAA

Most often, the photo jet was likely to be hit by AAA. It was first to enter the combat area and not able to jink due to the necessity of keeping steady and level in a photo run. However, escorts were hit also. From the same fighter squadron, VF-191, as the previous story, Lieutenant Dave Leighton tells how he was hit and survived:

> When the Vietnam War comes up, often someone asks "Did you ever get hit?" Yah, they hit me during a photo escort of VFP-63's OinC, Lieutenant Commander John Nork, over Vinh Son. We thought they had their anti-aircraft school there. The photo jet, running understandably "hot" about three or four thousand feet and me up above a thousand or two, weaving back and forth watching… Then it came! A bunch of 85mm bursts marching right up his tail. I radioed, "Corktip break! You're locked… coming up your six!" Watching him, naturally, I wasn't looking around (What did they say about not paying attention?) Wham! Wham! Wham! A burst of a half dozen 85mm surrounded me. Blew a big hole in the tail (missed the vital stuff).
>
> Quickly, I selected afterburner, made a barrel roll, then punched out chaff at the rate about 4,000 a minute.[xxxv] Wham! Wham! Wham! Again, flak right in my face. It was like being thrown in a small

xxxv Chaff/Flares were "aftermarket" items added as SA-2 SAMs and radar-guided AAA became more of a problem. They were like shotgun shells, loaded in packs and installed in the belly of the airplane. There was an added "punch button" above the throttle.

closet with someone slapping your face, then dropping a dozen cherry bombs in with you. Wham! Wham! Wham!

Both of us chastened and needing a smoke, joined up, headed out over the water and checked each other for damage. As he dropped under me and came up on my other side, I swear I could see his eyes get big. Nork called, "Do you feel anything on your controls?" Now that he mentioned it, the rudder pedals seemed to be "buzzing" a bit. Nork again called, "Slow down Feedbag, you got a big hole in your tail" I thought, Oh…Nice! I Think.

I slowed down, swallowed convulsively and limped back to the ship and made a normal landing. I observed numerous deck guys pointing. Fine, point away, I'm just happy to be back. After, shutting down, I observed, with mixed emotion, the significant hole in my tail (a hole which has no doubt gained stature over the years).

I retired to the Ready Room told my story a half dozen times and finally went down to my room to borrow my roommate's camera to take a picture to send to my girl—look like a hero, etc. I went up to the hangar deck and couldn't locate my airplane. The crew said, "Oh Yes, Mr. Leighton, we bent the edges back in, speed taped it and put in a few cold rivets—she went out last launch. We did tell the pilot to 'Take it easy.'" So much for serious battle damage…so much for a picture. My wife is still skeptical.

Operation Rolling Thunder *Ends on October 31, 1968*

In October, President Johnson's presidency was nearing an end, but he thought he could still use the remaining months to once more attempt peace negotiations to entice the North Vietnamese with a bombing halt. *Rolling Thunder* ended on October 31, 1968. However, air operations over North Vietnam did not come to a complete stop. American jets still flew sorties, albeit at a slower pace, and still faced hostile defenses. Richard Nixon won the presidency, but Lyndon Johnson was still commander-in-chief.

There is no record that a SA-2 missile ever shot down a RF-8G. That success largely was due to the Electronic Countermeasures gear in the RF-8G that Lieutenant Jim Ozbirn from Det. 43 on board the *Coral Sea* thinks back on. However, after being alerted, the pilot facing SAMs required extreme courage and skill to defeat their deadly accurate threat. Ozbirn describes when he had to face multiple SAM attacks:

I reported to VFP-63 in Dec. 1967 after going through the F8 RAG [training squadron]. I went through a training syllabus that involved a lot of low-level photo hops over the southwest—a really cool flying time. I was then assigned to Det. 43 and we became part of airwing 15 assigned to the *Coral Sea*. Our det consisted of Lieutenant Commander Stan Betts, the officer in charge, Lieutenant Dave Beam, Lieutenant Charlies Rudd, Lieutenant Harry Fulton, myself, and two photo Intelligence [PI] officers, Lieutenant Dan Schneible and Warrant Officer Chuck Sterling. We also had 29 enlisted personnel to maintain our four aircraft. We left CONUS [Continental United States] in August 1968 and headed to WESTPAC [Western Pacific] and arrived on Yankee Station on September 1968. Our primary mission was to take pre-strike photos of possible targets and post-strike BDA. The pilots and our PIs worked closely with the ship's air intelligence team to determine targets to be hit.

After our first line period, President Johnson declared that a complete bombing halt over North Vietnam would go into effect on November 1, 1968. My reaction was, "Alright no more exposing ourselves in the North." We were in Hong Kong when the word came out about the halt, but

A VFP-63 RF-8G NL 10 (Bu. No. 144618) hurtles down the track of the waist catapult during a launch from USS Coral Sea *(CVA-43) in 1967. Note the "Eyes of the Fleet" squadron logo on the raised wing surface. The safety net along the angled deck has saved many sailors from a fall into the water. (Cmdr. Peter Mersky)*

we VFP-63 pilots were still tasked to continue reconnaissance flights over North Vietnam. Our first flights were fairly uneventful, but when the North Vietnamese realized we were unarmed, they took advantage and started throwing everything at us. It now became a serious threat to our safety. We had the full support of the airwing and started planning what we called Photo Alphas. Each flight involved two F-4 escorts, an EA-3 Whale for ECM support, an A-4 Shrike aircraft [anti-radar missile-equipped A-4 Skyhawk], an A-4 RESCAP [Rescue Combat Air Patrol] and E-2 Hawkeye, an all-weather, carrier-capable, tactical early-warning aircraft for radar coverage.

The problem with the F-4s was that they carried drop tanks and were speed limited. Because I could go faster, and believe me, speed was life over there, I would brief them on the route and have them rendezvous with me in the turns. I am not sure when the bombing halt ended, but the photos we took showed a tremendous increase in goods, ammo and

As a "jaygee" in 1968, James Ozbirn dueled with a SAM. Here, ten years later, now-Cmdr. Ozbirn strides toward his RF-8G at NAF Washington. (Cmdr. Peter Mersky)

In a cloud of exhaust smoke, an NVN SAM lifts off, circa 1967. (Lt. Phil Sherman)

personnel moving south. It also showed a huge buildup of AAA and SAM sites in the North.

I had an encounter with a SAM on December 3, 1968. As I was approaching the mouth of the Ca river to begin a photo run, I started to get ECM warnings of a SAM radar pinging me and then the tale-tale warble sound of a missile launch. I then saw an orange fire ball and missile rising out of a low-lying ground fog near Vinh. It was far enough away so I had time to take evasive action. It exploded in a large ball of fire a couple of hundred feet from my aircraft. I was about 2 miles from the coast at that time and turned back inland and finished the photo run. I was told later that a second missile was also launched, but apparently it failed and I never saw it.

We had some fairly sophisticated ECM gear for that time. I felt our most important piece was the ALR-45 which was a small screen mounted above the instrument panel. It would give us strobe indications and show a line from which we could see where the SAM radar site was located. From that, we could see

An RF-8G from USS Coral Sea *(CVA-43) took this BDA shot after CVW-15 strikes near Haiphong. BDA was the RF-8G's "bread and butter" and, because of the predictability of its role after the strike, the photo-Crusader could usually expect a hot reception from gun and SAM batteries. (Cmdr. Peter Mersky)*

where the threat may come from. Tied to that was a SAM alert which would give us a warning that a SAM may be launched. If I remember correctly, an intermittent warble sound was an indication that the SAM site was painting us. A continuous warble sound indicated that they had launched a SAM. At that time the SAMs were the size of telephone poles and once picked up visually, it could be out maneuvered—the SAM could not turn with us. What hurt us, however, was that they would launch multiple SAMs and force us to fly the aircraft at a lower altitude and from there, AAA was now the bigger threat

As I said before, speed was our savior. I would try to pick routes that would initially take me over safer areas at a higher altitude, and then as I approached the target area descend and go as fast as the aircraft would let me, usually around 500–600mph. The nice thing about our photo camera system was we could synchronize the cameras to our speed and take pictures with the proper overlap that the PIs needed. We had very few SAM encounters, but more AAA encounters.

Discovery of a Hidden POL Storage Site That Leads to a Bronze Star

Lieutenant Gary Ruesling was the PI officer on board *Ticonderoga* October 15, 1966–May 29, 1967. He provides the following insightful account that demonstrates the value of photo-reconnaissance:

The Bombing Encyclopedia, a basic intelligence resource, among other things, listed old and new information on targets, including precise information on geographic location, as well as, pictures for bomb damage assessment and other intelligence useful in identifying target status. It was used by both PIs and pilots. Even with assets such as this, the North Vietnamese became masters at camouflaging and hiding the war materials they were sending south. It was difficult, at best, for American pilots to fly straight and level at speeds over 500mph while avoiding NVN defensive measures, such as, AAA, SAMs and much more infrequently MiGs. So, American photo doctrine changed as a result of high attrition to pilots and aircraft. The photo birds and their escorts abandoned straight, level and low for jinking and flying higher. As a result, flight casualties dropped. However, the biggest deterrent to visual observations was trying to see through the jungle's leafy canopy. This is where the PI's value came into play. They had the luxury of avoiding AAA, SAMs and MiGs and had the time to assess the target area.

The photo birds were usually the first aircraft given preference in landing aboard their carriers, to allow for the film they had taken to be quickly pulled and examined. Once the aircraft was stopped, the process of removing the film and getting it to the photo intelligence office began in earnest.

All officer and enlisted photo interpreters were knowledgeable, had been trained, and took part in "reading" the film. Before the first line period was over, all the detachment PIs, officer and enlisted, were as familiar with the terrain and targets as any of the pilots flying over it. The NVN air bases' runways and hangars in our operating area had been hit so many times they were inoperable and easily identified. Roads were heavily cratered, and in constant state of repair. It would be safe to say that nothing moved during the day and very little at night. Rail lines were totally destroyed, as were coastal and interior waterways' launching and egress points. Piles of dirt and gravel used to fill in road craters and river fords became a common sight, as did ruined and bombed-out military bases.

Other Installations, supply and other transshipment points, became easily identifiable. Still the POL (petroleum, oil and lubricants), arms, ammunition, other ordnance, as well as soldiers, continued to flow to the south in spite of our best interdiction efforts. Locating and destroying POL was high on the list of targets in the monthly Photo-Tasking requirement from CINCPAC [Commander-in-Chief, Pacific].

One target listed in the Bombing Encyclopedia and on our Photo-Tasking Message from CINCPAC was the Vinh Army Barracks, an old French army base which was in ruins, having been destroyed in some earlier war, military action or insurrection. It was located on the elbow of a bend in a river which ran south before turning east and ultimately flowing out to the Gulf of Tonkin, a distance of about 20 miles. The Barracks was also a junction for the only North-South running railroad connecting the Hanoi-Haiphong area with Saigon and the South. A major highway paralleled the railroad. The area had been rendered useless as a transshipment point, by continued heavy bombing from American Navy aircraft operating from carriers in the Gulf of Tonkin, as well as, gunfire support from some of the destroyers.

The VFP-63 photo plane piloted by Lt. William Kocar and his escort were part of the first launch of the day along with some fighters and attack aircraft on separate missions. Its photo mission was to run road recce from south of the Hanoi-Haiphong area, turn east at the Barracks, then exit at Vinh on the coast and return to the carrier. Lt. William Kocur purposefully let his cameras run while making his turn east over the Barracks area and in the process, picked up pictures of part of the ruined military installation. The pictures were quickly developed and I looked at the negatives of the first half, the road recce. There was nothing significant to report. I then assigned the short portion of the negatives [containing pictures of the Barracks] to enlisted PT Marvin Covey for training purposes.

About an hour later, Covey called me over to look at something he was seeing through the patchwork of openings in the forest canopy. Neither of us had seen anything quite like it before. It was a patchwork pattern of, row upon row of "dots" about the size of pinheads, which we finally guessed it to be part of a POL storage area. Ha! What we were looking down on from the camera's perspective, was a virtual 2,000 feet of 55-gallon drums of POL stored and hidden for the first part of their trip south. The negative images were quickly scanned and annotated and sent to the photo lab for prints. [Annotation called attention to important intelligence.]

I had Covey continue scanning the film and to begin writing up the rough draft for the Intelligence Report [IPIR–Immediate Photo Intelligence Report] to be reported to Fleet Intelligence Center Pacific (FICPAC), for further analysis. I took the duplicate, positive pictures and headed down to the Air Intelligence Spaces to show the ship's air intelligence officer what we had found.

Unbeknown to us at the same time the fighter and attack pilots were debriefing their squadron air intelligence officers on the other side of the room, about some secondary explosions they had gotten when they had dropped and cleared hung ordnance, preparatory to returning to the ship. This was all occurring during the second launch cycle, so there was no time to divert that launch to attack the barracks, but the cycle-three aircraft could be re-armed and briefed to carry out attacks, which is what happened with great success!

The attacks continued over the next three days, until there were no more secondary explosions to be observed. FICPAC reported back to the carriers a week later about a new trans-shipment point in the Vinh Barracks area they were analyzing. A column of smoke could be seen rising through the haze, from the deck of our carrier (about 25 miles away). And, ICS3 Covey was flown off the carrier that week to help brief the MACV [Military Assistance Command, Vietnam] team in Saigon. I wrote Covey up for a Bronze Star which he received when our detachment returned to NAS [Naval Air Station] Miramar after the cruise was over.

Another PI officer, Lieutenant (junior grade) Louis R. Mortimer, began his Navy career as an enlisted reserve plane captain, drilling at NAS Willow Grove, near Philadelphia, He was also attending Temple University. Upon graduation, he entered post-graduate work at Penn State, then the Navy's Aviation Officer Candidate School (AOCS) in Pensacola and received his commission as a reserve ensign in 1965. He then went to Lowrey AFB (Air Force Base) in Colorado to begin his education as a photo interpretation officer and was ultimately ordered to a VFP-63 detachment on board the *Coral Sea* Vietnam deployment August 1967–April 1968. It was to prove a long, extended, and very busy cruise. A month into the cruise his officer in charge, Lieutenant Commander Milton James Vescelius, was hit by AAA and ejected over North Vietnamese dikes north of Haiphong Harbor. His Crusader exploded soon after his ejection. He was seen to land but was apparently killed resisting capture (see following memorial). First to know, Lieutenant (junior grade) Mortimer called then-Lieutenant (junior grade) Jay Miller (later Rear Admiral), the det operations officer, in his stateroom with the news the "Boss" was down. It was a hard introduction to Vietnam combat for the air wing and the photo det.

Mortimer and his men were deeply involved in gathering photo intelligence for the Fleet strikes, not only from the *Coral Sea* but the other air wings scattered around the Tonkin Gulf. They were especially on the lookout for indications of how North Vietnam was sending supplies south into South Vietnam to support Viet Cong missions. By early January 1968, it was plain something was building around the American Army and Marine Corps base at Khe Sanh.

By February 1968, the *Coral Sea*'s aircraft and crews were finding enemy positions and related gun and defensive positions all around the besieged camp whose occupants would endure 77 days of hard, often hand-to-hand, combat. Even though the carrier's air wing was looking at the end of its deployment, to the North, the North Koreans had other ideas and were engaged in capturing the spy ship, USS *Pueblo* (AGER-2) on January 23, 1968.

The unprecedented action resulted in an extension of U.S. Seventh Fleet ship deployments, including the *Coral Sea*. Finally, the ship returned to the U.S. in late March with Mortimer now an experienced PIO ready to assume the lead in his next deployment's intelligence department to another detachment, this one on the *Ticonderoga*, "Tico," with its air wing, CVW-16, preparing to depart San Diego in February 1969. He was now head of the Tico's VFP-63 det's photo intel department.

Although President Lyndon B. Johnson had instituted a bombing halt the previous October, combat operations continued, though at a lesser pace. However, on April 14, when the North Koreans shot down a Navy EC-121M Warning Star (an airborne early warning and control, AWACS, aircraft) flying in international airspace over the Sea of Japan, with the loss of 31 crewmen, there was the almost instant fear of a major confrontation such as a blockade or strikes against the rogue rulers of this constant thorn in the world's side. Navy ships were quickly sent up to Korea, ready to begin combat operations. One of the major results of the shootdown was a drastic alteration to *Ticonderoga*'s air wing complement. Several squadrons were sent off to Yokosuka, Japan, leaving a mainly Vought wing with the two F-8 squadrons, and the one RF-8G photo det, as well as two A-7B squadrons and one A-4C squadron.

Thus, (now) Lieutenant Mortimer and his shop were still on board writing reports and looking at a potential additional combat theater. However, negotiations brought the building crisis to a halt, and eventually the other squadrons were brought back, and the "Tico" finally returned to the U.S. in September.

Louis also worked on and received his PhD in American Studies from George Washington University. Retiring from both the Naval Reserve in 1993, and then Civil Service in 2001, he filled his remaining years with the family activities of his three sons and six grandchildren. Unfortunately, he passed away on February 21, 2021 before the completion of this book.

The Thanh Hoa Bridge: Bane to Many U.S. Pilots

The reader may recall the many times "Thanh Hoa" is mentioned while reading the explanations for the VFP-63 shootdowns in the area where the infamous "Dragon's Jaw" bridge seemed to defy all attacks by American pilots; all wanted to be the one to take it down. The photo pilot was part of this quest and Lieutenant Andre Coltrin had his turn in the barrel:

The infamous Thanh Hoa Bridge during a CVW-16 strike in 1967. An old railway crossing, this bridge became a symbol of the frustration felt by many navy and air force pilots. It also highlighted the North Vietnamese resilience and ability to repair damage to major facilities seemingly overnight. (Cmdr. Peter Mersky)

> The Thanh Hoa bridge was always the prize target every bomber pilot wanted, in fact, every air wing wanted to claim it. One day a three-carrier alpha strike was launched against the bridge. We were the second of the three to attack. CAG gave me a special briefing. He told me I was to be launched a little early so I could be in the area of the target as the first attacking air wing was finishing their arrack. My photos were to prove if the bridge was still standing or not, when it was our turn to attack. I was then to stay in the area until after we were off target to acquire BDA photos to show we had downed the bridge before

The pilots and intelligence officers of Det. 43 on board USS Coral Sea *(CVA-43), 1967–68: Front row: Lt. (j. g.) Phil Sherman, Lt. Curt Eininger, Lt. Cmdr. Bill Rosson Standing: Lt. (j. g.) Jay Miller, Lt. (j. g.) Gordie Paige, Lt. (j. g.) Lou Mortimer, and Lt. (j. g.) Will Gray. Eininger and Mortimer were the det's intelligence officers. (Cmdr. Peter Mersky)*

the third air wing started their attack. It was quite a sight watching all the action.

Since photo birds were the least threat to the defenders of the bridge, we had little attention and ammunition expended on us. When our air wing was off the target and the smoke and dust cleared, the pride of the North Vietnam nation was damaged but still standing. As it was when the third air wing pulled off target. As a side note, at my next duty station, NAF [Naval Air Facility] China Lake, I was the project pilot for a special weapon that was developed there and called Bomb-Winder. It was specifically developed to take down the Thanh Hoa Bridge, but that never happened either. [That weapon may never have been used but the technology improved and became part of what is referred to as "smart bombs" that eventually brought the bridge down. See details in Chapter 7.]

1967–68 Non-fatal Combat Losses

On June 5, 1967, an RF-8A (Bu. No. 145614) from USS *Bon Homme Richard* (CVA-31) was shot down by AAA and VFP-63 Det. L pilot Commander Collin Haines captured and held prisoner until March 4, 1973.

On May 22, 1968, an RF-8G (Bu. No. 146830) from the *Bon Home Richard* was shot down by AAA. Det. 31 pilot Lieutenant (junior grade) Edwin Miller ejected and was captured. He was released on March 4, 1973.

Commander Roy McDermid provides some additional information:

> Lieutenant James Esco, a squadronmate in VF-51 flew the photo escort for Lt. (j.g.) Edwin Miller. Jim received a Distinguished Flying Cross for his actions following Miller's shootdown. Jim made some low passes over the North Vietnamese approaching him on the ground, hoping to drive them off while waiting for a rescue chopper to arrive—to no avail.
>
> The closest I ever came to being shot down was also on a photo-escort mission, weaving from side-to-side at a very high rate of speed. The North Vietnamese fired a burst of three very large caliber AAA rounds at us, which exploded in the exact space I'd occupied just seconds before. I never knew it until we debriefed at the end of the mission.

On July 21, 1968, an RF-8G (Bu. No. 145642) was lost due to mechanical failure. Its VFP-63 Det. 11 pilot, Lieutenant Fred. W. Pfluger, ejected and was rescued.

Lieutenant Phil Sherman provides more details:

Lt. Fred Pfluger left NAS Cubi Point in the Philippines on a test flight and encountered radio problems and, without an emergency radio, he couldn't find the ship. Out of fuel, he ejected over an island, landed in a tree, causing serious wounds to his leg. Villagers managed to get him to medical help and he eventually made it back to the ship.

Operation *Rolling Thunder* ended on October 31 but, under a new president, the war would drone on and new air war operations of varying names would replace it. In fact, the air campaign would become more brutal with the introduction of gigantic Air Force B-52 Stratofortress bombers over North Vietnam.

During the three and a half years of *Rolling Thunder*, Navy and Marine aircraft flew 152,399 attack sorties, dropping 864,000 tons of bombs and missiles on North Vietnam. During the war, 600 Navy and 271 Marine aviators were lost, most during *Rolling Thunder*.

In Memoriam

Captain James Milton Vescelius Jr.
November 16, 1934 –September 21, 1967
Milford, Michigan

Lieutenant Commander James Milton Vescelius Jr. was the officer in charge of Detachment 43 and the pilot of a VFP-63 RF-8A (Bu. No. 144623) on a combat mission over North Vietnam on September 21, 1967. He launched from the *Coral Sea* and was "about 5 miles west-southwest of the city of Quang Yen, near the borders of Thai Binh and Quang Ninh Provinces, when his aircraft was hit by enemy fire and crashed.

He was seen to eject, and other pilots in the area reported that when he reached the ground he was surrounded by Vietnamese. The following day, a Radio Hanoi broadcast described the incident and stated that the pilot had been captured. The U.S. classified James Milton Vescelius as a Prisoner of War [POW].

For the next 6 years, Vescelius' family waited for the war to end. In 1973, when 591 Americans were released from POW camps in North Vietnam, Vescelius was not among them. The Vietnamese denied any knowledge of him."[4]

Did Lt. Cmdr. James Milton Vescelius Go Down Fighting?

"In September 1972 an NVA rallier reported that in September 1967 he had seen a captured American pilot in North Vietnam near the vicinity of grid coordinates (GC) Xi 765 105. The pilot had reportedly shot a militiaman and was then beaten when captured. The pilot was evacuated from the area in a vehicle."[5]

"For a period of time hostile threat in the area precluded any visits or ground inspections of the sites involved in this case. Details of this case together with information indicating enemy knowledge of the case were turned over to the Four-Party Joint Military Team on November 7, 1973, with a request for any information which would assist in determining status and resolution of the Vescelius case. No response was forthcoming.

Then in August 1985, the Vietnamese "discovered" the remains of James Milton Vescelius and returned them to American control. For 28 years, he had been considered a prisoner of war—alive or dead. The U.S. gratefully accepted the "gift" of the remains of Lt. Cmdr. James Milton Vescelius and others, which should have been returned decades ago. Some hold the belief that we allowed the Vietnamese to politically choose the moment it complied with that section of the agreements which ended American involvement in the war in Vietnam."[6]

His remains were buried at Arlington National Cemetery, Plot Section 60 Site 110030.

He was posthumously promoted to captain. He is honored on the Vietnam Veterans Memorial Wall, Washington, D.C.: Wall, Panel 26E, Line 109.

Commendations

- ★ Prisoner of War Medal
- ★ Combat Action Ribbon
- ★ Vietnam Campaign Medal
- ★ Navy Presidential Unit Citation
- ★ Navy Expeditionary Medal
- ★ Purple Heart
- ★ National Defense Service Medal
- ★ Vietnam Service Medal
- ★ Vietnam Gallantry Cross

Testimony and Memories

Lieutenant Commander James Milton Vescelius, Jr. was flying an RF-8A of VFP-63 (Det. 43 on *Coral Sea*) on a bomb damage assessment reconnaissance flight in support of an Air Wing 15 strike on the Kienan bridge at the city limits of Haiphong. Chris Hobson tells part of the story:

> As Lt. Cmdr. Vescelius was making his run over the target at 3,000-feet and 600 knots, just as the last of the strike aircraft left the target area, his aircraft was hit by AAA and the starboard wing burst into flames. The aircraft commenced a shallow starboard turn and the pilot ejected just to the north of Haiphong harbor. The aircraft exploded shortly afterwards.[7]

Lieutenant Commander Scott Ruby adds this:

> I was playing golf with Commander Dutch Schultz one day when he was skipper. He and Lieutenant Commander Vescelius were officers in charge of different detachments at the same time and very good friends. We were discussing various shootdowns and he told me Vescelius was alive on the ground and talking to the guys overhead. His last transmission was words to the effect, "They are coming to get me, I am destroying the radio." He never made it to Hanoi.

The carriers *Intrepid* and *Coral Sea* were in the Vietnam theater at the same time. Lieutenant Andre Coltrin was on the *Intrepid* and offers this:

We were into our fifth month (September, 1967) when [officer in charge] Jim Vescelius was shot down and I got orders to transfer to the *Coral Sea* and replace him until a more senior officer could finish his training and get out there. Funny, as I sit here right now, I cannot remember how I got from *Intrepid* to the *Coral Sea*! Must have been by helicopter. I know damn well it was not by high-line [transfer by basket from ship to ship in close formation]. I definitely would remember that.

I knew Jim at the home squadron but not well. I had just returned from *Oriskany* [CVA-34] cruise and was put in *Intrepid* Det. 11. *Intrepid* was home-ported in Mayport, Florida, so we were doing a lot of cross-country time and not around Miramar much. One of my first tasks that needed to be taken care of after reporting to *Coral Sea* was to inventory and pack for shipping home all of Jim's personal belongings. I was contacted about ten years later about that inventory. I received a call from an individual in Washington, D.C. who was connected with the POW/MIA organization. They told me they had noticed the inventory had included underwear shorts and wanted to know if any of the shorts were camouflage material. I replied "No, they were all white. Why?" They said that according to Jim's wife he had a pair of camouflage shorts. Therefore, if they were not inventoried, Jim must have been wearing them. They also said they had a person who claimed to have witnessed a shootdown on that day and at the location where Jim was shot down. It was reported the pilot was captured, stripped down to his shorts and beaten to death. He was wearing camouflage shorts. It is my understanding Jim was shot down doing BDA on a recently hit target and the people were pissed.

Doctor Yvonne Kleine, N.D., PhD:

I have had your POW MIA bracelet since 1973 when my husband and I were at Shaw AFB as he went through RF-4 flight school. My wish for you is that you are in the palm of God's hand, that your family is comforted by our respect and gratitude for your sacrifice, and that someday we will all meet in a better place. I am so happy that you were found and rest in our sacred soil. I will never give up that bracelet.

Stan Jensen:

I was stationed at NAS Miramar from 1967–1970 as a plane captain. We lost too many brave souls in Vietnam. When a family member of VFP-63 dies we all grieve as one.

In Memoriam

Commander Michael Walter Wallace
September 12, 1936–March 28, 1968
Salt Lake City, Utah

Lieutenant Commander Wallace was a member of VFP-63 Detachment 14, Carrier Air Wing 19 on board the aircraft carrier *Ticonderoga*. On March 28, 1968, he was the pilot of an RF-8G (Bu. No. 144616) on a photographic mission 15 miles west of Khe Sanh, South Vietnam.

Wallace rolled in with the bombing group and then pulled off the target. His aircraft was observed in a tight spin with the nose 60 degrees below the horizon. The aircraft did not appear to be on fire, nor did any disintegration take place. The aircraft continued to spin until it struck the ground still in the nose-low attitude and burst into flames. The crash site was in Laos.

The strike was discontinued while the other aircraft circled the crash site. No parachute was seen, nor was an emergency radio beeper heard in the vicinity. It is believed the pilot was still in the aircraft when it crashed. The aircraft was consumed by fire.

Initially, Wallace was reported missing in action, which was changed on April 17, 1968, less than a month after his loss incident, to Killed/Body Not Recovered based on all the known facts at the time. As with any multiple-plane loss incident, Wallace's family wondered for years if he had managed to bail out of the crippled aircraft unnoticed, as others had done.

In the summer and fall of 1988, the U.S. helped ease the way for a private humanitarian concern to build medical clinics in Laos. The Lao, in their appreciation, agreed to assist in performing a limited number of crash-site excavations in their country.

In December 1988, American and Lao technical teams excavated the site of Michael Wallace's aircraft crash in Savannakhet Province, Laos. This excavation effort yielded bone fragments and, on March 13, 1989, these were identified as being those of Lieutenant Commander Wallace. Commander [post-mortem promotion] Wallace is buried and memorialized at Courts of the Missing at the Honolulu Memorial. This is an American Battle Monuments Commission location.

Michael is honored on the Vietnam Veterans Memorial in Washington, D.C.: Wall, Panel 46E, Line 60.

Commendations

- ★ Purple Heart
- ★ Combat Action Ribbon
- ★ National Defense Service Medal
- ★ Vietnam Campaign Medal
- ★ Navy Presidential Unit Citation
- ★ Navy Expeditionary Medal
- ★ Naval Aviation Wings
- ★ Vietnam Gallantry Cross
- ★ Vietnam Service Medal

In Memoriam

Lieutenant James Lee Merrick, Jr.
September 21, 1943–October 3, 1968
Ames, Iowa

On October 3, 1968, Lieutenant James Lee Merrick, Jr. was serving with VFP-63 Det. 19, CVW-21, on board *Hancock*, TF-77, Seventh Fleet, off the coast of South Vietnam. On that day, he died in a non-hostile related crash at sea of his RF-8G (Bu. No. 144620), while returning to the carrier from a mission over North Vietnam. His body was recovered.

James L. Merrick Jr is honored on the Vietnam Veterans Memorial in Washington, D.C.: Wall, Panel W42, Line 70.

Commendations

★ Combat Action Ribbon
★ Vietnam Campaign Medal
★ Navy Presidential Unit Citation
★ Navy Expeditionary Medal
★ National Defense Service Medal
★ Vietnam Service Medal
★ Vietnam Gallantry Cross
★ Navy Aviation Wings

Memorials and Tributes

After graduation from Ames High in 1961, James Merrick went to Iowa State University, where he joined Delta Sigma Phi fraternity and enrolled in the Naval Reserve Officer's Training Corps program. Merrick graduated from Iowa State in the spring of 1965. He was commissioned as an ensign, U.S. Navy, in August 1965. Merrick's training as a naval aviator took place in Pensacola, Florida, and Corpus Christi, Texas. He received his wings in March 1967 and was assigned to VFP-63 on the carrier *Hancock*.

CHAPTER 7

1969–72: The Final Years

Air War Continues, Protests Become Deadly, and POW Freedom

On January 20, 1969, Richard Milhous Nixon took the oath of office to become the 37th President of the United States. His inaugural speech soared with his confidence in the people to unite and overcome the nation's division over the war. The word "Vietnam" was never mentioned. Despite his campaign promise to end the war with honor, it droned on for his first term without resolution.

During 1969, the air war for VFP-63 noticeably operated at a less deadly pace. The only combat-related casualty was on December 16 when young Lieutenant Victor Buckley mysteriously crashed at sea. His body was not found. Sadly, another VFP-63 pilot became a prisoner of war (POW).

The nation would have to wait for Nixon's second term before the POWs would come home. Five of them were VFP-63 pilots—the last one was from these final years. The complete story of Lieutenant Commander Gordon Paige's shootdown, capture and release is included in great detail in the following history.

Unlike President Johnson, Nixon gave military commanders more freedom to select targets and run the air campaign. Previously forbidden targets would receive severe punishment and air losses would climb.

On April 30, 1970, President Nixon made a television address announcing American and South Vietnamese troops would be conducting operations in the North Vietnamese occupied sanctuaries along the border between Cambodia and South Vietnam. He justified the action as a concern for the safety of American troops in South Vietnam. However, ten days prior he had announced withdrawing an additional 150,000 troops from South Vietnam.

The Cambodian action was perceived by student protesters as increasing the war and protests on college campuses became more aggressive. On May 1, students at Kent State University, in Kent, Ohio, conducted protests and on May 2, the ROTC (Reserve Officers' Training Corps) building was set on fire. Ohio National Guardsmen were moved on to campus.

On May 3, confrontations between students and the Guardsmen continued. On May 4, marching and counter-marching evolved into students throwing rocks and the Guardsmen chased them and fired tear gas up a hill. Then the confrontation turned deadly. The Guardsmen pointed their M1s with bayonets fixed and started firing. Nine students were injured, one with permanent paralysis, and four killed.

It was the first deadly anti-war protest and sparked massive college walkouts all over the country. Everyone watched graphic television video coverage showing the carnage. "The most poignant visual icon was the Pulitzer-Prize winning photo by Kent State photojournalism student John Filo, showing Mary Ann Vecchio screaming as she kneels by the body of a slain student. Her arms are outreaching and evoke a visual plea, 'Why are you doing this?'"[1]

After the Easter invasion of March 1972, many previously restricted targets were hit in an all-out campaign against the road and railways systems that carried supplies south. Although the 1966–68 Rolling Thunder *strikes had damaged many of these supply arteries, the 1972 strikes saw greatly intensified attacks, including this one in April 1972 by aircraft from the* Hancock *against the Dong Phong Thuong Bridge area. (Cmdr. Peter Mersky)*

Air Force Exchange Pilot Joins VFP-63 Det. 3

The Navy and Air Force had a pilot exchange program, and one of the participants was USAF then-Captain Jim Morgan. That experience gives him a unique perspective on naval aviation during the later years of the war. He describes his tour:

> My own cruise was aboard the *Midway* (CVA-41, VFP-63, Det. 3) in 1971. We had a very lucky cruise for several reasons. Det. 3 lost no one, though we came close to losing Jimmy D—l to the Sasebo brig after the cruise was almost over! But that's another story. That particular period was during one of the insane "bombing halts," which we all knew was just an opportunity for the North Vietnamese to go on R&R—Rest and Reload.
>
> I was an O-3 while I was with VFP-63. We in the Air Force call this a captain, but most of my Navy buddies of the same rank were lieutenants. I was very careful in the use of my rank on the phone on a naval installation, to make sure those on the other end knew I was an O-3, not a Navy O-6! The captain of the ship was walking on the hangar deck before we left Alameda when he saw

Capt. Jim "Mugs" Morgan, USAF, on the tail of VFP-63 Det. 3 aircraft 601 (Bu. No. 146856), 1971. Note "Recon Reptile" on the tail. Jerry Nolan came up with it as a variation of the lizard characters in cartoonist Vaugh Bode's underground comic strips. The Airframes guys and Jerry did the stencils up in the PI shop; hard to see here but it looked hand-painted on the tail. (Jerry Nolan ISC)

my name on the canopy rail of RF-8G 602, reading CAPT JIM MORGAN. He asked who this captain was. Finding out it was an Air Force exchange officer, he said something to the effect of, "Well, we'll have to change that. There's only one captain on this ship!" So, our guys changed it to "CAPT JIM MORGAN (USAF)," which was fine with me! That captain, by the way, was Capt. Eugene Carroll, later rear admiral. A couple of days after that, I was walking along the pier when this car pulled up and offered me a ride. It was Captain Carroll, and we had a very nice talk as he gave me a ride!

I had come to VFP-63 from the RF-4C photo-Phantom (see next chapter), and had already completed one combat tour. I was very excited about the Navy assignment, as I had applied for an exchange tour, but I had never heard of an RF-8. I was actually out on a weekend cross-country at McConnell AFB [Air Force Base] when I got word of the assignment. I changed my itinerary to go to NAS [Naval Air Station] Dallas because I knew they had F-8s there, and I wanted to see one up close. I was able to do that and even got a picture of one. One of the requirements of accepting the assignment was agreeing to another combat tour, which I did.

I didn't really have any difficulties transitioning into naval aviation. The obvious great difference was carrier aviation, and I think my checkout was a bit different from other incoming pilots. I didn't go through the F-8 RAG [Replacement Air Group] for training, except for the Tactics syllabus. All the rest, including carrier operations, except for the instrument training, was done through the squadron, VFP-63. The instrument training was at, what I think they were calling, VF-126 flying the TA-4J, which I thought was pretty cool! I can say that I was very well received. I suffered through Air Force (AF) jokes from time to time, but I gave as good as I got, and I loved that tour. I consider my two years with VFP-63 and naval aviation one of the two best tours in my 27 years in the Air Force, and I still maintain ties with my det mates from the cruise aboard *Midway* in 1971, as well as the skipper of the squadron. The other really enjoyable assignment was a flying tour with the 38th Tac Recon Squadron in Steinbruck, Germany. That was great on a bright, clear day over the Black Forest, or chasing U.S. Navy carriers down in the Med—until the day when an F-14 actually shot one of our USAF RF-4C's down, on purpose, in an exercise! (That was September 22, 1987, if you want to look it up.) We thought *That* was a bit overdone! The differences in combat missions with the Navy and the Air Force: You might say the difference was night and day. As I mentioned, most all of my combat missions in the RF-4C were at night. In the RF-8G we never flew at night, except for general proficiency when in port. There was no point in flying combat missions at

VFP-63 Det. 3 aircraft 601 (Bu. No. 146856) cat-shot off USS Midway *(CVA-41), 1971. A good view of the RF-8G's impressive afterburner. (Jerry Nolan ISC)*

VFP-63 Det. 3 aircraft 601 (Bu. No. 146856) about to launch from USS Midway *(CVA-41), 1971. Recon Reptile's face is on the wing bulkhead. The sailor in the green jersey monitors the catapult steam gauges. (Jerry Nolan ISC)*

Capt. Jim Morgan, a USAF exchange pilot with VFP-63 Det. 3, USS Midway *(CVA-41), 1971, with plane captain ADJ-AN J. Christensen. The plane captain performs the most vital role of pulling the safety pins from the ejection seat prior to launch. The pilot counts them to ensure a safe ejection. The bond between pilot and plane captain, often the least senior enlisted man, can be very close. (Col. Jim Morgan USAF)*

There was one period of time when Det. 3's RF-8G 601 was the only "Up" airplane. It flew its wings off during that period, completing 35 combat sorties in a row, being dubbed "The Cast Iron Crusader" in the process. The airplane received a hangar deck celebration to mark the event and the ship's captain attended! Front (L–R): Chief Ed Murray cutting the "Cast Iron Crusader" cake, Capt. Harris, and OinC Lt. Cmdr. Scott Ruby, with Det. 3 crew behind. (Col. Jim Morgan USAF)

The huge Soviet Tu-95 Bear *was a frequent "visitor" over the Sixth and Seventh Fleet during the Cold War. They tested the carrier's security but were always "greeted" by one or more fighters and photo-Crusaders. The RF-8G, from USS* Midway's *VFP-63 Det. 3, is loitering below while another takes this photo. (Col. Jim Morgan USAF)*

night because the airplane was not capable of it in any real reconnaissance sense [See discussion in Chapter 3]. The other big difference was that virtually all our Navy reconnaissance missions had F-4 escorts assigned, while I never had a fighter escort on an AF recon mission. The F-4 escorts were only loaded with air-to-air weapons, but the guys on the ground didn't know that. In talking to AF recce guys, they were going the same places we were, and they were getting hosed down on occasion. I never saw a shot fired on 40-plus combat missions.

I guess you could say that 1971 was a kind of lull before the storm of the final days. We didn't have all that many missions into North Vietnam because there was a bombing halt. When we did go north, it was completely different from anything I had experienced in the Air Force. All of those had been single ship reconnaissance missions, and all were at night. When we went into the North with the Navy, it was daytime and it was kind of like an Alpha Strike without the strike part. But there were armed fighters and a whole support package. It was sort of like trolling with a recce mission to see if anybody would shoot, then using that as the basis for attack. But even that was very limited on the 1971 cruise. Also, we were restricted to a minimum of 4,500 feet AGL, so there wasn't much danger of small arms ground fire. Det. 3 flew probably about the standard VFP-63 three-airplane rate, about 3–4 sorties per day for each line period. I wound up with about 540 hours in the RF-8G in two years, which is a fairly decent yearly average.

We got home to Miramar in November 1971, but Det. 3 turned around and went back out on *Midway* ahead of schedule in 1972. Only one of our pilots turned around with the det. That was Lieutenant Paul Ringwood (Worm). He was the one who was shot down on June 16, 1972, near the Thanh Hoa bridge and was (Thank God) picked up [details follow].

Overall, I would like to say what an honor it was for me to serve with VFP-63! I came away with nothing but admiration for naval aviation and the U.S. Navy.

A Fighter Pilot's Memoir of Life and Combat Operations in 1972

Lieutenant Pete Phelps of Fighter Squadron 24 (VF-24), on board USS *Hancock* (CVA-19) in 1972, kept a logbook with short notes describing his life in a warzone. His meticulous notes, excerpted here, portray the stress buildup when multiple disasters strike friends and unknown colleagues. Some deployments were more routine, but others, like during 1972, after the North Vietnamese marched into South Vietnam in force in March, were far more demanding and perilous. His notes reveal the volume of disasters that happened on a daily basis. Each pilot copes with the carnage and loss but has to get up each day and fly into the same danger zone, not knowing if he will be next. His notes are presented here to help us appreciate that struggle during the late months of the war:

My Dad would have understood my Vietnam combat experiences. On July 9, 1943, his best friend and co-pilot, Frank Hare, was killed by 50-cal machine gun fire through his seat, just 2 feet to the left of my father, during a PBY Catalina bombing run on a German sub off of Brazil—also wounding Dad. However, my dad never said anything about that incident to me. Dad and his other best friend, the pilot-navigator that day, continued the attack and were credited with a sub kill. Ten years later (1953), Captain Mike Argento, that third pilot in the PBY, by then CO NAS Jacksonville, flew a F-9F Panther jet into Teterboro New Jersey Airport and took a 7-year-old kid on a high-speed taxi down the runway, returning me to the flight line, then flying off into the wild blue yonder! You think that didn't influence an impressionable young kid into going to the Naval Academy, flying fighters in Vietnam, and followed by 40 years of flying jets?

I was a slightly young (28) and naïve fighter pilot headed off to war for my second cruise in 1972! After all, I had lost my first two roommates in 1972: the first, during my third day in the squadron, killed by a ramp strike [crashed into the fantail of the carrier] off the Farallon Islands, during December buildups. The second was shot down east of Hanoi and became a POW on May 24 east of Hanoi. My third roommate showed up on the *Hancock* that same day and was cautious after I told him, "He was number 3 on this match!"

Saturday April 15, 1972:

- Yesterday an Air Force F-4 Phantom was shot down just west of Dong Hoi. I think the pilot got out but was captured.
- Today the *Kitty Hawk* [CVA-63], *Coral Sea* [CVA-43] and Air Force conducted strikes on Vinh and Dong Hoi airfields, SAM sites and transshipment points.
- There was some talk that a Navy A-7 went into the water just east of the DMZ [Demilitarized Zone]—no further word.
- I manned for the next photo escort and went with Joe Reeves again to that area near Firebase Carroll, west of Dong Ha and Cam Lo. They had about 12 A-4s in there and wanted the photo bird to take BDA [Bomb Damage Assessment] photos. The strike attacked at least three 57mm AAA sites and numerous other smaller AAA. There were flak puffs everywhere.
- After the photo run, Joe, as lead, maintained a slow pattern at 21,000 feet, too slow! We got a warning call: "Singer High—SAM! SAM! SAM!" That same SAM site shot at us yesterday and fired three more SAMs at us over a period of 10 minutes. Mike Falcon from VA-212 shut the radar guidance down with a Shrike shot at them, yelling "Shotgun! Shotgun!" (He had launched a Shrike anti-radiation missile back at the SAM's radar trailer). I was all over the sky trying to spot where the missiles were coming from. We get low on gas and headed back to the boat. I was relieved: I didn't want to take low-level photos of AAA anyway!
- CAG [Commander, Air Group] Barth was moderately shot up by AAA but got the plane to Da Nang, where he commandeered his wing man's plane and flew back to the boat.

Sunday April 16, 1972:

- Well, it's really getting hot and heavy now! Eighteen B-52s with some Standard Arm anti-radiation missiles on Navy A-6 Intruders, went into Haiphong Harbor and dropped their 106 500-pound bombs each, knocking out more than 60 percent of North Vietnam's POL storage. By 8 AM we did a weather recce thru the harbor. Secondary explosions were still going off.
- I'd kind of like to do something to end all of the s—t. Of course, on the other hand, I'm now only contributing to it.

Wednesday May 24, 1972:

- A VA-56 A-7B Corsair II off *Midway* was down in the water—picked up within minutes. *Midway* got two MiGs yesterday.
- I go on the second hop: TARCAP (Target Combat Air Patrol) to Haiphong's Cat Bi airfield. The God damn SAMs [surface-to-air missiles] were thick as flies (at least a dozen)—they were everywhere. We dodged and ducked like a roller coaster—no one was hit thank God. A SAM usually leaves a cloud of dark smoke or dust on liftoff, but in flight they are like angry,

fast little bees, with bright-pink little fire trails coming at you. When they get up high, they can leave white contrails until exploding in a puff of gray smoke! Smoke color is significant; SAMs explode in bright gray-white puffs of smoke. AAA [anti-aircraft artillery] caliber can usually be identified by shades of white, gray, dark gray, and even almost black puffs of smoke, depending on the caliber of the round.

- A photo bird's tail hook came off on arrestment but boltered OK [took off again] and went to Da Nang.
- VA-55's Lt. Chuck Carroll listed officially as missing in action. Damn!

Thursday May 25, 1972:

- We were told we would have two alpha strikes today. I flew a photo escort on the first one—target was supposed to be Hai Dong (west of Haiphong), but we were diverted to Vinh. With most of the heavy air defenses pulled back to Haiphong and Hanoi, the southern part of the country is supposed to be relatively safe, but there was a hell of a lot AAA there. We used to joke that Vinh was where the North Vietnamese Army AAA training school was located! They were calling AAA all around the target—then we flew thru for pictures and saw nothing, but our TARCAP said there was a white wall of flak following us.
- The second alpha strike was the real bad news: An A-7 off the *Midway* was hit near Vinh and made it back just aft of our ship before he ejected and was pulled out of the water!
- Our second strike went back to Vinh—Commander Hank Strong (CO VA-212) disappeared in a cloud of flak in his bombing run—never seen again—presumed hit and lost. (An A-4 with his name and squadron markings is on display today at the San Diego Air & Space Museum.)
- Commander George Fenzel, XO VA-55, was hit during his first bombing run on a TER (Triple Ejection Rack for ordinance). Blew a couple hundred small holes in the rightwing and a few in the fuselage. He made it back to the ship OK (the A-4 is a great little airplane).
- Rob Barber (VA-164) was hit in the centerline buddy tank—a 2-foot hole on one side and a hundred or two out the back—was burning like a torch off the target—a 50-foot flame behind him until all the gas burned out and then all was OK. The wet-wing tanker plugged him en route back to the ship and he landed OK.

Friday May 26, 1972:

- Flew a TARCAP west of Quang Tri (Laos) with three Eagles (VA-212) and a Nickel (VF-211) as the A-4s bombed some enemy locations in support of the RESCAP [Rescue Combat Air Patrol] of Gunsmoke 02 (AF F-4) who was down—both of the crew were OK.

Sunday May 27, 1972:

- The carnage continues. Planned the fighter portion of the second alpha strike, which was diverted from Hai Duong to a railroad yard half way between Vinh and Thanh Hoa. Looked for lucrative targets but no luck. Then it started: Jack Zerr (VA-55) punched out 30 seconds after the cat shot about 2-3 miles ahead of the ship—engine exploded.
- A day ago, the two Barons were the last ones to leave the target (Vinh), rolled in to drop the two MK 82s they had. Tom Latendresse was hit (wing separated?) and punched out. Eric Burns, his wingman, dropped to 500ft circling him. Tom came up on Guard channel yelling for ordnance—said the gomers were all around him, then said his papers etc. were in his safe and finally that he was about to be captured and even if it sounded corny, to tell his wife that he loved her. Damn! Eric saw one guy on the ground in a large group, come forward and

grab Tom's arm. God Damn that really hurts—Tom is a really great guy—he's alive—but? Eric was almost crying. Ray Winn (VA-212) turned in his wings—is anything worth this? I believe Ray reconsidered, and returned to flying later.

- Yet I continue! Judy if it happens to me—forgive me.

Pilot Discussion on Fighter Escorts

By this point in the air war story, the tactic of the unarmed RF-8G having a fully armed fighter escort, both F-8 Crusader and F-4 Phantom, was an integral part of the photo recon effort. For a single-seat photo jet, having an extra pair of eyes over a target bristling with radar guided AAA and SAMs, is common sense—and with the Phantom, you got two pairs of eyes. Add the potential of MiG attack, what makes it controversial? Photo pilots to this day disagree on the tactic. By the time this book's manuscript was reaching completion, an impromptu, vigorous discussion erupted online. It provided an excellent revelation into how pilots viewed their survival over dangerous territory. Air Force two-seat RF-4C Phantoms rarely had escorts, although they were unarmed. A summary of the discussion follows:

Captain Will Gray (RF-8 photo pilot):

> I guess there is not a day that passes that I don't think about the Crusader. I remember finishing VT-26 training in the F-11 Tiger (*Blue Angels* were flying them). I was sure that I had flown the sweetest machine ever built. When I got to VF-124 and ready to go flying … I wasn't sure how I would like the Crusader. It was big, heavy, and the flight controls felt stiff and heavy, too. Rolling down the runway at NAS Miramar on FAM-1 [first familiarization flight], I realized that the bird was coming alive in my hand like nothing before … Right about then I realized that the F-11 was just a toy compared to the Crusader, so smooth and so powerful, like an extension of my fingers.
>
> For the photo pilot, [our real] enemy was bad tactics (going in low early in the conflict), slowing down so the escort could keep up, and the insane idea that taking BDA photos, within four minutes of the last bomb from an alpha strike, which led to many losses. Escorting photo birds was a useless exercise (calls like: 'they are shooting' were of no help). MiGs and SAMs were not the threat, it was gunfire that got you shot. Using any [fighter] aircraft for flak suppression was just plain stupid.

Lieutenant Pete Phelps (VF-24 F-8 fighter escort pilot):

> Will Gray obviously is no fan of photo escorts, but I think he was commenting more on his F-4 escorts and maybe the F-4s had other issues, like higher fuel-burn rates to maintain higher speeds (more than 600kts) and I'm not sure if the F-4s tanked before going feet dry like we did. The F-8 was a cleaner airplane, less drag, with similar flight characteristics as the photo bird. I do know that we had to keep up a higher speed than the photo to keep up with his ground track as we S-turned over him to keep an eye on both sides and rear of the flight path.
>
> As far as Will having little concern of a MiG-17 or MiG-19 sneaking up behind him and shooting him down with an Atoll missile, that's probably true, but one MiG-21 did sneak in from the deck under Al Molinare and "Tooter" Teague (flying F-4s), pulled an Immelmann [an aerobatic maneuver that results in level flight in the opposite direction at a higher altitude] and bagged Al from behind. Top speed of a MiG-21 is 1,300mph, max F-8 speed is a bit over 1,200mph, and an F-4 can do 1,475mph, you do the math, we did! I'm not sure if the photo bird could fly any faster

than the F-8 fighter, it might have been slightly lighter, but it had older engines with less thrust (16,500-pound thrust, I believe). Our newer F-8Js had 19,500-pound thrust, but we were heavier. Of course, those numbers don't mean as much as the dynamics of a dogfight, but the winner of a straight-line photo-run race down Highway 1, from Thanh Hoa to Vinh, might just be predicted by thrust and "slickness" (and the F-4 was never considered slick).

Lieutenant Roger Crim (photo pilot):

I can assure you that one can be hit at 600 knots. I lost one third of the starboard wing outer panel due to, AAA just north of Thanh Hoa [see Chapter 3]. Even if they couldn't see you until the last minute, they were able to throw a lot of flak up, which you might fly into. As has been stated, it may be comforting to have someone along to relate what happened but they could not effectively do anything about it. After all, the escorts weren't going to circle back and hose the now known flak sight. I was fortunate that my aircraft was still flyable, though at an increased landing speed, as light as possible and 145 knots, the RF-8A was still barely controllable.

Will Gray:

There was the case of an F-8 using his guns to prevent the bad guys from capturing one of our photo pilots after he ejected and landed in Haiphong Harbor. I don't recall the names but that F-8 driver kept the boats away and "encouraged" our helicopter pilot to rescue him. F-4 escorts had no guns for such a defense and only contributed their smoke and large radar cross section to the situation, while running out of fuel and calling, "BINGO," stopping the photo pilot from continuing his work.

Commander Paul Ringwood (photo pilot):

The bad guys were actually frightened of the F-8, and we photo guys benefited from that because they did not know we were unarmed.

Will Gray:

The Phantoms were plenty fast enough to stay with us but had to be in minimum afterburner to kill the smoke and really needed that to stay with us. They often had racks and of course the big centerline tank. I think it had a 550 KIAS [aircraft's indicated airspeed in knots] limit but they ignored the limit when necessary.

The Phantoms smoked a lot and had a large radar return, there was no way the gomers could miss seeing them. They were forever bitching about the speed in what they called low threat areas—nuts to that! I did all my work at 3,500–5,000ft more than 600KIA. I jinked all the time, making sure my flight path did not indicate what my target might be. Only had a couple of SAMs shot at me. Watched them come all the way from the cloud of dust at launch until they went by (good sonic boom). If I was to do post-strike BDA, I waited a good long time after the strike—since my first Haiphong BDA ride nearly got me—lots of bullets going by close enough to hear. Three days later my OinC got bagged flying the same mission. I stopped doing immediate post-strike BDA. I usually just milled around out over the gulf and finally picked a time and went downhill to get some smack [energy for speed] and then flew the route or point target. It seemed that most people turn left off a strike (right-handed I guess). I made a point of turning right when I could.

This pilot discussion illustrates the bold, independent, self-confident nature of fighter pilots. However, this book also makes clear that fighter-escort pilots also had mixed feelings about their role. They felt responsible for the photo pilot and suffered a deep sense of loss and self-doubt when an RF-8 was shot down. Some have even harbored a mis-appropriated sense of failure or guilt for decades. The F-4 escort pilots were frustrated their jet did not have the capability to thwart the radar systems of the guns shooting at them.

1972 Non-Fatal Combat Losses

On June 16, 1972, a VFP-63 Det. 3 RF-8G (Bu. No. 145613) was hit by AAA near the Thanh Hoa Bridge. Lieutenant Paul Ringwood ejected and was rescued.

On board *Midway*, Ringwood sat in his Crusader waiting for his turn to launch and proceed on a routine river-reconnaissance mission. His F-4 Phantom escort pilot would launch with him and join on a tanker overhead for a quick fuel top-off. The high drag from tanks, bomb and missile racks was the one reason why the Phantom did not have the range or speed of the slick and clean RF-8 when flying reconnaissance missions, which demand low, high-speed flying. As opposed to most air wings equipped with the RF-8, *Midway* had F-4 fighters instead of F-8s. With an F-8 as escort, the RF-8s had the luxury of flying much faster, thus much safer, runs in a heavy AAA environment.

Lieutenant Ringwood was about five-to-seven miles from the Thanh Hoa Bridge that had resisted years of bombing attacks but still stood tall, proud and defiant. It was fortified with an extensive array of 37mm and 57mm guns and the gunners were very proficient after years of practice. Many aviators and aircraft were victims of the air defense deployed around the area. That day, the bridge was not part of the mission. Ringwood hadn't yet finished his planned mission, when his escort warned, "AAA—Jink!"

Unfortunately, in a RF-8 photo run, the pilot cannot jink if he expects to get 100 percent coverage of his assigned run. Soon thereafter though, he was finished with the run, turned his cameras off and started heavy jinking. At that point he felt a thump and realized he had been hit. The irony is that the pilot expects trouble when one is most vulnerable (straight and level). While jinking, a pilot normally assumes he had dodged the bullet—not in this case.

The heavy maneuvering had slowed him down, so he selected afterburner to gain back some airspeed; the fire warning light immediately illuminated. His escort confirmed his aircraft had been hit at the tail break area and that he was on fire. The Crusader's tail section slides over the rear area of the engine and can be removed during an engine-pull for maintenance. The seam of connection is called the "tail break." Unfortunately for Ringwood, that is also the area where fuel lines pass through to feed the afterburner and as soon as he selected afterburner he fed raw fuel to the fire. This all happened at about 4,000 feet and he was able to head out to sea and safely commence a climb.

When he got 10 miles from shore, and at 10,000 feet altitude, Ringwood decided to eject. As he descended in his parachute towards the water, he noticed a circle of fish beneath him. His first thought was, "Sharks!" He felt very young and vulnerable and tried to remember, from his training, how to control his path by pulling on the chute lanyards. It didn't work. He landed in the middle of the fish and beat the world's record for climbing into a raft. As he settled down, he noticed that the "fish" were swimming up and down—they were actually porpoises. There have been observations that porpoises have exhibited protective behavior around people in trouble. They showed interest in him and swam in a tighter circle around his raft.

Soon, a Vietnamese fishing fleet noticed him and headed his way. When they were about a mile away, an A-7 Corsair circling above as RESCAP (rescue patrol) dove and dropped a 500-pound bomb in their midst. They got the message and immediately made a U-turn for the beach. Being that close to an exploding bomb was an impressive and shocking experience. Paul didn't complain.

It took about 20 minutes for the SAR (Search and Rescue) helicopter to arrive. After getting him aboard, it made a brief stop at a nearby cruiser and then returned him to the *Midway*.

Eventually, (now) Commander Paul Ringwood would accumulate 164 combat missions in Vietnam.

★ ★ ★

Lt. Cmdr. Gordon Paige's RF-8G (Bu. No. 146873) was lost in his shootdown on July 22, 1972. (Lt. Phil Sherman)

On July 22, 1972, VFP-63 Det. 3 was on board *Midway* and Lieutenant Commander Gordon Paige's RF-8G (Bu. No. 146873) was hit by AAA; he ejected and was captured. He was released on March 29, 1973.

Commander Gordon Paige Details His POW Experience:

The Background

In 1972 VFP-63 Detachment 3 was attached to Carrier Air Wing Five embarked in *Midway*. Planning a June deployment, the air wing was involved in training operations off the coast of southern California in early April.

The detachment consisted of four pilots, two chief petty officers and 28 enlisted personnel of various rates. We had four RF-8G Crusaders assigned. The det flew to the ship on April 5 expecting to conduct CARQUALs [Carrier Qualification], but after the first trap, we learned the aircraft and crew were being kept aboard and some aircraft were moved to the hangar deck. Arriving in the ready room I was told that the ship was returning to Alameda and that there were rumors of an early deployment. As *Midway* steamed at high speed back to port, VFP-63's commanding officer informed us that we had been ordered to sea and that we could expect to deploy within the next couple of weeks. Later, of course, it became obvious that this was all in preparation for Operation *Linebacker* which would involve the mining of Haiphong harbor in early May.

Midway ultimately deployed on April 10, 1972, five days after we got word. To say the det's loading aboard was chaotic would be a serious understatement. The tremendous effort put out by the Home Guard squadron was nothing short of heroic.

USS Midway *(CVA-41) leaving San Francisco Bay for WESTPAC, April 10, 1972. (Robert L. Lawson Collection, National Naval Aviation Museum, Pensacola, FL)*

The Setup

From VFP-63's first operations in Vietnam tactics began to evolve. At first the early tactics employed over Cuba [very low altitude, high speed] were employed. In Vietnam the resulting losses from small arms fire made us reevaluate. As the war progressed, tactics were developed which still involved very high speeds but mid-altitude [3,000 to 7,000ft above ground level] recon with unpredictable flight paths [jinking]. This generally served well throughout the remainder of the war.

On *Midway* the fighter squadrons were operating F-4Bs. While the F-8 was capable of speeds in excess of 500kts in basic engine, these speeds required the F-4s to use at least min-burner which was consuming a lot of fuel. This resulted in a cascading effect of additional tanking required and occasionally an additional tanker airborne.

At a July skipper's meeting with CAG, the high speeds were called into question. I argued that we had learned from hard experience that they were necessary due to the unique requirements of photo recon. However, I did ultimately agree that in low-threat areas we would experiment with lower speeds, but that I would make the final determination as to what constituted low threat on a mission-by-mission basis. All agreed and my mission on July 22 was the first test of this program.

The Mission and The Shootdown

My mission on July 22, 1972, was routine *Blue Tree* recon in Nghe An province. *Blue Tree* was the term applied to missions to update the status of road traffic, storage facilities and general operations, a general airwing strike was not involved. The area was determined to be low threat by the standards that we'd set. I don't recall the actual targets involved. On this mission I was escorted by an F-4B from VF-161 piloted by Lieutenant Pete LaChat and his radar intercept officer, Lieutenant Jimmie Bragdon.

We both launched and Pete hit the tanker outbound which was the normal procedure. We flew outbound at around 15,000ft. Approaching the coast just north of Brandon Bay, we descended, with Pete in combat spread on my wing, and accelerating toward 350-400kts which was the new low-threat speed. Shortly after crossing the beach, in the vicinity of highway one, I felt a thump and Pete immediately called, 'You're hit!' I said I was coming back toward the beach and started a left turn. Through about 45 degrees of turn the aircraft exploded. I estimate that we were about 4,000–5,000ft AGL at that point.

The cockpit began tumbling and I remember seeing fire around it. I was pressed up against the canopy and having difficulty reaching the face-curtain handle, so I switched to the alternate handle on the front of the seat, pulled it and ejected. My chute opened normally and, as I was descending, I could hear small arms fire which I hoped was not directed at me.

Paige's F-4 escort, Lieutenant Pete LaChat from fighter squadron VF-161, provides more information on the shootdown:

I was the escort and my RIO [Radar Intercept Officer] was Jimmie Bragdon. As we approached feet dry, I was on his right, starboard, side in a loose echelon. I decided that since the main threat would be from the north, I wanted to be on his port side. So, I initiated a canopy roll over him in order to be on his left side, looking through him to the north for threats.

Just as I was starting down his left-hand side, I saw a huge fireball on his right outer wing panel. I keyed the mike and said, "Baby Giant, you've taken a hit, let's come port for the beach." Gordie did not answer. The fire went out almost immediately and there was fuel trailing from the wing panel. [Otherwise,] all looked OK.

North Vietnamese radar-guided Quad ZSU anti-aircraft artillery (AAA) site. (Lt. Pete LaChat)

His plane started a shallow roll to his left, and then there was a HUGE ball of flame, an explosion on the bottom of the fuselage, beneath the wing. The wing came off the fuselage, still in one piece, and for a moment was suspended over the fuselage so that the two pieces of plane were separate and still completely recognizable. It was like they were dissembled in a hangar for maintenance. It's a sight that is seared in my brain and will be forever.

At that time, neither showed any signs of damage other than the fireball under the fuselage. Almost immediately, the fuselage jackknifed, the nose and tail both came up [nearly equal parts] and then the entire fuselage exploded in a ball of flame and unrecognizable wreckage. It fell to the ground. We could see the wreckage on the ground. There was not much left. Neither Jimmie nor I ever saw a chute nor did we see Gordie on the ground. Neither of us believed at the time, that anyone could have survived. I don't have a specific recollection but I think we were likely between 4,000 and 6,000 feet.

We did one turn over the site and left. I reported Gordie KIA. However, by the time I was back aboard there was the news that there had been an ELT (Emergency Locator Transmitter) broadcast from the area of the shootdown. Within a short time, the North Vietnamese reported him captured.

It was a definite point of remembrance in my life. I feel guilty for not having seen his chute. I was there to protect him and he got shot down.

However, that said, there are some other issues that I have pondered over the years; I am sure that the AAA that got him was the ZSU type [Soviet-built self-propelled anti-aircraft mount] —I do not know the caliber but likely 37mm—those guns are radar guided, so no tracers nor puffs, and no way to know that they are shooting at you. We did not have any ECM [Electronic Countermeasures] equipment that would either detect or jam—completely defenseless. And they were easy to hide. On one photo recce, Lt. Paul Ringwood and I flew right over a battery of four emplacements and never knew it until the recce photos were developed back aboard *Midway.*

I always wondered why they shot at him. I was the much more valuable target. Then it suddenly occurred to me that they were likely shooting at me. When I did the canopy roll over Gordie, the radar guns locked on his RF-8, instead of me, and he got hit.

Commander Paige continues:

I was only in the chute briefly and hit the ground uninjured. I removed my parachute and flight gear, hid them in some bushes and moved down towards a nearby river with the idea of crossing it. When I got to the edge, I realized that it was not only too wide, but that there were too many people in the vicinity, so I hid in some undergrowth hoping to wait out daylight and move after dark. That plan went south after about 20 minutes, when I was discovered by a couple of locals who yelled for the militia. I was now officially a POW.

All that evening we hiked along the dikes to a small group of buildings, which I assumed was some military outpost, as I could see a Soviet AN-2 Colt [aircraft] sitting in the grass nearby. Through that night, although shackled to the bed, I entertained plans to hijack the airplane and fly to Da Nang. I never had the chance and discovered many years later, in talks with an owner of the type, that they were well known for being cranky, noisy, and difficult to start.

The next morning a truck appeared and, escorted by two uniformed soldiers, we resumed the journey north. In the late afternoon we arrived at a second military outpost where I was given a wrapped Granola bar to eat and put on a cot in a small cave. I dozed off but was awakened to the sound of rifles being cocked and [was] pulled from the cave, blindfolded and hands tied. I was pushed against a wall and figured that this was it. After a few moments, several flashbulbs went off and my blindfold was removed. As I was being pushed back to the cave, I saw that the rifle was being held by a small girl wearing an army helmet. I was apparently the subject of a photo-op: 'Small girl single-handedly captures Yankee air pirate.' In the morning we loaded up and started north again, this time arriving at Hoa Lo [A.K.A. Hanoi Hilton] prison in the early afternoon.

The Hilton

Introduction to POW life at the Hilton started with an interrogation. Two NVN [North Vietnam] soldiers asked me the expected questions Name/Rank/Serial No. and then what unit I was attached to, the ship I came from, etc. All questions that, having my flight suit and access to the aircraft wreckage, they already knew the answers to. This was primarily a sizing up operation to decide how cooperative I was going to be. I stuck with the Military Code of Conduct: Name, Rank, Serial Number and was a bit surprised that I wasn't pushed very hard for more.

That night was spent sitting on a six-inch-tall stool, hands tied behind me, in the interrogation room. Whenever I'd doze off, I was awakened by the guard in the corner. In the morning, I was moved into a solitary cell in what I would learn was the infamous "Heartbreak Hotel." However, by this time, while the interrogations continued on a regular basis, they were not pursued with the vigor experienced by the earlier shootdowns.[xxxvi] The Vietnamese had a pattern of a midday meal break and siesta, which lasted about an hour. During this time, it was possible to communicate by whispering through the barred transom of the cell. I could see and talk to Captain Kevin Cheney in the cell across from me. Kevin had been shot down in early July. He could see and talk to me, as well as, Captain David Grant and his GIB,[xxxvii] Captain Bill Beekman (all USAF). Both shot down in late June.

This early contact established the essentials of the communication process that would continue through the next eight months. It was a tremendous morale builder and while in Heartbreak, we had little information about the camp; we at least were able to establish a picture of the daily routines of the guards.

Time in Heartbreak proceeded day by day. I watched Cheney, Grant and Beekman removed to, where? Another prison, taken out and shot? I had no idea. The original three were replaced by later shootdowns and over time I became the "old hand" in Heartbreak. After thirty days, to the day, I was told to "put on long clothes,"[xxxviii] and to also bring my sleeping mat and metal cup. I was marched out of Heartbreak and around the corner into the main camp. I went into a large room, which at the time housed about nine POWs—all FNGs [F—ing New Guys] shot down in the last few months, including, Grant, Beekman and Cheney.

This room was "home" for the next seven months. The senior officer in each room was in command; in our case, Lieutenant Commander Hank Lesesne, shot down in early July in an A-4F from the *Hancock*. As operations in *Linebacker* [President Nixon's new bombing campaign] spooled up, we would eventually grow to about thirty POWs in the room.

Communication between prisoners was the most important issue in the camp. It maintained a flow of information and boosted morale wonderfully. In the early years, the North Vietnamese did everything they could to prevent comms. (In those years it was a torture offense.) In 1972, leadership was segregated in a separate area and screens were in place around the "front yard" of each room denying any visual contact with prisoners in the other rooms. However, the enforcement was more lax by 1972 and we learned that we could transmit information to the room directly across from us by standing in the barred windows at the top of the room and using "Flash Code." This was the traditional tap code adapted to the hand fan, that was given out in lieu of air conditioning. Ultimately, there was no place in the camp that could not be communicated with in some way.

As rookies, we weren't too fast with the flash code, so usually the communicator would simply recite the number of flashes and a decoder would turn that into letters and words. I was communicating one day and received a message, which I dutifully passed to the decoder. At the end, I asked what the message was and he said, "I swindle." We looked at each other for a minute and he said: "Tell him you pick pockets," maybe you can get something going. It was, of course, Marine Captain Orson Swindle.

As we got into the rhythm of communications, passing information from the upper leadership, sending reports of interrogations [quizzes] and camp observations upstream, it became apparent that the FOGs [F—ing Old Guys] were starved for ordinary information. Having been fed nothing but a nonstop stream of propaganda and with no new POWs in the last four years, they had no idea of the political situation with the war and what was going on in the States. We did our best to bring them up to date, eventually establishing a midday "news" program during the quiet time. Questions about

---

xxxvi Since there had been essentially no POWs arrive at the camp since about 1969, the shootdowns prior to that time were referred to as the FOGs [F—ing Old Guys] while we were known as the FNGs [F—ing New Guys].

xxxvii "Guy in Back"—jargon for navigator, radar intercept officer in rear seat.

xxxviii This meant long pants and long sleeve shirt, "formal attire" and usually meant an interrogation.

daily life in the U.S. began to come in. Squadronmates would want to know information about their families, which fortunately we sometimes had. Also, who won the Super Bowl, the World Series, The Masters, etc. Guys just trying to touch base with their previous lives.

The old guys were the backbone, keeping us on track and spirits high. More than once I heard: "If I can do six years, you can do another day." But if there was a single achievement that I feel that the FNGs contributed to the camp, it was providing this contact with everyday American life.

We were fed twice a day. Part of the year it was pumpkin soup, tea and bread. [xxxix] The remainder of the year we got "sewer greens," another soup but made with some sort of bitter green plant. One day the bread was suddenly replaced by rice which, as a staple of Asian life, was not considered suitable for prisoners. When we asked why the change, the answer was: "Americans bomb bakery."

The room had frequent chores. Emptying the 55-gallon drum that served as our toilet was one of them. This was taken out into the central yard of the camp and dumped into a sewer drain. It offered a chance to see and be seen by the other POWs and occasionally an opportunity to pass a short message.

There were occasional interrogations, usually pressure to make statements or fill out personal information. For most of us there wasn't serious pressure. However, this was about the time that the USAF began using the Laser Guided Bomb (LGB). The NVN knew about the weapon and were dead serious to get more information. One of the guys in the room was from a squadron that had employed the LGB and was taken out for a few days and tortured for information. To my knowledge that was the only time one of us was tortured. F-4 pilot Lieutenant Jack Ensch (shot down while aboard *Midway*) had been shot down by a SAM and a piece of shrapnel had nearly severed his thumb. He was denied treatment for several days until a "doctor" finally cut it off completely without benefit of anesthetic. Later Jack acquired the callsign "Fingers" due to the lack of a thumb.

Although we were not being tortured the way the old guys had been, we were still subject to the uncertainty. What if the talks broke down? What if the North Vietnamese decided to "disappear" a few of the MIAs out of convenience or as bargaining chips? Since the only news coming out of the camps were what the NVN wanted out, we were pretty much pawns in the bigger game.

Filling the time

We didn't have a lot, but we did have plenty of time and the POWs devised many ways to pass it. Chess pieces made from bread or rice and chess boards scratched into the floor under a bed board. A duplicate bridge tournament was painstakingly conducted between rooms through flash and tap code. (Did I mention, we had plenty of time?) Playing cards drawn on toilet paper (more like commercial paper towels than T.P.) provided poker, pinochle, and other card games.

Then there was "dinner and a movie." A couple times a week two or three guys would get together and take us all out on a "date." This involved describing an elaborate meal either from experience at a particular restaurant or simply created out of imagination, followed by a (usually dramatic) retelling of a movie. Often others who had seen it would shout corrections or insert their own impressions of the actors.

It wasn't all fun and games. Many of us attended or taught school. Nearly all the POWs were college grads and commonly with non-aviation degrees: oceanography, history, literature, and foreign languages were all represented in the room. Discussions would break out, sometimes spontaneously, about subjects which took us far away from the present world. One guy with a remarkable photographic memory was able to recreate chapter after chapter of Russian language text.

---

xxxix This may sound like fine dining but in fact the soup was just a watery broth with pieces of pumpkin floating in it. The tea, also thin, came in a large tub. The bread was edible but was filled with weevils.

The guards were not drawn from the cream of the North Vietnamese military. Some were well known as energetic torturers and had nicknames to reflect that. Few of the guards spoke any sort of English and communicated with grunts and gestures. A couple, however, did seem to have a humane streak. One in particular we called "Good Neighbor Sam" would often do his best to report an injury or illness if a POW required help.

The screens come down

One day in October 1972 there was a lot of activity in the camp and it was soon obvious that the bamboo screens surrounding each room were being removed. No explanation as to why, but it could only be seen as a positive move. In the near term, nothing else changed, we still went out individually, but we could now easily see who was in each room and even pass a wave or thumbs up to an old squadron buddy. A lot of time was spent trying to identify POWs among the FOGs and compare them to the list we'd all been tasked to memorize.

Christmas 1972

We always knew when a strike was inbound. Sirens would sound and, at night, the power to the city was shut off plunging the camp into darkness. One night the sirens went off and shortly after an increasing rumble started and went on and on. Out of the dark one of the POWs said: "Pack your bags guys, that's an *Arclight*[xl]—If the Buffs [B-52s] are coming downtown, someone has decided to get serious about this war." I can't describe the relief that we felt, or the heroism involved by the B-52 crews. Apparently briefed to expect up to 30 percent losses in the opening nights of the campaign they pressed on and delivered the goods.

It was the turning point in the negotiations in Paris and the effect was obvious inside the camp. In the morning the North Vietnamese officers had to come to each spot where a guard was hiding and pull him out, often by force. They were terrified and I'm sure the same held true in the city outside the gate. The bombings went on for 11 days from the 18th to the 29th of December. Through that time B-52 crewmembers began arriving, some severely burned, in the room next door to ours. We volunteered to help out and a few of our guys were tapped to shuttle food, and dress and clean wounds and burns. They also picked up as much intel as they could about the strikes.

By mid-January 1973 the camp changed dramatically. POWs were allowed outside together for extended periods. For the first time, we could chat freely with the old guys, some of whom we hadn't seen for almost eight years. Also, POWs from the other camps began arriving in the Hilton.

One of the cardinal tenets of the 4th Allied POW Wing[xli] was release order by date of shootdown. This demand had been passed to U.S. leadership by a couple of POWs who had been released, notably Doug Hegdahl.[xlii] It had apparently been incorporated into the agreement because toward

xl Arclight was the code name for B-52 bombing strikes. These had typically been confined to the area right around the DMZ and in very southern NVN. That changed with Operation *Linebacker II*.

xli This was our official military organization. "The prisoners formally organized themselves under the 4th Allied POW Wing, whose name acknowledged earlier periods of overseas captivity among American military personnel in World War I, World War II and the Korean War. This military structure was ultimately recognized by the North Vietnamese and endured until the prisoners' release in 1973" [Hubbell, POW]

xlii Douglas Brent Hegdahl III is a former United States Navy Petty officer second class who was held as a prisoner of war by North Vietnam during the war. After an early release, he was able to provide the names and personal information of about 256 fellow POWs, as well as reveal the conditions of the prisoner-of-war camp.

the end of the month, the big reshuffling took place. The FNGs were all moved to 'The Zoo,' another camp on the outskirts of Hanoi.

On the 12th of February we heard the unmistakable sound of a C-141 and its four turbofan engines. We knew at least some of the FOGs were going home. After three releases, and a long wait hoping that nothing derailed the agreement, our turn came on April 28, 1973.

We were loaded onto busses and driven through the city, which had obviously suffered from the bombings. Notably as we passed the railyard, we could see that it had been the recipient of a lot of B-52 attention. One locomotive was literally standing on end.

At Gia Lam airfield we got off the bus, moved from NVN control to a group of U.S. officers and on to that big beautiful C-141. The takeoff was greeted by cheers, but the loudest celebration greeted the captain's announcement that we were 'feet wet.' We were over the Tonkin Gulf and out of Vietnam.

First stop was Clark AFB in the Philippines. Physicals, debriefing, uniforms and best of all Hot Showers! We were at Clark for a few days before we were again sorted out by destination and sent onward. Honolulu, Travis AFB and, in my case, to Andrews AFB for transfer to Bethesda Naval Hospital. My parents were living in Alexandria, Virginia at the time.

I spent 30 days as an in/outpatient at Bethesda while I was poked, prodded, psychiatrically evaluated and rid of parasites, which we all brought back. After which, I returned to San Diego for another 30 days of leave.

We were offered our choice of orders following repatriation. Since I had been a NavCad and had come to naval service unencumbered by higher education, I asked to go to post-graduate school to finish a bachelor's and get a master's degree. I received those orders and reported to Monterey in August of 1973. I graduated in 1976 and received orders back to VFP-63 as the officer in charge of Detachment 5 assigned to CVW-6 on USS *America* (CV-66). (Keep doing it until you get it right.) *America* completed a very enjoyable Mediterranean deployment in 1977–78. The det had no accidents or incidents, some great port calls and returned to Miramar at the end of April 1978.

The life of optical photo-reconnaissance was coming to an end. Commander Dave Beam, an old friend was the last CO of VFP-63 and presided over its disestablishment. Without a warfare specialty, I didn't screen for an operational command. The idea of a training command squadron wasn't particularly appealing and with my newly minted MS in Aero Engineering I applied for the Aeronautical Engineering Duty Officer [AEDO] program and was accepted.

I spent three years as the powerplants officer at ComNavAirPac at North Island, Coronado, CA. Followed by another three as the Flight Clearance Officer at NavAirSysCom in Washington, D.C. I retired in September 1984 as a Commander and live with my wife, Wendy, in Arizona.

★ ★ ★

On September 5, 1972, Lieutenant Commander R. W. Harrison from VFP-63 Det. 1 on board *Hancock* was involved in a three-aircraft mid-air collision; he ejected and was rescued.

The one danger that lingers in the back of every pilot's mind is the threat of a mid-air collision. In combat, this danger lurks with the crowded skies and confusion while evading enemy defenses. As we saw in Lieutenant Commander Len Eastman's shootdown, the chaotic dogfight of MiGs and F-8 Crusaders maneuvering for advantage over a foe led to a lost aircraft and pilot. Military aviation, in contrast to its civilian counterpart, regularly requires close formations, so well-demonstrated by the Navy's flight demonstration team, *The Blue Angels*. While they take it to a stunning new level, fleet aircraft execute their basic techniques.

A three-aircraft mid-air accident happened over the Gulf of Tonkin on September 5, 1972, as told here by Lieutenant Pete Phelps of fighter squadron VF-24 on board *Hancock*:

> I've seen some accidents, notably F-8 ramp strikes during ship recoveries that were fantastically violent, but this accident was amazing because everyone lived. It started with the launch of two photo-mission sections from *Hancock* during foul weather. They included VF-24's Lieutenant Jack Shultz, the F-8J photo escort for Lieutenant Commander R. W. (Yogi) Harrison, VFP-63's Det. 1 officer in charge, the lead element for our four-aircraft photo mission. I was the escort for VFP-63's Lieutenant Doug Little, the second section for the mission. Additionally, there was a cast of *Hancock's* helicopters and Lieutenant Skip Lewis, our VA-55 A-4 tanker.
>
> After launching, we met a thunder squall that made visibility very poor, so we climbed out using instruments. The tanker guy (Skip Lewis) found a hole between two cloud layers, and radioed a rendezvous point 12 miles northwest of *Hancock* to meet up. The undercast was at 9,500 feet, with an overcast just above and cells all around the rendezvous point. We had to rendezvous just north of the ship due to a thunder bumper over the ship.
>
> As I approached the rendezvous circle from the inside, I saw Jack beginning to refuel from Skip's A-4, with Yogi's RF-8G outside the rendezvous circle. Unexpectedly, Yogi decides to get some close-up photos of Jack's F-8J tanking from the A-4 and crossed over the top of Jack and Skip. Unbeknownst to anyone, Skip tightened-up his turn to avoid a thunder cell, without mentioning it—he was the lead, after all. Yogi was above the two, but couldn't see the two aircraft in his camera viewfinder. He rocked back and forth a little, but ended up settling into Skip's tanker and Jack's F-8J, as the turn tightened. Yogi's RF-8G split the A-4 from just aft the intake and broke off its left horizontal stabilizer, then toasted Jack Shultz's helmet top as Yogi's tail crashed down into the F-8J's nose. Yogi pitched up and Jack snap rolled left. There was at least one explosion, followed immediately by two simultaneous ejections a couple hundred feet apart.
>
> With sheet metal, smoke and debris everywhere in front of me, I felt some superficial hits from the debris. I orbited and became on-scene commander and called John Harshberger, flying a VA-55 A-4, whom I believe was the second tanker for our mission, and told him to orbit our position below the overcast—wide enough to await the chutes. Meanwhile, Skip went into a death spiral, with no remaining left horizontal stabilizer for control. I told him to eject several times, but he got control of it after entering the undercast, in a near vertical dive. Once below the overcast, Skip limped back to *Hancock* on the wing of another A-4 that picked him up after descending thru the clouds. They made a direct beeline to *Hancock*'s TACAN (navigational aid system for aircraft).
>
> I called in for a helo, notified ship's strike operations and orbited the two chutes until they disappeared into clouds at 9,500 feet. John said two chutes came thru at 2,500 feet. I circled down when the helo came in and picked up Jack. They couldn't find Yogi. Then, the helo experienced engine trouble and headed back towards the ship. I called the helo and they said they only had Jack, but there were several small rain squalls in the area. I was afraid Yogi may have "streamed" (chute failed to open), in the clouds or was pulled under by his chute. However, John had said he saw two chutes hit the water, so I went back to where the helo's smoke marker was. One of those

small squalls was right in that area, so I circled around it at 1,000ft to see its back side. As it moved southward a very small bright discoloration in the water appeared on its edge as it moved away. About a mile away I saw green dye and dropped to 200 feet and saw Yogi waving. I called the ship's helo pilot, who had regained the engine, and vectored them back to pick up Yogi. Both pilots were in good shape.

Skip got his aircraft aboard *Hancock* but just barely. He almost had another mid-air with another section of A-4s approaching the ship on a CCA (Carrier Controlled Approach) from astern!

The squadron maintenance crew examined the A-4, found it had major damage along the entire fuselage, damage into the engine, and the port stabilizer hanging from just its cables. They were going to pull the intact nose for spare parts, then push the hull over the side, but they transferred the hull to NAS ATSUGI Japan for transfer back to the States. It was decided to total it when they found major structural damage to the wing spar and interior structure.

Skip Lewis adds the following:

When the collision happened, my first thought was that someone outside the flight had hit us. I observed that my plane was oscillating, suggesting stability, so I let it settle, then tried the controls. At that time, I observed an F-8 just entering underlying clouds and a nearby chute entering the clouds soon after. I radioed the situation to Rampage [*Hancock*]. The pilot who checked me over understated the damage as "a piece of your stabilizer is hanging down." He later stated this was so I wouldn't be nervous, or words to that effect. So, nobody else knew the scope of the damage yet.

On approach I dirtied up early to see if I could and what effect it would have. When the flaps were down, I had very little available back stick and chose to do a no-flap landing which is about 10 knots faster than normal. On the first pass the LSO waved me off (pitching deck). I was told that Skipper Fenzl jumped out of his seat when I flew by on the PLAT [flight deck live video display], revealing my [F-4] Phantom-like tail. The second pass was successful.

I was stunned by the damage. The left stabilizer was hanging down and moved easily when I pushed on it. There was a large gash on the right side of the fuselage through which I could see the engine. The skin of the fuselage was wrinkled from the twist.

Later I saw the plane on the hangar deck with two F-8 silhouettes painted on the side.

Pete Phelps concludes the story:

Excitement over, I rendezvoused with VFP-63's Doug Little, got an "UP" damage inspection of my F-8J, and we flew our photo mission (modified to merchant ship surveillance) off Vinh. Upon return to the ship, we were met by very high winds, up to 35–40kts but got aboard safely.

The next day, September 6, an A-6 was hit near the "Hour Glass" area. He managed to go feet wet in time to eject, but high winds blew him back to the beach where he was captured—poor bastard.

Hancock's attrition saga continued the next day over the "Hour Glass," when Jim Loughmiller's wingman warned of a SAM tracking them and they barely beat it. Then, Will Pear of VA-55 got hit by AAA southeast of Thanh Hoa. With his aircraft on fire, he made it to the water and ejected 2 miles off the beach. SAR forces gathered overhead and the SAR helo (Big Mother) was vectored in by his wingman, Ray Winn. Within one-half hour, they picked him up, as the winds blew him back toward shore. Shore batteries and AAA fired at the rescuers, but the RESCAP bombed the crap out of them! Will Pear was OK!

Two VFP-63 Det. 19 RF-8Gs from USS Hancock *(CVA-19) refuel from VA-55 A-4s, January 1970. (Robert L. Lawson Collection, National Naval Aviation Museum, Pensacola, FL)*

USS Hancock *(CVA-19) in the Tonkin Gulf, March 17 1971, as a VF-24 "Red Checkertails" Crusader makes a flyover. The squadron was the first ace squadron with four MiG kills. (Robert L. Lawson Collection, National Naval Aviation Museum, Pensacola, FL)*

★ ★ ★

On December 13, 1972, a VFP-63 Det. 4 USS *Oriskany* (CVA-34) RF-8G (Bu. No. 144608), piloted by Lieutenant T. B. Scott, crashed in a recovery accident. He was rescued. The aircraft had a remarkable history.

Marine Corps Major John Glenn (a future astronaut, who was the first man to orbit the earth, and, later still, became a U.S. Senator) used an F8U-1P (later, RF-8A) photo-Crusader (Bu. No. 144608) to perform his record-setting cross-country flight during *Project Bullet* on July 16, 1957. At a time, when speed records were deemed to be an important thing for aircraft to achieve, the U.S. Navy was excited to try to beat the previous USAF transcontinental speed record, which averaged 672mph, held by the Republic F-84F Thunderstreak. More importantly, the F8U-1P was able to prove that its J-57 turbojet engine could handle maximum combat power (in afterburner) for long periods of time at high altitude. Lieutenant Commander Charles F. Demmler flew an F8U-1 (later, F-8A) fighter as a backup during the record attempt.

The pilots had to refuel three times during the flight using U.S. Navy piston-engine AJ-2 Savage tankers, which had a ceiling of 25,000 feet and a top speed of 300mph. That meant the Crusader pilots had to reduce their speed from more than 1,000mph and descend from their cruising altitude of 50,000 feet to refuel. On one of the tanking evolutions, Demmler damaged his refueling probe and had to abort, leaving Glenn to finish the race alone.

The flight took off from NAS Los Alamitos in California and landed at Floyd Bennett Field in New York City. Glenn turned his cameras on to produce photo coverage of the coast-to-coast 2,446-mile course. He achieved a new speed record by averaging 725.5mph, or Mach 1.1, at 35,000 feet during the flight's duration of 3 hours 23 minutes. This meant Glenn had completed the crossing faster than the muzzle velocity of a .45-caliber bullet.

Flying at supersonic speeds (the speed of sound varies at different altitudes, being 761mph at sea level and 68 degrees Fahrenheit, and 670mph at 30,000 feet), the F8U-1P was laying down sonic booms along the way. When an aircraft travels through the air, it produces pressure waves much like the bow of a boat makes waves as it plows through the water. As the jet approaches the speed of sound, the waves are forced together and merge into a single shock wave traveling at the speed of sound (Mach 1). This is perceived on the ground as a loud boom. Altitude and atmospheric conditions can affect the strength of the sonic boom, which can break windows if strong enough.

In later history, this F8U-1P was acquired from Naval Air Test Center (NATC) by VFP-62 for Cuban Missile Crisis Operation *Blue Moon* missions in October 1962. After its assignment to VFP-62, it was returned to NATC and eventually transferred to VFP-63. Unfortunately, VFP-63 pilot, Lieutenant Thomas B. Scott, crashed on a landing attempt aboard *Oriskany* in the South China Sea on December 13, 1972. The doomed jet hit the flight deck round-down, damaged the landing gear and went into the sea. The pilot survived. Had it not been so, Bu. No. 144608 would certainly have

In 1926, Congress authorized the Distinguished Flying Cross (DFC). In this photograph, Secretary of the Navy Thomas Gates presents the DFC to future astronaut Maj. John Glenn USMC, for his record-setting transcontinental flight in an RF-8A Crusader on July 16, 1957. (National Naval Aviation Museum, Pensacola, FL)

Maj. John Glenn USMC in his Project Bullet *RF-8A Crusader July 16, 1957. He beat the previous USAF transcontinental speed record averaging 725.5 mph or Mach 1.1 during the flight's 3 hours 23 minutes. The object above his right hand is the photo view-finder hood.*

been a strong candidate for preservation in the Udvar-Hazy National Air and Space Museum at Dulles International Airport, Virginia.

The Project Bullet *RF-8A (Bu. No. 144608) was destroyed in a landing accident on December 13, 1972. The pilot, Lt. T. B. Scott, ejected and was rescued. This photo also clearly shows the camera bay windows (dark rectangles).*

Thanh Hoa "Dragon's Jaw" Bridge Finally Falls

The Thanh Hoa Bridge, a frequent target for the Navy and Air Force for seven years, still stood as proud and defiant as the government in Hanoi on the morning of October 6, 1972. That day, four A-7C Corsair II jets from Attack Squadron 82 (VA-82) launched from USS *America* (CVA-66) and headed for the bridge. The A-7C was a Vought manufactured attack aircraft and had design features that resembled a mini-Crusader. At quick glance, one can mistakenly confuse one for the other, but they are drastically different in mission and design. Two of the A-7s were loaded with two 2,000-pound Mark 84 general purpose bombs and the others with two 2,000-pound Walleye "smart" bombs. When launched, the Walleye would follow a radar beam, directed by the pilot, to the target. One of the pilots flying with the Walleyes was (then)

VFP-63 Det. 4 aircraft 601 (Bu. No. 144608) over Mt. Fuji, Japan, en route to USS Oriskany *(CVA-34) from Atsugi in 1972. This was Maj. John Glenn's (future astronaut and senator)* Project Bullet *jet. This may be the only photo of it in its combat configuration. This aircraft was also used by VFP-62 during the Cuban Missile Crisis recon missions. (Lt. Rick Fessenden via Jerry Nolan ISC)*

Lieutenant Commander Leighton "Snuffy" Smith, later promoted to four-star admiral, took part in the strike that brought down the Thanh Hoa bridge. Here's his story.

> Regarding the Thanh Hoa Bridge, I was in the flight of four that put it in the water. That occurred on October 6, 1972. A book, *The Dragon's Jaw: An Epic Story of Courage and Tenacity in Vietnam*, was published in 2019, written by Barrett Tillman and Stephen Coontz (*Flight of the Intruder*). It is a very good account of the many strikes on that bridge. I have never figured out how I seem to have gotten much more credit than due for knocking down the bridge. There is a story there, though. I had led a strike on the bridge a couple of days before. We did not achieve the desired results (crap, nobody had for seven years) so the bridge came up on the target list for the 6th. On the earlier strike, our CO, Commander Don Sumner, a good guy, had been grounded with a cold. On the 6th, he got an "up chit" and decided to go on the strike that day. He asked me to brief the hop, since we would fly almost the same track as the earlier strike, so I did. He, however, was the division leader. He and [Lieutenant (junior grade) Jim Brister] carried two, 2,000-pound GP bombs. Enter our CAG, Commander Jim Joy, as a flak suppressor. Being the senior guy, he became the strike leader. So, the line-up was CAG as leader, Sumner as division leader, and I was the section leader of the two Walleye II strike aircraft.
>
> We flew the strike as planned. After we had all gotten feet wet, Skipper Sumner flew back towards the bridge to assess the damage, but there was so much smoke around the bridge, he could not get any BDA. Not planned, was a photo recce of the bridge, however: a RA-5C pilot from RVAH-6 named Wes Rutledge had been on another mission up near Hanoi and decided to make a run by the bridge on his way out. That film was developed about 6pm and shortly thereafter I got a call from the ship's Intel Officer to come down to IOIC, as there was something that he wanted to show me. I did and he did: photo evidence of the bridge in the water. The four strikers had quite a celebration that night.

Loaded with bombs, an A-7A Corsair II of VA-27 prepares to be catapulted off the flight deck of USS Constellation *(CVA-64) steaming in the waters of the Tonkin Gulf off North Vietnam in 1968. The first operational deployment of the A-7A was in combat operations the previous year. The Corsair resembles the F-8 Crusader. (National Naval Aviation Museum, Pensacola, FL)*

Operation Linebacker II – *B-52 Christmas Bombing*

By late 1972, it was apparent the war was coming to an end, one way or another. President Nixon largely failed to get North Vietnamese leaders to negotiate during his first term and approved Operation *Linebacker II* which involved B-52 Stratofortress bombing of major Hanoi and Haiphong targets from December 18–29, the so-called Christmas Bombing. The largest bombers in the U.S. arsenal were sent in and had to contend with the SA-2 SAM defenses: never varied their flight routes and altitude, did not have ECM gear tweaked for the threat—hence, shockingly vulnerable. U.S. Air Force B-52 pilot Major Robert Clark provides his insight on mission planning:

> The crews were concerned about running airplanes together. By not having the knowledge of the capabilities, SAC [Strategic Air Command] Headquarters' mission planning for the first three days was fairly basic: same altitude, same routes, and a ninety degree turn off target. Ninety degree turns after bomb release highlighted an aircraft to enemy radar because its ECM gear wasn't pointed at the threat. The mission planning cell at both U-Tapao Thailand and Anderson AFB, Guam was finally

> included in building the frag [daily operations order] after day three. They varied the attack routes, altitudes, timing and a host of other things. They were the people who had redone the mission planning for *Arclight* [*Linebacker I* B-52 bombing of South Vietnam] and were familiar with what the crews were capable of and operational capabilities of defenses up north.
>
> At 35,000ft, the 85mm and 100mm flak couldn't touch us. They could only reach to 25–26,000ft. That left the SAMs to contend with. Some missions ran north of Thud Ridge [northwest of Hanoi] and turned south to their targets. I was the lead cell with the third wave of B-52Gs, and my cell's attack route came down on the southern slope of Thud Ridge. With the duty SAM site at the foot of Thud Ridge, there was no way to avoid it, and there were five cells behind us. The SAMs were quiet, however, when we attacked. We were the third wave of B-52Gs and the B-52Ds, out of U-Tapao, had been attacking before us. In retrospect, I think they held fire until they had figured out how to deal with our ECM and number of Buffs attacking, or were reloading.

Eighteen B-52s were shot down. However, President Nixon's bold move worked and the Paris Peace Accords were signed in January 1973. By April, all 591 of America's known POWs were released. For the United States, the war was over.

In Memoriam

Lieutenant Victor Patrick Buckley
August 4, 1944–December 16, 1969

On December 16, 1969, Lieutenant Victor P. Buckley was assigned to VFP-63 Det. 19, Carrier Air Wing Twenty-One (CVW-21), deployed on *Hancock*. He was the pilot of an RF-8G (Bu. No. 145611, call sign: Cork Tip 600) and disappeared over the Gulf of Tonkin while returning to *Hancock* from a photo-reconnaissance mission.

Buckley advised the approach controller he was unable to hear flight instructions. The fighter escort took the lead and gave the standard lead change signal, which Buckley acknowledged. His aircraft was then observed to drift aft into a loose cruise position as the fighter escort descended for refueling and rendezvous with a tanker. The KA-3B tanker crew never saw the second aircraft, only the fighter escort when it came in to refuel, despite good visibility. Following refueling, less than ten minutes after they had switched positions, the escort was unable to locate the RF-8G either visually or via radio, nor was *Hancock*.

Search efforts by aircraft, search and rescue helicopters, and surface units, over a 54-hour period, found no evidence of the missing pilot or aircraft. During the search, one naval vessel recovered an apparent nose wheel from an aircraft within one of the search areas, but were unable to say with any certainty if it came from his aircraft. They terminated the organized search. The U.S. Navy requested all units to maintain electronic-search alert for any evidence related to the missing aircraft or pilot.

On January 21, 1971, the Department of Navy determined Lieutenant Victor Buckley was killed-in-action. The Joint Casualty Resolution Center designated this air-loss incident as Reference number (REFNO) 1537

Commendations

- ★ Purple Heart
- ★ Naval Aviation Wings
- ★ Vietnam Campaign Medal
- ★ Navy Presidential Unit Citation
- ★ Navy Expeditionary Medal
- ★ Combat Action Ribbon
- ★ National Defense Service Medal
- ★ Vietnam Service Medal
- ★ Vietnam Gallantry Cross

Memorials and Tributes

Author, from online tribute:

> Pat came from Virginia to the Naval Academy as no stranger. His brother was in the class of 1964 and his father was graduated in 1939. After graduating from Annapolis in June 1966, Pat was assigned to training as a Naval Aviator. He qualified to fly the RF-8 fighter and eventually deployed in *Hancock* in a photo-reconnaissance detachment.

Memories from Darlene McPhee Simeone, December 15, 2016:

> My fiancé, Lt. V. Patrick Buckley, disappeared returning to *Hancock*, in the Gulf of Tonkin, on Dec. 16, 1969. His remains have never been recovered. I remember that day like it was yesterday. The sadness just never leaves you. I held on to the hope for years that his plane somehow made it to land and he was captured. I hoped and prayed that he would be returned to us. But the POWs eventually came home and he wasn't among them. I wish that I had the words to describe to you what a handsome, bright, dynamic individual he was. He just loved life and had so much to offer. I tried without success to find out what happened to him. I know that if the situation were reversed, he would never have stopped looking for me. I hope that he knows that with the little resources that I had at my disposal, I did try my best and I continue to try. I hope that whatever happened to him was quick and that he did not suffer. It is said that pain eases with time, but I still feel his loss so acutely to this day. I hope that he is somewhere where there is no pain and suffering and if I pray really hard, I will someday see him again.

Memories from an escort pilot, Captain Charles L. Robinson USN (Ret):

> I was on my first cruise in VF-211 in *Hancock*. I didn't know Pat very well since we were in different squadrons, but we saw a lot of each other on the ship. I was supposed to be Pat's wingman the day he disappeared. Pat flew the photo bird (RF-8 from VFP-63) and was to be escorted by a VF-211 F-8J. We briefed for the mission, I don't recall the target, but it was likely the Mu Gia Pass in Northern Laos. We always briefed with a spare pilot/aircraft in case one had problems. The spare would brief/man-up/start and then shut down if the go-bird launched. On this day my aircraft wouldn't start properly so the spare, Lieutenant Chris "Boomer" Wilson, launched in my place.
>
> The RF-8 carried more fuel than the fighter, so after feet wet from the mission, they joined on a tanker en route to the carrier so the fighter could take on fuel. Boomer joined on the A-4 tanker and took his fuel while Pat was supposed to fly loose wing on them. When Boomer disengaged and looked around, Pat was gone. He and the A-4 searched for him and made radio calls on Guard channel, but no trace was ever found of him.
>
> We had lost other guys, but this one really hurt. There were no answers. If he had suffered unknown battle damage while feet dry, why didn't he make a Mayday or other radio call when he

realized it, unless it was catastrophic. Perhaps he loosened his oxygen mask as we often did while cruising around and the cockpit air was contaminated and he passed out. Both the A-4 and F-8 are single seat so the pilots would have been too busy during the refueling evolution to watch for Pat. After refueling, if he had been going the opposite direction at the fueling speed of 250kts, they could have been separated by 80 miles.

But still so many questions. Did he fly west over North Vietnam, north to Chinese Hainan Island or south/east over open ocean? More likely, since we didn't use autopilot, the aircraft, if uncontrolled, would have soon spiraled down into the water. With all the ships in the area, why was there no radar contact?

I think about it often. It's over 50 years ago, Boomer's gone, and there are still no answers.

Harold Ferguson, January 15, 2007:

After Pat graduated from the Naval Academy, he began flight training and was stationed at various bases throughout the U.S. Months would go by when their only communication was through letters or expensive phone calls. When Darlene finished college in May of 1969, Pat finished flight training and was due to deploy that summer for an eight-month cruise as a carrier jet reconnaissance pilot in *Hancock* in Vietnam. They spent as much time together as they could and before he left, Pat proposed. Darlene accepted and they envisioned getting married when he returned.

Yet, as Pat began preparing for a tour in Vietnam, reality set in. "He often spoke of the mortality rate of pilots, and he worried about breaking my heart if something happened to him," [his fiancé] Darlene said, "I truly believed that we were meant to be together and that he would make it back."[2]

On December 16, 1969, my ship the USS *Dennis J Buckley* (DD 808) was sent to search for a pilot that had went down in the Tonkin Gulf while coming back from a mission over Vietnam. We broke off from the aircraft carrier we were working with and proceeded to the site where the plane went down. Captain Luskin announced the pilot's name was Victor Buckley [a strange coincidence]. We spent three days looking for him, but to no avail. We did find a nose wheel off of a plane, but had no idea whether it came off of his plane. It was a tremendous let down to the crew when we were ordered to return to the carrier.

Tom Porter, November 13:

Victor (Pat) was a true friend; we shared many classes at the Naval Academy. It's so sad he left us so early. May God continue to bless his soul.

Bill Cowan, USMC (Ret), July 19, 2004:

Although he was tragically lost in Vietnam, I'm not able to think about Bucs without instantly remembering his ever-present smile. He was a friend to all who knew him, a confidant to those who needed help or advice, and a professional when it came to doing his work. These days, Bucs surely sits somewhere close to God, so that he can be called on to cheer things up when even God is dismayed about happenings here on earth. A wonderful person, part of the tragedy of his loss is that others never had the chance to meet him.

From *Daily Breeze* on May 23, 2015. Quote from Steve Wilson:

"A couple of these guys never came back. I worked on the flight deck of an aircraft carrier and would just watch them leave and never come back," the Torrance resident said, walking to another section [Vietnam Veterans War Memorial Wall] and landing his finger beneath the name Victor P. Buckley. "We searched three days for him and never found him."

In Memoriam

Lieutenant Joseph R. Klugg
July 30, 1943–November 14, 1970
Okemos, Michigan

Lieutenant Joseph R. Klugg was a pilot assigned to Light Photographic Squadron 63, Detachment 34, on board the aircraft carrier *Oriskany*. At 3:03 pm, on November 14, 1970, he was preparing to launch in his RF-8G Crusader (Bu. No. 145624). During the catapult launch, the aircraft's right tire blew and the starboard main landing gear collapsed, causing the aircraft to roll to the right and skid off the end of the carrier.

Klugg had the presence of mind to initiate a seat ejection from the aircraft as it rolled off the deck, but he did not have enough height to separate from the ejection seat prior to impacting the water. Either the weight of the seat took him down too quickly for him to recover or he sustained injuries rendering him unable to surface. No trace of him was recovered.

He was listed with honor among the missing in Southeast Asia because his remains were never recovered. His carrier was over 100 miles offshore, just north of the DMZ, and this death is not considered battle related.

Lieutenant Joseph Klugg is honored on the Vietnam Veterans Memorial, Washington, D.C.: Wall, Panel W6, Line 60.

Commendations

★ Purple Heart
★ National Defense Service Medal
★ Vietnam Service Medal
★ Vietnam Gallantry Cross
★ Combat Action Ribbon
★ Vietnam Campaign Medal
★ Navy Presidential Unit Citation
★ Navy Expeditionary Medal

CHAPTER 8

Other Navy and Marine Corps Photo-Reconnaissance Aircraft

The North American RA-5C Vigilante

"The Navy gave North American Aviation the go-ahead for two prototypes in mid-1956. The first prototype of the YA3J-1 Vigilante, as it was formally designated, was rolled out on May 16, 1958. Initial flight was on August 31, 1958, with North American chief test pilot Dick Wenzel at the controls.

The Vigilante was long and sleek, with a relatively small high-mounted swept-back wing and powered by twin General Electric YJ79-GE-2 engines, with engine bays made mostly of titanium, and covered with gold film to reflect heat. The aircraft had a large fuel capacity to give it long range and permitted extended flight in afterburner.

The decision to develop the Vigilante strictly as a reconnaissance aircraft was taken at a time when efforts were already being made to enhance its attack abilities, as well as adapt it to the reconnaissance mission. An improved attack variant, the A3J-2 (later A-5B), and a reconnaissance version, the RA-5C, were both built. The RA-5C was developed in parallel with the A-5B, and first flew on June 30, 1962.

...The major difference from the A-5B was the RA-5C's equipment fit, which featured a suite of reconnaissance gear that was state-of-the-art for the time. The TV camera under the nose became part of the reconnaissance suite, but most of the gear was carried in a long slender 'canoe' on the bottom of the aircraft's fuselage and running from the nose gear back towards the tail. Antenna for the Westinghouse AN/APD-7 'side looking airborne radar (SLAR)' system, which shot radar pulses out to the side of the aircraft and stored the return echo on a long film strip, permitting all-weather, day-night imaging.

An electronic strobe flash pod, powered by a spinner on its tail, could be carried under one wing to provide illumination for night reconnaissance. The sensor systems on the RA-5C worked in conjunction to bring back a flood of information from a reconnaissance mission, stored on magnetic tape and photographic film.

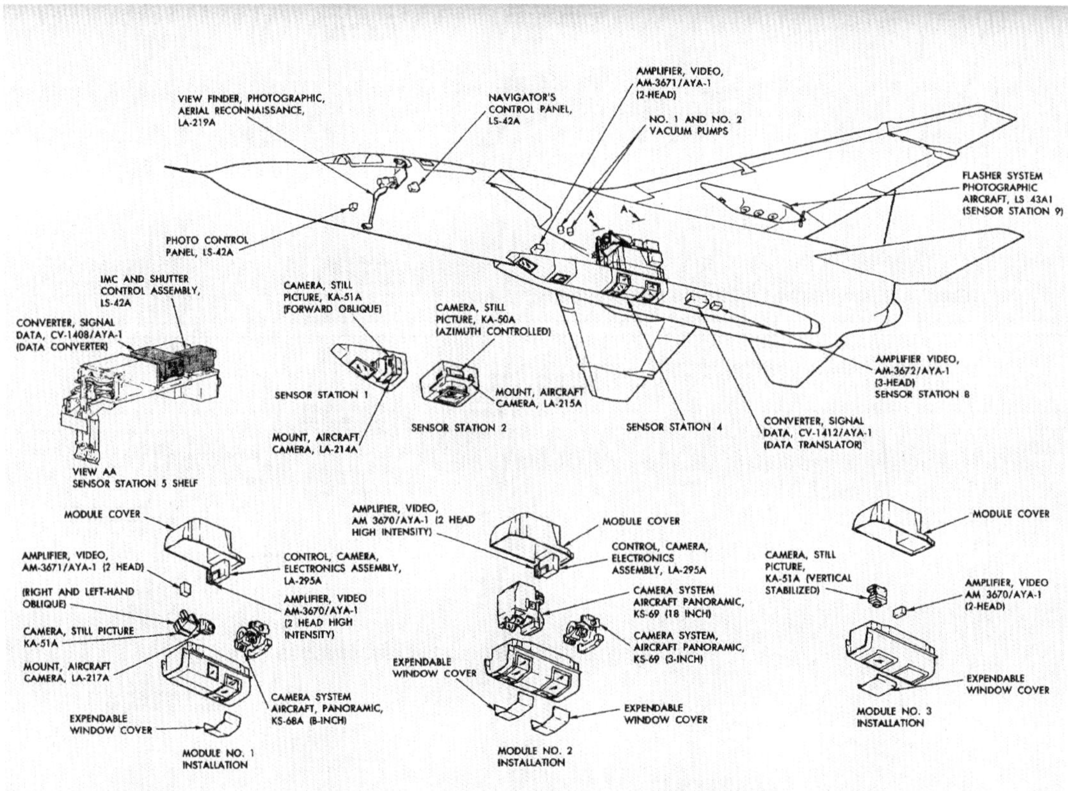

RA-5C sensor stations with camera configurations and electronic modules. (Art Jorgensen PHCS)

The RA-5C's reconnaissance systems were under control of the back-seater, who was designated the 'reconnaissance-attack navigator (RAN)'. The AN/ASB-12 system was retained, to be used for navigation and camera targeting.

An RA-5C's mission was conducted by an aircraft carrier's Integrated Operational Intelligence Center (IOIC). Electronic intelligence experts studied the information stored on magnetic tape, while the [photographic] film was passed through a one-hour film processing system, which at the time was a classified system. The processed film was then inspected by photographic intelligence specialists.

The RA-5C entered fleet service in 1964. Forty-three RA-5Cs were built, following the 12 A-5Bs that had been completed as RA-5Cs. After this batch of 43 was completed, the 43 surviving A-5As and A-5Bs were rebuilt to RA-5C standard, and the production line was shut down.

The RA-5C proved so useful in Vietnam that the Navy ordered 46 more RA-5Cs in 1968. Only 36 were actually completed, however, with the last rolling off the production line in August 1970. This final batch featured J79-GE-10 engines with 79.46kN (8,100kgp/17,860lbf) afterburning thrust, as well as a leading-edge wing extension trailing back from the air intakes, plus slightly modified air intakes. By this

An RVAH-12 North American RA-5C Vigilante, October 12, 1970, NAS Astugi, Japan. The so-called "canoe" under the fuselage carries the cameras and sensors. (Saburo Inoue)

An exceptional view of the mighty engines of an RA-5C Vigilante clearing the carrier deck as it heads out on a mission. (National Naval Aviation Museum, Pensacola, FL)

time, the RA-5C had plenty of power and it was no longer such a handful on carrier deck landings."[1]

The RA-5C: An RF-8 Pilot's Perspective

Lieutenant Commander Scott Ruby provides some history of the RA-5C on board carriers and a comparison with the RF-8:

Photomates working on the RA-5C sensor station. Note the size of the unit. (Art Jorgensen PHCS)

> The RA-5C was a spinoff of the A-5A and designed to be a replacement for the A-3, which had a nuclear delivery capability. It was designed with a unique delivery approach where the bomb bay was horizontal with the fuselage, and would kick the weapons out the rear end and theoretically let the weapon fall straight down. The problem was that it never worked. The weapons would not come out of the bird, the track alignment refused to align, and any weapon became stuck in the tunnel.
>
> Now the Navy is stuck with a bunch or A-5As without a mission. A-Ha, let's make them photo birds! So, they modified the aircraft, adding a ton of weight and they became RA-5Cs. At first, they started with six birds to a squadron, eventually it went to four. Six was a good number because then they could be called a squadron and not a detachment. As I have said before, their objective was to put light photo-reconnaissance out of business. At some meeting early in the game where both light photo and the R-A5C community were in attendance, the skipper of the RA-5C "wing" turned to Lieutenant Commander Dutch Schultz, later VFP-63's skipper, and told him out loud, "You are our enemy!" The operating cost of an RA-5C was two and a half times that of an RF-8. An RF-8 detachment deploys with four pilots, one PI, 43 enlisted and five officers. The RA-5C deploys with seven crews, two PIs, a Maintenance Officer, 17 officers, and approximately 165 enlisted. Think about space aboard a carrier.

An RF-8 detachment deploys with a family of KA-series cameras with an additional panoramic camera. The RA-5C deploys with the same series of KA cameras, plus the SLR [Side-looking Radar], and a long focal length folded-optics camera. However, I was up at OP-05 one day and had an opportunity to go through some cruise reports. A *Ranger* [CVA-61] cruise report stated that the SLR wasn't worth a s—t and could have been left at home. The folded optics camera—the wing had a grand total of three of them: one for deployment on the East Coast, one for the West Coast, and one for training—a very limited number of assets—so, you have a high priced, over-weight, over-manned, ungainly bird around the ship.

Most carriers have a deck multiple of around 110. A number is assigned to each type of bird by size. Add up the total deck multiples of each bird/squadron, and when it gets to 110 or so, that is how many aircraft total you can put aboard. An RF-8 has a deck multiple of 1. Therefore, you can put 110 Crusaders on a boat, if you so choose. An RA-5C has a deck multiple of 2.25—total deck multiple of an RA-5C squadron works out to a total of 9.0. A RF-8 detachment has a total deck multiple of three. Therefore, you can put three photo detachments on a boat in the space of one RA-5C squadron.

Having been a catapult officer, there are restrictions on use of the gear. The arresting gear cabling,[xliii] with the exception of cross deck pennants, is good for 1,500 hits. Cross deck pennants are good for 100 hits or you get too many broken wires. For RA-5Cs and A-3s, the arresting gear cabling limitation for these birds is 100 hits before it has to be replaced. There is something like 1,500 feet of cabling that has to be replaced if that becomes necessary. That is at least a two-day evolution. No admiral, CAG [Commander, Air Group], or boat skipper wants to be non-operational for that long. Each arrestment is counted/logged during a deployment. Toward the end, we would pull cross-deck pendants during a day recovery, if the number started to get too close, we left it on for night recoveries.

The so-called official count of RA-5C Losses during the war was 18. This resulted in 35 MIA/KIA/POWs. This means 35 extra people in the replacement pipe line. You may ask, why the replacement number was not 36 [2 times 18]? It seems that when one RA-5C was shot down, the flight crew was captured on the beach area and were being frisked and stripped for transfer to the Hanoi Hilton. Some RESCAP [Rescue Combat Air Patrol] showed up and the GIB [Guy in Back] managed to escape and make it out into the water on a sand bar. He also had a second pistol that the bad guys had not found yet. The RESCAP people were doing their thing, and he kept away from the Vietnamese long enough for the helos to show up. However, one of soldiers had followed him into the water and was getting close for a recapture. The GIB pulls out his pistol and shoots him between his eyes. He is then picked up by the helo. The pilot did not make it to Hanoi. The Navy did not know if they should give the GIB a medal or court martial him—they finally just let it go.

The RA-5C was unwieldly around the boat. Worst aircraft to bring aboard. I had a friend of mine, Tom "H," who was with me on my first deployment to the *Ranger*. He ended up as an executive officer of one of the RA-5C squadrons. He was not a particularly good naval aviator. He was really bad around the boat. Rumor had it that the RANs did not like to fly with him. One dark night, he is trying to get aboard and the LSO [Landing Signal Officer] is shouting "Power, Power, Power!" The RAN in back ejects. Tom traps. Later on, Tom hits the ramp and kills himself along with his RAN.

I was launching an RA-5C one day, always unwieldly around the cat, and the fuel dump valve for some reason came open. The RA-5C fuel dump valve is located between the twin engine exhausts.

xliii Cross deck pendants are steel-braided cables on the aft flight deck and used to stop landing aircraft. Navy aircraft have tail hooks that catch the cable. Arresting gear cables connect to either end and connect to the pneumatic arrestment system.

The bird is dumping raw fuel down into my R&T[xliv] spaces. I decide to go ahead and launch him. Primary is yelling at me. Right after launch, the first fire ball goes about ten feet or so above the JBDs [Jet Blast Deflectors]. The second fire ball is more or less right beside me. It did not singe me much.

The RA-5 is faster than the RF-8—only good thing about it. I had to TRANSPAC [Trans-Pacific Flight] an RF-8 to Cubi one time. An RA-5C was in my cell [group of aircraft]. They loaded up the bird with six external fuel tanks. They had to tank [refuel] twice to make it to Hawaii. I only had to tank once. They didn't make it to the second tanker and got wet. There are other things, but this is the most problematical of them.

The McDonnell RF-4C (U.S. Air Force)/RF-4B (Marine Corps)

"Although the Air Force had some entirely understandable resistance to acquiring a Navy fighter, after adopting the Phantom the USAF quickly became very enthusiastic about the type. Shortly after ordering their first production Phantom fighters, the service decided to acquire a reconnaissance variant to replace their McDonnell RF-101 Voodoo. The following discussion on the [Air Force] RF-4C applies to the [Marine Corps] RF-4B as well.

The RF-4B actually followed the F-4C into service, reversing the usual sequence of subvariant codes. The RF-4B was strictly a Marine machine; the Navy did not use the type since that service had no requirement for it, relying on the RF-8A/G Crusader and RA-5C Vigilante for the reconnaissance role. Forty-six RF-4Bs were built. The last ten were odd hybrids, with the original RF-4B nose, RF-4C fuselage and tail, and F-4J wings. In the last half of the 1970s, the RF-4Bs were given a substantial update under Project SURE, involving structural strengthening, new reconnaissance systems, datalink, defensive-countermeasures, and other avionics.

The RF-4C's[xlv] nose and reconnaissance gear were fitted to the F-4B airframe to yield the RF-4B for the U.S. Marine Corps, with initial flight on March 12, 1965, leading to operational introduction in May 1965.[xlvi] The equipment fit differed slightly from the RF-4C's in that the station two cameras could be rotated in flight.

The recce Phantom was originally designated the 'RF-110A', but was re-designated RF-4C in September 1962. The Phantom was adapted to the reconnaissance role through fitting a new forward fuselage to carry cameras and other reconnaissance gear. Initial flight of the first of two 'YRF-4C' prototypes was on August 8, 1963. Five-hundred-five RF-4Cs, including the two prototypes, were built to 1974.

---

xliv R&T Stands for the Retract and Tension gear. For each catapult there is a R&T room that is used to retract the catapult pistons to get them back in battery for the next launch. When an aircraft is spotted on the catapult, the tension part of the R&T is used to take tension on the aircraft in preparation for launch.

xlv The specifications for the RF-4B and RF-4C are similar.

xlvi Marine Corps VMCJ-1 transitioned from the RF-8A to the RF-4B in October 1966.

A Marine Corps VMCJ-1 RF-4B Phantom II on approach to Yokota AB, 1971. (Saburo Inoue)

The cameras were fitted in a new nose that stretched the aircraft's length by 84 centimeters (33 inches). The wing-mounted pitot tube was moved to the nose from the leading edge of the tailfin as well, resulting in a total increase in length of 147 centimeters (57.8 inches). As noted, a modified version of this nose was fitted to the F-4E to accommodate the M61 cannon, and resulted in the same increase in length.

The RF-4B/C's nose featured three camera stations that could be configured by ground crews with different camera fits:

- Station 1, or the forward camera station was just under the radome and stared forward at an angle. It could accommodate a KS-87 or KS-72 camera.
- Station 2 was behind Station 1, and included a camera port staring downward, as well as camera ports staring off to each side. It could accommodate various combinations of KS-72, KS-87, or panoramic KA-56 cameras in vertical or oblique (angled to the side) mountings.
- Station 3 was behind Station 2, and included two vertical ports. It could accommodate a KA-91 or KA-55A high-altitude panoramic camera; dual KS-87s with different focal lengths; or KC-1A, KC-1B, or T-11 mapping cameras.

In addition to the cameras, the RF-4B/C carried electronic-reconnaissance gear, as well as systems to support the reconnaissance mission:

- A Goodyear AN/APQ-102 side looking airborne radar (SLAR) that shot radar beams out to the sides of the aircraft and recorded the echoes on a long film strip, giving an all-weather view of the terrain alongside the aircraft's flight path.
- The AN/APQ-102 also had a moving target indicator (MTI) capability that picked out any vehicle moving at more than 9.25kph (5.75mph or 5 knots) perpendicular to the aircraft's flight path, highlighting the target on the film strip. The SLAR was mounted under the pilot's position, with the SLAR antennas fitted unobtrusively into the fuselage at that location, forward of the engine intake ramps.
- An AN/AAS-18 infrared line scanner was mounted under the back-seat position and stared out of the belly vertically. It recorded infrared imagery on a film strip to provide a thermal map of the terrain below the aircraft's flight path.

- An AN/ALR-17 radar homing and warning system (RHAWS) that located, identified, and targeted adversary radar stations, marking them on film imagery. RHAWS antennas were mounted on either side of Station 1 and on the wingtips.
- An auxiliary data annotation set (ADAS) that marked camera film with such useful data as date and time, radar and barometric altitude, latitude and longitude, heading, pitch, roll, drift angle, and unit identification.
- Two photoflash cartridge dispensers, fitted underneath the fuselage at the tail for night photography.

The RF-4B/C could also be fitted with electronic-intelligence (ELINT) systems carried in pods on stores pylons.

The RF-4B/C was not equipped to get into fights. Fire control systems were deleted; the recesses for Sparrow missiles under the fuselage were faired over, since the RF-4B/C didn't have the radar to guide the Sparrows; and the pilot's weapons sight was replaced by an LA-313 optical viewfinder to help target camera shots.

Instead of an AN/APQ-100 radar set, the RF-4B/C was fitted with a more compact Texas Instruments AN/APQ-99 forward-looking radar set, intended to support air navigation instead of combat. The AN/APQ-99 provided a ground mapping capability, along with terrain-following and terrain-avoidance modes. The RF-4B/C also featured an improved AN/ASN-56 INS, and a long-range HF communications system. Although in Air Force terminology the back-seater was still known as WSO, since the RF-4C didn't have any weapons, he was more often known simply as the 'navigator'.

Following the Vietnam War, USAF RF-4Cs were given various upgrades to keep them up to date, the most important being fit with the AN/ALQ-125 ELINT system."[2]

Comparison of RF-4B/C to RF-8A/G

U.S. Air Force exchange pilot Captain Jim 'Mugs' Morgan flew the RF-4C (Air Force version):

> The RF-8G was a fine day reconnaissance platform in the same way the Air Force RF-101 was. But the RF-4C was a much more capable reconnaissance airplane than either of those. That was primarily because of the improved navigation capabilities due to the inertial navigation system and the radar, which made all-weather and night reconnaissance possible in a tactical environment. For the most part, that was a no-go for the RF-8, as navigation by moonlight was virtually impossible, especially if you had to take any kind of evasive action or were operating in an area of questionable chart accuracy, as we were in Vietnam. Also, in the RF-8 you had to remove the Radar Homing and Warning gear to install the photoflash cartridges that were used at night. That would not have been a good thing in an intensive-threat environment like North Vietnam. The Air Force RF-101s were not used at night for essentially the same reasons. I did see some testing of photoflash strobes on the RF-101s back at Shaw AFB [Air Force Base] in late 1966. At the time I thought that was an advance in technology, but after I had some experience in night photo in a lethal environment, I realized that using strobes to activate cameras at night in the air defense environment of North Vietnam would have been suicidal.

My first combat tour in Southeast Asia (SEA) was in the RF-4C based out of Tan Son Nhut in Saigon. That was with the 16th Tac Recon Squadron, the first deployment of the RF-4C to Southeast Asia. We had a few daytime sorties every day, but by far, most of our sorties were at night. We primarily used the infrared line-scanner sensor in the south and photoflash cartridges for photography in the north. I went TDA [temporary duty assignment] to Udorn, Thailand, when the RF-4Cs first got over there and spent a couple of weeks flying night sorties into "The Barrel." My assumption is that the RA-5Cs were also capable of that because of their navigation capabilities, but I'm not really knowledgeable about their systems or how they were used.

The final product of the reconnaissance missions in the daytime, so far as I could tell, were virtually the same. The American philosophy was that we used a large enough film format that the interpretation began as soon as the film was developed and the film was put on a light table. It was interpreted using the film directly in both the Navy and Air Force. Other countries had a different philosophy and used a smaller film format, such that they had to develop the film then print it out on paper in a large enough size to interpret. That, of course, takes longer to get to the interpreter.

I would also say that the RF-4C had one other advantage in a high-threat combat environment, and that is another set of eyeballs for threat avoidance. That alone enhanced the survivability somewhat. The GIB, or the Weapons Systems Officer (WSO, pronounced "Wizzo"), as the AF called them, were really the heart of the mission, especially at night or bad weather. The state of the art being what it was in the F-4 days, there's no way one man could have been successful in those conditions doing all the required tasks. But to put the emphasis where it should be placed, the WSO is basically what made the RF-4C more capable than the daytime reconnaissance platforms.

I had 540 hours in the F-8 in two years with VFP-63 and had just over 2,600 hours in the F-4, flying it on and off over 20 years. My choice of the airplanes would depend on the mission. As I have said, the RF-4 was a superior airplane for the reconnaissance mission for a number of reasons. I've already discussed the navigation capabilities that allowed it to fly recon missions at night and to penetrate weather. It also had expanded sensor capabilities which included an infrared line scanner, later improved over the initial units in Vietnam, a Side Looking Airborne Radar sensor (SLAR) with multiple modes, a Tactical-Electronic-Reconnaissance ELINT sensor (TEREC) that would pinpoint radar emitters. It did have more power than the F-8, but that came with a detraction: A clean F-8 had the legs of an F-4 without three external tanks. So, if you had a daytime target a long way away, especially if you could accept high altitude photo, the RF-8G was your bird. For pretty much every other recon mission, it was the RF-4C. Having said all that, for sheer fun of flying, I'd take the F-8! Was the RF-4C a steadier platform? My guess is that it had a higher wing loading, so in that sense it was more stable, but that wasn't a significant factor in any comparison of the two. Neither airplane had any problem with that.

Side Looking Airborne Radar—we called it "SLAR" for short—when it first came out, as in Vietnam, the resolution wasn't very good. It was good enough for radar mapping and picking up water-borne traffic, but not much else. By the eighties, resolution had increased to about 10 feet, so it was more useful, particularly in a theater like Europe, where armor was expected to be heavily used. We used it to keep track of what was going on across the borders of friendly countries, and it was particularly useful in the "Solidarity" uprisings in Poland in about 1981 when U.S. intelligence wanted to keep an eye on what the Soviets were doing. One of the drawbacks, though, was the maintenance involved. That was very intensive, and that, in turn, caused the in-commission rate to suffer.

When the war kicked off, there weren't any RF-4Cs available, so the RF-101 bore the brunt of the AF intel collection. The first squadron of RF-4Cs deployed to Tan Son Nhut in late 1965, and they built up from there. As more RF-4Cs became available, they started phasing the RF-101s out.

The Douglas RA-3B Skywarrior

"The A3D-1 was originally designed as a bomber. From that initial design, numerous variants evolved. The A3D-1 was quickly replaced in production by an improved model, originally to be designated the A3D-1B but actually rolled out as the A3D-2. One of the A3D-2s was modified by Douglas as the effective prototype (YA3D-1P) of a photo-reconnaissance variant of the Skywarrior. It could carry up to 12 vertical and oblique film cameras in a pressurized compartment in the forward bomb bay, with a store of photoflash flares for night observations in the rear bomb bay. The YA3D-1P retained the tail cannon, but the gunner took on the auxiliary job of photo tech and could access the cameras in flight if need be.

The A3D-2P was a photo-reconnaissance variant, effectively the production version of the one-off YA3D-1P, featuring the same general arrangement. A total of 30 A3D-2Ps were built, with the first performing its initial flight on July 22, 1958. All were fitted with mid-air refueling probes, but only two had the modified wing with full span leading-edge slats. All were built with tail cannon, but were eventually refitted with the ducktail fairing for ECM [Electronic Countermeasures] gear.

The A3D-2P (later designated RA-3B) was capable of landing and launching from carriers and were breathtaking to watch. They were nicknamed, 'The Whale,' but were actually a beautiful two-jet aircraft. There were no ejection seats, the crew entry hatch instead being used as an escape chute. The ejection seats were left out to save weight, the assumption being that the A3D would generally operate at high altitude. The lack of ejection seats was not appreciated by aircrews since it ensured that the likelihood of survival in a low-level accident was poor, and the A3D was nicknamed 'All 3 Dead.'"[3]

Memories of the RA-3B from a VAP-61 Crewmember

Commander Frank Peele enlisted in 1958 as a Navy photomate, advancing to chief petty officer, then a commissioned warrant officer and retired with a senior rank of commander in 1988. The so-called "Mustang" officers, or formally LDOs (Limited Duty Officers), were highly respected by enlisted crews. He flew in VAP-61 RA-3Bs as Crewman/Navigator (C/N) from 1962–64. VAP-61 was the Heavy Photographic Squadron flying RA-3B Skywarriors in the Pacific Fleet. In May–June 1964, he made a detachment to the USS *Kitty Hawk* (CVA-63) participating in a massive Operation *Yankee Team* photo-reconnaissance effort. The classified missions were tasked with getting photo-reconnaissance of North Vietnamese infiltration through Laos (See Chapter 1). He describes his duty and the RA-3B:

> We were a three-plane detachment that flew from Guam to Cubi Point, Philippines, to await further orders. After what I think was about two weeks, we flew to *Kitty Hawk* for operations over SE Asia. When *Kitty Hawk* was relieved on station by *Constellation* [CVA-64], we cross-decked

An RA-3B Skywarrior of Heavy Photographic Squadron (VAP-61) on the ground at Agana, Guam, on October 9, 1969. Standing in front of the aircraft are Photographer's Mate First Class R. Laurie, Lt. (j. g.) D. Schwikert and Lt. Cmdr. Charles D. Litford. Arrayed in front of them are the cameras the aircraft could carry on missions over Vietnam. (National Naval Aviation Museum, Pensacola, FL)

to "Connie" and continued operations. We were deployed aboard the two CVAs for about two months total.

I can certainly vouch for the enemy's AAA [anti-aircraft artillery]. Before our first night mission, the briefings were very emphatic about one aspect of our ECM gear. As we'd been told repeatedly ever since the gear was installed, under no circumstances were we ever to go into "Transmit" mode. Yes, we could use "Receive" to see what radar threats were out there, but if we jammed the radars the enemy could use our transmissions to figure out how the ECM gear worked and develop counter-countermeasures. Of course, these emphatic briefings had all been given by bureaucratic weenies who would never face the threats the gear was designed to counteract.

When the briefings wrapped up, as we aircrews were about to head to the flight deck, Admiral Thomas Moorer, who was Commander, Seventh Fleet, spoke up and called those of us who operated the ECM gear to follow him. In a small room off to the side, he said, (and this vivid memory is burned into my brain, so this is pretty darn near a word-for-word quote), "Now boys, you've heard what the experts from Washington have said about not revealing the classified capabilities of our ECM setup by using it to jam the enemy's radars. But I have to tell you, if it was me and my crew, and the gear warned of imminent threat of being blown out of the sky, I'd have to think seriously about going into transmit mode."

After launching, my crew and I were making our first night photo run using flash cartridges. Doing so requires flying in a straight line, probably increasing the odds of getting hit if there was AAA. As the C/N [Crewman/Navigator] I sat behind the pilot, facing aft. About the time my ECM panel started to look like a pinball machine of flashing lights, I began to see tracers coming toward us from the ground. They were coming right up our flight path, and Admiral Moorer's words rang in my ear. I switched the appropriate set to transmit, and within moments the tracers simply stopped their advance. The whole thing was over in a few seconds, and the remainder of the flight was without any unusual drama. I don't remember for sure, but I don't think I ever told my crew what had almost happened. "Plausible deniability" seemed like a good idea; in case I got caught, at least the pilot and right seater wouldn't be culpable.

Admiral Tom Moorer went on to become Commander-in-Chief, Pacific Fleet, and eventually Chief of Naval Operations. I am steadfastly convinced that his comments after the briefing saved at least one crew and aircraft that night. Fact is, I was a dedicated sailor, and probably would have obeyed the strict orders to never transmit with the ECM gear had it not been for his guidance.

Some days later, on a day photo mission, we experienced the "popcorn" of AAA bursting in the air all around us. One camera chose that moment to fail, and I had to unstrap from my seat and go into the photo compartment to fix it. We were flying low and fast, and if we'd been hit, there's no way I could have gotten strapped back in to my parachute quickly enough to bail out. Fortunately, nothing serious happened. But as we were pre-flighting the aircraft for our next mission, I found a hole in the starboard wingtip about the size of a 30-cal shell. Seems we had been hit, but it caused no significant damage. It was the first time an RA-3B had been hit by combat fire.

The occupant of the third seat was designated Crewman/Navigator and was typically, but not necessarily, a PH [photomate]. The primary responsibility of this crew member in VAP-61 was celestial navigation. Operating all over the Pacific, and with no electronic navigation gear except VOR [Very high frequency Omnidirectional Range] and TACAN, neither of which had value beyond 200 nautical miles from a VOR or TACAN ground station, celestial navigation was our normal mode. We were quite proud of qualifying as celestial navigators, partly because in most US military aircraft navigation, it was done by an officer. I went through six months of training at NAS [Naval Air Station] Whidbey Island, WA to learn celestial navigation. In addition to photomates, we had a small number of other ratings flying as C/Ns: AT [aviation electronic technician], AQ [aviation fire control technician], PT [photo interpreter] and AE [aviation electrician]. In truth, it was no harder to teach these non-photomate types to handle the photographic duties than it was to teach the photomates how to navigate.

Some of the photographic duties included thorough knowledge of the entire photo system and the ability to troubleshoot it when deployed without maintenance personnel. Of the 12 camera positions, 10 had manually-operated doors over the camera windows, and operation of these was up to the C/N. Likewise, changing film magazines and adjusting certain camera operating parameters also was done by the C/N by leaving his seat and going into the photo compartment.

Long-range radio communication via HF radio was also done by the C/N. Each of the three crew positions had the ability to operate the UHF, VHF and HF radios, but most HF transmissions involved position reports, and it made sense for the navigator to do those. In about 1962 our aircraft were equipped with four types of highly classified electronic countermeasures (ECM) gear. This was also operated by the C/N. Its function was to detect radars of four different types and, if necessary, to jam them.

The Skywarrior was easily the most versatile photo recon aircraft ever built. From low-level high-speed combat recon to precision high-altitude cartographic mapping, it was all in a day's work. We used black and white, infrared, color infrared, normal color negative and transparency. Cameras ranged from 35mm motion pictures to 5 × 5, 9 × 9 and 9 × 18" format stills, with lens focal lengths up to 36" (914 mm).

While the lack of ejection seats meant low-level failures usually led to fatal consequences, high altitude bailouts should have (theoretically) been survivable. Much would have depended on sea state, water temperature and such details as the crew member's ability to avoid getting tangled in parachute shroud lines once in the water, absence of sharks, etc. I don't have reliable numbers to know if the Skywarrior's fatal accident rate was higher than other aircraft, but its word-of-mouth reputation in the fleet wasn't good in that regard. From my perspective, it was one heck of a capable vehicle and photo system, and I enjoyed most of my 688 hours of flight time in it. It was in some ways the most challenging of my Navy tours, and that just added to the value of the experience.

CHAPTER 9

Summary and Conclusions

"Any man who may be asked in this century what he did to make his life worthwhile … can respond with a good deal of pride and satisfaction, 'I served in the United States Navy.'"

PRESIDENT JOHN F. KENNEDY, ADDRESS AT THE NAVAL ACADEMY'S GRADUATING CLASS, 1963

During 1964 to 1972, VMCJ-1, VFP-62, and VFP-63 provided fleet commanders with the information that improved bombing performance and improved the chance of survival for fighter and attack aircraft—the first surface-to-air missile (SAM) site was found by VFP-63's photography. VMCJ-1's Electronic Warfare capabilities also located and thwarted Soviet-supplied SAM and AAA (anti-aircraft artillery) radar systems. In addition, the shore and carrier-based reconnaissance squadrons provided, otherwise unobtainable, evidence of the infiltration effort of the enemy.

During the Vietnam war, VFP-63 detachments lost 31 RF-8s, 25 percent of all Crusader losses. VFP-63's pilot casualties included: ten fatalities (eight combat related and two noncombat incidents) and 21 nonfatal ejections (fifteen rescued and six prisoners of war). VFP-63 deployed 42 detachments to 11 carriers from October 1963 to January 1974, making it the only squadron to have at least one unit in the theater from 1964 until the end of hostilities in Vietnam.

In Paris, on January 27, 1973, representatives of the Democratic Republic of Vietnam (North Vietnam), Republic of Vietnam (South Vietnam), the United States of America, and the Provisional Revolutionary Government (Viet Cong) signed the Paris Peace Accords. United States prisoners of war were released and all U.S. forces were removed from South Vietnam, Laos, and Cambodia. Later history would show that only the United States kept its agreement. The war would go on until the fall of Saigon in April 30, 1975.

With VFP-62's disestablishment on January 5, 1968, VFP-63 found itself providing detachments for both Atlantic and Pacific Fleets. Eventually, the squadron split into a shore activity parent command and a sea component of five numbered detachments, two for Atlantic Fleet operations and three for the Pacific Fleet. Logistically, the East Coast commitment was very difficult. For comparison, it was a major operation to move a VFP-62 detachment from its NAS Cecil Field, Florida home base to either Norfolk, Virginia, or Mayport, Florida, where the aircraft carriers were docked. Normally, before a six-month deployment to the Mediterranean Sea, there would be several shorter qualification exercises in the Atlantic or Caribbean Sea. Each VFP-63 deployment involved two transcontinental moves of aircraft, men, personal belongings, and maintenance equipment. Commander Peter Mersky provides the final history:

> By September 1972, VFP-63 assumed responsibility for all Crusader training, both fighters and photo aircraft. Thereby leaving VF-124 to concentrate on the upcoming F-14 Tomcat program. The dual training continued until July 1975 as the F-8 fighter made its last deployments and left the Fleet. VF-191 and VF-194 sailed in the *Oriskany* [CVA-34] in September 1975 and returned in March 1976 to close out the fighter's Fleet career. VFP-63 reverted to all-photographic training, although it retained a few of the fighter-Crusaders for proficiency flying. On August 26, 1975, Lieutenant Jerry Tucker, already a combat veteran in the fighter-F-8, became the last aviator to graduate from VFP-63's training syllabus. Coincidentally, the Marines' VMCJ-1 was disestablished in September 1975, ending a long and proud history of aviation photo-reconnaissance and electronic warfare service.
>
> During the remainder of the 1970s, VFP-63 provided light photographic detachments in the Mediterranean and Pacific areas, with an additional theater of operations opening in 1979 with the Iranian Hostage Crisis, and the growth of U.S. presence in the Indian Ocean. Detachment 5 left NAS Miramar in August 1979 bound for an Atlantic deployment in the USS *Nimitz* (CVN-68). However, when the Iranian crisis broke, Det. 5 and the *Nimitz* sailed for the Indian Ocean, remaining on station for several months. When the *Nimitz* was relieved, Det. 5 cross-decked to the *Coral Sea* [CV-43] to serve alongside that ancient carrier's assigned Det. 2, which had left Miramar in November 1979.
>
> The two detachments remained with the *Coral Sea* until she returned in June 1980, thus making a ten-month cruise out of what originally would have been a routine six-month deployment.[1]

The End of Dedicated Light Photographic Squadrons

Detachment 2 departed Miramar in August 1981 to make the last Crusader deployment in the Fleet, returning in March 1982. The date was set for VFP-63's disestablishment, June 30, 1982, although the squadron was ordered to maintain a contingency detachment—ready for deployment should the need arise—until April 1982. The squadron's last RF-8G was transferred to desert storage (Davis Monthan "boneyard") on May 28, 1982. After 33 years of dedicated photographic reconnaissance service, VFP-63 was disestablished in June 30, 1982. There were no more dedicated Navy-photographic squadrons.[2]

> Today, as we mark the end of VFP-63, the Navy's last dedicated photographic reconnaissance squadron, we must pay tribute to the many thousands of men and women who have served in the command, and without whose dedication, the contributions the "Eyes of the Fleet" made to world peace would not have been possible.
>
> Remarks made at VFP-63's disestablishment ceremony

End of an Era

The photo-Crusader had a full career in the Naval Air Reserve from 1970 to 1987, equipping two squadrons at Naval Air Facility, Washington, D.C. VFP-206 and -306 carried on the traditions of the fleet photos, initially attracting many former fleet Crusader drivers, both fighter and photo, as well as many younger aviators who were anxious to add Crusader time to their logbooks.

A Reserve Squadron VFP-306 RF-8G. (Capt. Len Johnson)

A New Generation of Photo-Reconnaissance Jets

Without VFP-63 RF-8s, the retirement of the RA-5C Vigilante in November 1979, and having no RF-4B Phantoms, the Navy found itself without a tactical reconnaissance capability—the first time since 1949. It had to find new photo-reconnaissance capabilities.

On March 29 1987, Light Photographic Squadron 206 (VFP-206), the last squadron of its type in the navy, was disestablished. It also marked the end of F-8 Crusader operations in American naval aviation. In this photograph, a pair of VFP-206 RF-8G Crusaders flies over Monument Valley, the backdrop for many a John Wayne western. (National Naval Aviation Museum, Pensacola, FL)

In 1974, the twin-engine, two-seat Grumman F-14 Tomcat entered the fleet as a replacement for the aging F-4 Phantom II. In 1981, the F-14 gained a photo recon capability when fitted with the Tactical Airborne Reconnaissance POD System (TARPS)—similar to the RA-5C's "canoe"—housing electronic sensors and cameras on the exterior of the aircraft. It was intended as an interim solution for the lack of a photo-reconnaissance capability, anticipating the arrival of the F/A-18 Hornet. TARPS was an 1,800-pound 17-foot portable container that contained three camera stations and two stations for electronics and systems components. With the assistance of a special hydraulic skid, photomates mounted it on the starboard side of the tunnel between the engine nacelles normally used for a Phoenix missile. TARPS would be connected to the Radar Intercept Officer's (RIO) instrument panel by a cable. Initially, only certain

F-14s had the necessary TARPS connection cables and were designated as "TARPS F-14s." Maintenance or aircraft loss had the potential of limiting the number of photo recon F-14s available for mission assignments.

Second Class Photographer's Mate Kristopher Brewer claims the system was reliable and produced good photographs. He said photomates would practice rapid removal of film after an F-14 landed and still moving to a parked location. In addition to photomates, the fighter squadron would have several electronics technicians for repairs.

The F-14 had one advantage over the Vietnam-era photo jets: it needed no escort, having its own store of weapons. For that reason, it was favored over the still-deployed RF-4B/C Phantoms, which were unarmed. However, Commander Dave Baranek, F-14 RIO and author of four books on the subject, writes that in high threat areas an F-14 escort would be assigned. The F-14s with TARPS flew in the conflicts of Somalia and Lebanon (1983), Libya (1986), *Desert Storm* (1991), Bosnia (1995), and Kosovo (1999).

Later, TARPs had a digital image sensor employed which could download target data to a memory card or be transmitted directly to a carrier's intelligence officers while still in flight. Brewer says the early images lacked the resolution of photo film but had the advantage of getting quick or real-time intelligence to the air intelligence officers on board the carrier. The F-14's replacement, the F/A-18 Hornet, has a new generation of reconnaissance capabilities that are beyond the scope of this book.

Strategic Reconnaissance Over Vietnam

This book tells the story of tactical photo-reconnaissance over Vietnam, but there were strategic reconnaissance missions using the high-altitude (over 70,000 feet) U-2, first used in the fifties during the Cold War with the Soviet Union. By Vietnam, the U-2 had received many upgrades that improved its capabilities. Later, it was used in the Iraq and Afghanistan wars. Then there was the Mach 3+ SR-71 Blackbird flying at 85,000 feet. The SR-71 flew missions in 1968 and beyond and the North Vietnamese fired many SAMs at it but the jet simply outran them.

On top of that, Pentagon and Intelligence agencies relied on satellite imagery and data collection. None of the intelligence went directly to tactical commanders on the ground or at sea.

Vietnam: The Author's Personal Perspective

The military is not a democracy, far from it. We immediately become aware of that in boot camp where all our rights are stripped from us, and slowly, one at a time, returned as "benefits" for demonstrated professional accomplishments, advancements in rank and rate, dedication to duty, loyalty to country and service, work ethics, and concern for our shipmates. When fighter pilots circle a downed comrade waiting for rescue and get shot down in the process, that bravery is what makes the military so special.

In an unpopular war, the only choices we have are to respect the chain of command and follow faithfully the oath we all swear to upon entry into the service. However, whether for cowardice or principle, some aviators did give up their wings. Vietnam tested the military as never before. The frustration aviators felt with bombing pause after bombing pause only gave the enemy time to recover and improve its defenses, and the new medium of television brought the brutality and errors of warfare into our living rooms. Anti-war protests also frayed the morale of soldiers, sailors, and airmen. It was common to go home on leave without a uniform.

The post-Vietnam years were difficult as well. Military and civilian leaders were occupied with self-reflection and questioning command leadership at all levels. Thankfully, the military emerged with renewed pride, professionalism, confidence and reliance on the all-volunteer service we are all proud of. With that, world circumstances and terrorist threats continue to mire the military into perpetual combat, in places reminiscent of Vietnam, with the same dreadful loss of lives and brutal personal suffering. The public now realizes, however, that if they aren't willing to fight, who will? For that, gratefully "thank all veterans for their service."

A hundred years from now many of our tombstones may go unattended. I believe the great black wall in Washington, D. C. will not. The stark blackness of the Vietnam Veterans War Memorial Wall seems to extend into eternity representing our eternal mourning of the dead, but the 58,318 etched names also represent our national memory and honor for their lost lives—lives that did not experience walking a daughter down an aisle; seeing children develop into adults; the joy of grandchildren, and a nation that is finally grateful to the military. They and the living survivors gave all for: "Duty, Honor, Country." Without words, the wall gives us a warning: "Those who don't know and learn from history are doomed to repeat it."

In 1968, the Department of Defense completed an eighteen-month study of "United States–Vietnam Relations. 1945–67," popularly known as the "Pentagon Papers." After it became available to the public in June 1971, the Committee on Foreign Relations began a detailed study into U.S. involvement in Vietnam.[1] One of the resulting papers to evolve from that work is: "Bombing as a Policy Tool in Vietnam," which is included in its entirety in Appendix 2. It is provided as an additional resource.

We were sailors once, gone ashore for good, wistful about our Navy days,
when the seas belonged to us and a new port of call was ever over the horizon.
Remembering this, we stand taller and say with pride and satisfaction,
"I WAS A SAILOR. I WAS PART OF THE NAVY AND
THE NAVY WILL ALWAYS BE PART OF ME."

Anonymous

APPENDIX I

Analysis of the Bombing Effectiveness in Vietnam

Introduction

Presidential libraries and memoirs from key administration officials confirm that there was much debate, disagreement, and power struggles in the Johnson administration over the objectives and strategies of the Vietnam Air War. President Johnson was a hands-on commander-in-chief steering the various air-war campaigns. As brutal as the air war became, the strategy of gradual intensification failed to accomplish the administration's objectives. As early as 1965, one key advisor, Defense Secretary Robert S. McNamara, was concerned that the emphasis on a military-alone resolution to the crisis would not accomplish the American objectives outlined below. As the American ground presence in South Vietnam and the aerial bombardment of North Vietnam escalated, he and others lost more resolve in their tactics. Others did not, including the Joint Chiefs of Staff, Secretary of State Dean Rusk, and General William C. Westmoreland, Commander U.S. Military Assistance Command Vietnam, to mention a few that represented the "Hawks" advocating for ever more intensification of the military effort. At the same time, the "Doves" were lobbying President Johnson to test the bombing effectiveness resulting in numerous bombing halts. The stop and go pattern of the bombing campaigns frustrated the aviators, whose lives were in constant jeopardy. The merits of these herculean struggles, are still debated today. Could it have turned out differently? The following analysis attempts to answer that question.

U.S. Objectives for Bombing North Vietnam

1. Interdiction: Reduce the infiltration of troops and supplies into South Vietnam.
2. Make North Vietnam pay a high cost for supporting the war in the South.
3. Break the will of North Vietnam.
4. Affect negotiations for an end to the war.
5. Raise U.S. and South Vietnamese morale.[1]

Objective 1: Evaluation of Interdiction

Interdiction was an optimistic effort to weaken the communist fighting capacity in the South but largely failed. The ever-resourceful Vietnamese supplemented truck movement with modified bicycles that could carry supplies over rugged jungle paths and roads. Their movements were increasingly done at night, keeping their presence hidden from the prying eyes of recon aircraft and avoiding destruction from attack aircraft. The bombing attacks on the Ho Chi Minh Trail in Laos barely degraded the communist war effort: their troops' needs were minimal and they had no large military machinery requiring fuel and support systems to fight the Americans and South Vietnamese (SVN).

As early as January 18, 1966, Secretary of Defense Robert McNamara received an analysis verified by the CIA that "the North Vietnamese could infiltrate 4,500 men a month, along with supplies sufficient to support a substantial combat effort in South Vietnam despite the current interdiction campaign."[2]

Misguided efforts such as the aerial defoliation of undergrowth using Agent Orange, a chemical that caused injury to Vietnamese, Laotians, and Americans, only increased South Vietnamese peasant loyalty to the Viet Cong and fostered anger directed towards the Americans for being complicit with their failed and corrupt government.

Objective 2: Evaluation of Make North Vietnam pay a high cost

As for the second objective, North Vietnam provided a poor target for an air attack but did suffer from the bombing. One source estimates "The U.S. air offensive probably killed a hundred thousand civilians. North Vietnam was largely an agrarian society where most of its people were rice farmers, who worked the land with water buffaloes and hand tools. The loss of infrastructure, such as power plants, could be endured by its citizens or war-related light-industrial facilities and could be replaced by increasing support from their Chinese and Soviet patrons."[3]

"When NVN was first targeted, the JCS found only eight industrial installations worth listing on a par with airfields, military supply dumps, barracks complexes, port facilities, bridges, and oil tanks. Even by the end of 1965, after the JCS had lowered the standards and more than doubled the number of important targets, the list included only 24 industrial installations, 18 of them power plants which were as important for such humble uses as lighting streets and pumping water as for operating any real factories."[4]

The bombing campaign did not impact the ultimate outcome of the war nor did it break the will of North Vietnam. In fact, it had the opposite effect. As it did during the Nazi bombing of Britain during the Second World War, the populace stiffened their resolve and became more determined. With the help of the Chinese and Soviets, "they improved air defenses, laid aside economic development plans; bombed facilities were in most cases simply abandoned; and large vulnerable targets such as barracks and storage depots were dispersed and concealed. The North Vietnamese appeared willing to accept the loss of their small industrial base rather than reduce their support for the war in the South.

However, the President, his advisors, and the JCS felt, "it did not seem unreasonable to believe that NVN's leaders would not wish to risk the destruction of such assets, especially when that risk seemed easily avoidable by cutting down the insurgency and deferring the takeover of SVN until another day and perhaps in another manner—which Ho Chi Minh had apparently decided to do once before in 1954."[5]

Another hope of the U.S. war planners was that through bombing the North, it would reduce their capability to sustain supplying men to the South. This also did not meet expectations. "By 1968, as many as 475,000 to 600,000 civilians including women and children were working to repair the damage done by the airstrikes, while another 110,000 military personnel were assigned to air defense duties. A study by the Systems Analysis office of the Department of Defense reported that 90 percent of the North's manpower needs were met by normal population growth."

Here again, its Chinese ally provided an "estimated 40,000 Communist Chinese were thought to be employed in maintaining North Vietnam's Road and rail net … and the State Department concluded that there was no evidence that manpower shortages in themselves were becoming acute enough to prevent Hanoi from continuing its policies."[6]

The Americans underestimated the economic aid the North Vietnamese were getting from Communist China and the Soviet Union. The second JASON study, submitted in December 1967, concluded:

> NVN has transmitted many of the material costs imposed by the bombing back to its allies. Since the bombing began, NVN's allies have provided almost $600 million in economic aid and another $1 billion in military aid—more than four times what NVN had lost in bombing damage. If economic criteria were the only consideration, NVN would show a substantial net gain from the bombing, primarily in military equipment…NVN was a stronger military power than before the bombing.
>
> …A study by the Systems Analysis Office of the Department of Defense reached a similar conclusion: Over the entire period of the bombing, the value of economic resources gained through foreign aid has been greater than that lost because of the bombing. The study concluded that North Vietnamese standards of living may have declined but that food supplies had been maintained with only a slight decline. Overall, "the North Vietnamese are not badly off by past North Vietnamese standards or the standards of other Asian countries."[7]

Objective 3: Evaluation of Breaking Hanoi's Will

As far as the third objective, it is clear that those who adhered to this fantasy of breaking Hanoi's will, never studied Asian culture or Vietnam's long history of resisting foreign threats and conquests, not to mention the tragic experience of the French futile effort to subdue the will of Ho Chi Minh. "One of the most pervasive justifications for the bombing of the North is the belief that in some degree the bombing will put pressure on the Hanoi leadership to terminate the war. According to the Pentagon history of the conflict, this was the *original purpose of the sustained bombing of the North* [emphasis added] although the public rationale was generally put in terms of North Vietnam's capability to continue the war. An interagency task force known as the NSC Working Group concluded in late 1964 proposed that the nature of the war in Vietnam is such, that U.S. *ability to compel* the DRV [Democratic Republic of (North) Vietnam] to end or reduce the Viet Cong insurrection *rests essentially upon the effect of the U.S. sanctions on the will of the DRV leadership to sustain and enlarge that insurrection*, and to a lesser extent upon the effect of sanctions on the capabilities the DRV to do so [emphasis added]."[8]

The Joint Chiefs of Staff, continued to adhere to the belief that bombing, if severe enough, would subdue the North resulted in Operation *Rolling Thunder* (1965–68). As early as the end of the first year, Defense Secretary, Robert McNamara convinced President Johnson to approve the first bombing pause at the end of 1965—the first of many. President Nixon promised a negotiated settlement for his first term but followed the same play book and added B-52s to the air war. For a considerable time, Hanoi remained incalcitrant.

Objective 4: Evaluation of Bombing as an Aid to Negotiations

Breaking the will of NVN was thought to aid the fourth objective, to affect negotiations for an end to the war. From the previous discussion, it is apparent that the bombing campaign against the North was not going to pressure the NVN leadership to make fundamental negotiating concessions. This dreary conclusion was summarized in the Committee on Foreign Relations' study:

> Moreover, bombing appears to take second place to the military situation in the South in Hanoi's calculations. However, it appears probable that the desire to end the bombing played some role in the decision of Hanoi to accept the U.S. offer of negotiations in 1968...No doubt, the bombing of the North represents a bargaining chip in negotiations, but its value is uncertain. In spite of its prominence in public statements by both sides, the uncertain role of bombing in the course of negotiations from 1965 onward, the relative ineffectiveness of bombing in either stemming infiltration or breaking the will of the North, and the predominance of concern with the course of the war in the South indicate that in terms of extracting major concessions, bombing is a bargaining chip of relatively low value.[9]

Objective 5: Evaluation of Boosting Morale

The final bombing objective according to Assistant Secretary of Defense McNaughton, was to sustain American and South Vietnamese morale. To a degree this objective was achieved. The [Gulf of Tonkin] retaliatory strikes in 1964 and the sustained bombing in early 1965 probably contributed to some degree to boosting the morale of the hard-pressed South Vietnamese government. As the second JASON study found in 1967:

> There had been an appreciable improvement in South Vietnamese morale immediately after the bombing began and subsequent buoyancy always accompanied major new escalations of the air war. *But the effect was always transient,* (emphasis in original) fading as a particular pattern of attack became a part of the routine of the war. There was no indication that bombing could ever constitute a permanent support for South Vietnamese morale if the situation in the South itself was adverse."[10]

Caveats

This book's thesis is to illustrate and bring to light the bravery and sacrifice of naval aviators and enlisted men who faithfully and skillfully executed their orders, despite the Vietnam War's controversies, civilian disenchantment, and failed government leadership. The Foreign Relations Committee's study used in this section only analyzed the air war during 1965–68. It effectively exposes failures to assess the effectiveness of the air war with the objectives set and its failure to adjust or suspend when the costs of the bombing, mounting civilian casualties, captured and lost airmen, and the consequences within the United States, warranted a brave adjustment or reversal. The study's authors make some caveats:

- This study should contain two warning notes. First, the focus of this study has been on interdiction and strategic bombing of North Vietnam during the period 1965–68. It does not consider tactical air support, which has been relatively successful in achieving its goals. Neither does it consider the … [later years of the] air war against North Vietnam, which [were] far heavier than previous offensives.
- Second, the experience in Vietnam cannot be readily transferred to other situations. In overcoming the effects of the bombing, the North Vietnamese have had certain advantages which may not apply to other cases. The leadership has shown great tenacity and high motivation, as well as exceptional ingenuity and adaptability in coping with the effects of the bombing. The evident control and organization of the society, together with apparently high popular support have made possible this tenacity and adaptability. Equally important has been the willingness and ability of other communist countries to provide sufficient military and economic aid. The location of North Vietnam has also been of considerable importance. Bordering on an ally, China, North Vietnam could not be blockaded—land transportation routes were available. Moreover, the proximity to China long tended to moderate U.S. escalation of the air war because of the fear of Chinese intervention. The common border with South Vietnam and the relatively unpopulated and heavily foliated border area with Laos, facilitate infiltration and make interdiction bombing more difficult. The original guerrilla nature of the war long reduced the number of supplies which had to be infiltrated, thus reducing the burden on the North. And finally, the underdeveloped nature of the Vietnamese economy has provided relatively few valuable targets for bombing.
- These caveats notwithstanding, this study calls into serious question the efficacy of strategic and interdiction bombing against a highly motivated guerilla enemy in an underdeveloped country. Bombing appears capable of raising the costs of war to an enemy in such a situation, but it cannot be depended on to weaken his will or to substantially reduce his activity by interdicting his supplies. Compared to the damage to U.S. prestige and the internal division created by the bombing policy, its meager gain must be seriously questioned.[11]

Epilogue

The United States entered the Vietnam conflict in response to a free world fear of Communism. It was a time, not unlike today's fear of terrorism. At first, it received the support of most Americans. However, unlike modern conflicts, the United States government did not have complete European allied support. The government unwisely escalated the war effort without any military support from key allies. Today, the military resists entering into military action without having a clear understanding of how that action will come to an end—in other words, what defines success. Unfortunately, political leadership has not heeded the tragedy and miscalculations of Vietnam and have led us into never-ending military conflicts that resemble the failures of Vietnam. As this book goes to publication, the President of the United States is departing Afghanistan, leaving the fledgling government to fend off the Taliban by itself.

The veterans of the Vietnam War deserve our support and admiration for holding true to their oaths. The stories in this book show that we owe our gratitude to them for putting their grievances and cynicism aside to share with us their actions of bravery, professionalism, and sacrifice.

APPENDIX 2

Bombing as a Policy Tool in Vietnam: Effectiveness

In 1968 the Department of Defense completed an eighteen-month study of "United States-Vietnam Relations, 1945–1967," popularly known as the "Pentagon Papers." The existence of this classified 47 volume study became known to the public through newspaper reports in June 1971. In September the Defense Department declassified large portions of the first 43 volumes. The other four volumes remained classified on the grounds that disclosure of the materials they cover—the history of negotiations—would be detrimental to national interest.

In September 1971 the Committee on Foreign Relations began a detailed study of the Pentagon history and related materials. The study was initiated under the authority of S. Res. 140, agreed to July 24, 1971, for the purpose of inquiring into the origins and evolution of U.S. involvement in Vietnam, with particular reference to lessons for U.S. foreign policy making that might be drawn from the Pentagon history. Three staff researchers, Robert E. Biles, Robert M. Blum, and Ann L. Hollick, have been engaged in a careful review of the 7,000 pages of documents and analysis included in "United States-Vietnam Relations." They have had at their disposal both the classified and unclassified versions of the Pentagon Papers. In addition, they have drawn upon corroborative printed materials and interviews with individuals involved in the events under study.

"Bombing as a Policy Tool in Vietnam" by Robert E. Biles examines the effectiveness of the bombing of North Vietnam in achieving the goals set for it by those involved in making the air war policy. Focusing on the period of intense bombing from 1965 to 1968, the study examines the intelligence and defense community's own "in-house" studies of the air war. It finds that of the five major goals set for the bombing only one has been achieved. The bombing has succeeded in making North Vietnam pay a high price for her support of the war in the South. But the air war has not stopped the flow of supplies to the South, broken Hanoi's will, or forced the North Vietnamese to negotiate an end to the war. The gains in U.S. and South Vietnamese morale from escalation of the bombing have always proved fleeting. There are several reasons for the failure of the bombing to achieve its goals. North Vietnam, an agricultural country with little industry, provides few major targets for air attack; the North Vietnamese have proved highly determined and extremely resourceful in adapting to the damage done by the bombing; and North Vietnam's allies have provided sufficient aid to more than offset the losses from the bombing.

Throughout the war, the claims made for strategic and interdiction bombing have consistently exceeded their accomplishments, and the extravagance of the rhetoric supporting the current air offensive against the North has a familiar ring. The bombing of North Vietnam has been a costly one in terms of pilots lost, civilian casualties, damage to our international standing, and riches expended. The failure of the bombing to achieve the goals set for it makes that high cost a very sad waste.

Bombing as a Policy Tool in Vietnam: Effectiveness

Introduction

Bombing has served several functions during the course of the Vietnam war: close support of troops engaged in combat, interdiction of enemy supplies and reinforcements, and strategic bombing to reduce enemy capabilities. By far the most controversial aspect of United States bombing policy has been the interdiction and strategic bombing. In their name, the United States has bombed South Vietnam, North Vietnam, and supply lines in neighboring Cambodia and Laos. Critics have contended that interdiction and strategic bombing have been unsuccessful and immoral acts, that they cost too much, and that they do violence to America's reputation abroad. Supporters of the bombing reply that it has at the very least made it very costly for North Vietnam to support the war in the South and has saved American lives. If it has not been as successful as expected, it is because of restrictions on targets and the graduated increase in the bombing, which gave North Vietnam time to adapt. The purpose of this study is to evaluate these arguments and thereby to improve our understanding of strategic and interdiction bombing as a policy tool in the Vietnam war. The study covers the period from 1965 when the regular bombing of North Vietnam began, to 1968 when it was halted in an attempt to promote a negotiated settlement.

The objectives to be gained by bombing North Vietnam have varied during the course of the war, but they can be summarized as follows: (1) to reduce the infiltration of men and supplies into South Vietnam, (2) to make North Vietnam pay a high cost for supporting the war in the South, (3) to break the will of North Vietnam, (4) to affect negotiations for an end to the war, and (5) to raise U.S. and South Vietnamese morale. Individual objectives have been combined, downgraded, and re-emphasized. At times the official, public objective has differed from the Government's private objective. But each of these goals has played an important role in the debate over bombing policy.

Interdiction

Shifting Rationales

When the bombing of North Vietnam began in early 1965, the public rationale was the reduction of the flow of supplies and men to the South. In the words of the Pentagon history of the war:

> The public was told that NVN [North Vietnam] was being bombed because it was infiltrating men and supplies into SVN [South Vietnam]; the targets of the bombing were directly or indirectly related to that infiltration; and the purpose of attacking them was to reduce the flow and/or to increase the costs of that infiltration. Such a rationale was consistent with the overall position which morally justified US intervention in the war in terms of NVN's own intervention; and it specifically put the bombing in a politically acceptable military idiom of interdiction.[1]

In private, however, the rationale for the bombing was a mixture of complex and often conflicting objectives. The situation in South Vietnam seemed to be falling apart. The bombing of the North, it was hoped, would boost morale in the South, show the determination of the United States, and break the will of the North to continue its aggression. Again, in the words of the Pentagon history:

> Target selection had been completely dominated by political and psychological considerations... Relatively little weight was given to the purely physical or more directly military and economic implications of whatever target destruction might be achieved.
>
> With the gradual acceptance, beginning in March [1965], of the need for a militarily more significant, sustained bombing program, serious attention began to be paid to the development of a target system or systems that would have a more tangible and coherent military rationale. The first and most obvious candidate for such a target concept was that of interdicting the flow of men and supplies into South Vietnam by striking the lines of communication.[2]

Objectives and Methods

The objective of an interdiction program, of course, would be to reduce the capability of the Communist forces to operate in South Vietnam. Guesses as to the effect of the interdiction of aid from North Vietnam varied widely. Admiral Sharp, commander of Pacific forces, predicted in a January 12, 1966, message to the Joint Chiefs of Staff that a properly executed bombing program "will bring the enemy to the conference table or cause the insurgency to wither from lack of support."[3] A more moderate but still optimistic view was taken in a Special National Intelligence Estimate (SNIE) of July 23, 1965. The SNIE estimated that a bombing program which included destruction of the petroleum facilities and military targets in the Hanoi-Haiphong area together with sustained interdiction of the lines of communication from China could reduce communist capabilities in the South. It reasoned that:

> If additional PAVN [North Vietnamese Army] forces were employed in South Vietnam on a scale sufficient to counter increased U.S. troop strength [which the SNIE said was "almost certain"

> to happen] this would substantially increase the number of supplies needed in the South. The Viet Cong also depend on supplies from the North to maintain their present level of large-scale operations. The accumulated strains of a prolonged curtailment of supplies received from North Vietnam would obviously have an impact on the Communist effort in the South. They would certainly inhibit and might even prevent an increase in large-scale Viet Cong military activity, though they would probably not force any significant reduction in Viet Cong terrorist tactics of harassment and sabotage.[4]

The physical reduction of North Vietnam's support for the war in the South could be accomplished by four methods: (1) the destruction of war-related industry and war-supporting facilities such as weapons production and petroleum storage facilities; (2) general debilitation of the North Vietnamese economy and thereby its ability to support the war effort; (3) attacking the lines of communication so that supplies are slowed, stopped, or destroyed; and (4) destruction of the North Vietnamese military. During the course of the war, all four methods were tried, but as will be seen none proved successful in accomplishing the goal of reduced support for the war in the South.

The POL Debate

In the early stages of the bombing of the North, some critics claimed that the program had failed to achieve its objectives because of restrictions on the targets that could be struck and the piece-meal nature of the escalation. It was argued that because the increase in the bombing was gradual, North Vietnam had time to adapt itself to the bombing, replenish and disperse its stock, diversify its transportation system and improve its defenses.[5] One CIA report, for example, noted in early 1966 that—

> almost 80 percent of North Vietnam's limited modern industrial economy, 75 percent of the nation's population, and the most lucrative military supply and LOC targets have been effectively insulated from air attack.[6]

Most of this line of criticism of the bombing program stemmed, in the words of the Pentagon history—

> from basic disagreement with an air campaign centered upon a tactical interdiction rationale rather than a punitive rationale more in keeping with strategic uses of air power, a campaign in which the apparent target was the infiltration system rather than the economy as a whole…This kind of criticism of the bombing concentrated on the most conspicuous aspect of the program for failing to focus on the kinds of targets which strategic bombing had made familiar in World War II—power plants, oil depots, harbor facilities, and factories.[7]

In response to this criticism, Secretary of Defense McNamara at first questioned the effect strategic bombing would have on the infiltration effort and stressed the risks of widening the war if such targets were hit.[8] Eventually, however, he agreed to the bombing of North Vietnam's petroleum facilities. According to the Pentagon history, the failure of these attacks to reduce either infiltration or logistical support from the North apparently tipped the balance in McNamara's mind against any further escalation of air attacks against North Vietnam. "The attack on North Vietnam's POL [petroleum] system was the last major escalation of the air war recommended by Secretary McNamara."[9]

The Joint Chiefs of Staff were strong proponents of bombing North Vietnam's POL system. In November 1965, they proposed a major program of air attacks against it. "Attack of this system," they argued, "would be more damaging to the DRV [Democratic Republic of (North) Vietnam] capability to move war-supporting resources...than an attack against any other single target system."[10] As the Pentagon history explains:

> It is not surprising that the JCS singled out the POL target system for special attention. NVN had no oil fields or refineries, and had to import all of its petroleum products, in refined form... Nearly all of it came from...the USSR and arrived by sea at Haiphong, the only port capable of conveniently receiving and handling bulk POL brought in by large tankers. From large tank farms at Haiphong with a capacity of about one-fourth of the annual imports, the POL was transported by road, rail, and water to other large storage sites at Hanoi and elsewhere in the country. Ninety-seven percent of the NVA POL storage capacity was concentrated in 13 sites, 4 of which had already been hit. The other 9 were still off limits. They were, of course, highly vulnerable to air attacks.[11]

In making their recommendation that North Vietnam's POL system be attacked, the Joint Chiefs emphasized the interdiction effects. "POL-fueled carriers," they said, were the "principal vehicles" for transporting supplies to South Vietnam and Laos. Moreover, POL was becoming increasingly important to the effort in the South. With five confirmed and two suspected North Vietnamese regiments in South Vietnam, there was an increasing load on the supply system. Roads were being improved and increasing numbers of trucks were being imported. Finally, "recuperability [sic] of the DRV POL system from the effects of an attack is very poor."[12]

The record in the Pentagon history of what the intelligence community was telling policy makers during the POL debate is incomplete. Thus, we do not know the full range of debate nor the impact that intelligence may have had on the decision to increase the scale of bombing. Nevertheless, examination of the information available in the Pentagon history does provide some insights. The intelligence community was initially skeptical of the Joint Chiefs' claim that attacking North Vietnam's POL facilities as part of an intensified program would substantially reduce the North's capacity to support the war.[13] There was some dispute within the intelligence community as to just how effective the proposed bombing would be in interdicting the flow of men and supplies. But it appears that there was a tendency on the part of the intelligence agencies to accommodate their estimates to the growing pressure to increase the level of bombing.[14]

There is no indication in the Pentagon history that any of the major intelligence agencies believed that the bombing of the North could or would reduce the level of support for the war in the South below its then current level. Rather, the agencies placed their hopes in punishing North Vietnam and in possibly breaking her will. The most optimistic view of interdiction bombing was that the damage to North Vietnam's economy and transportation capacity might set an upper limit on the amount of support she could provide for the war in the South. Such a hope was predicated upon intensified air attacks, destruction of POL facilities, bombing both military and industrial targets in the Hanoi/Haiphong area, and mining North Vietnam's harbors. But even such a heavy program of attacks, the intelligence agencies concluded, would not prevent North Vietnam from providing levels of support for the war substantially higher than those in 1965.[15]

What, specifically, did the intelligence agencies feel could be accomplished by a more intensive bombing campaign? First, Hanoi would have to pay a high penalty for her support of the war. She would suffer considerable economic disruption and destruction. The Defense Intelligence Agency, the National Security Agency, and the three service intelligence agencies even held out the hope at one point that the intensified air strikes combined with the increased U.S. troop commitment might eventually break Hanoi's will.[16]

While all the intelligence agencies seemed to agree that the air attacks would increase the burden and costs of supporting the war, there was no agreement that they would break Hanoi's will. In December 1965, the Board of National Estimates characterized Hanoi's will to persevere in the South as virtually unshakeable in the short run and extremely tough even in the long run. In the words of the Board, "They continue to believe that time is their ally and that their own staying power is superior."[17] The Bureau of Intelligence and Research in the State Department argued that "Hanoi would be less and less likely to soften its opposition to negotiations and at some point, it would come to feel that it had little left to lose by continuing the fighting."[18]

The POL strikes finally began on June 29, 1966, and continued into the fall. They were initially hailed as highly successful. During the first month, for example they reportedly destroyed 70 percent of North Vietnam's bulk petroleum storage capacity.[19] However, as the Pentagon history relates, by September both the CIA and DIA were in general agreement as to the failure of the POL strikes."[20]

> What became clearer and clearer as the summer wore on was that while we had destroyed a major portion of North Vietnam's storage capacity, she retained enough dispersed capacity, supplemented by continuing imports (increasingly in easily disposable drums, not bulk), to meet her ongoing requirements. The greater invulnerability of dispersed POL meant an ever-mounting US cost in munitions, fuel, aircraft losses, and men. By August we were reaching the point at which these costs were prohibitive.
>
> ⋆ ⋆ ⋆
>
> It was clear in retrospect that the POL strikes had been a failure. Apart from the possibility of inconveniences, interruptions, and local shortages of a temporary nature, there was no evidence that NVN had at any time been pinched for POL.
>
> ⋆ ⋆ ⋆

> The real and immediate failure of the POL strikes was reflected…in the undiminished flow of men and supplies down the Ho Chi Minh trail to the war in the South.[21]

There were several reasons for the failure. First, "NVN's dependence on the unloading facilities at Haiphong and large storage sites in the rest of the country had been greatly overestimated."[22] Bulk imports continued; tankers simply stood off shore and unloaded onto barges. More oil was also brought in already drummed; thus, it was convenient for dispersed handling and storage. Second, "the difficulties of switching to a much less vulnerable but perfectly workable storage and distribution system, not an unbearable strain when the volume to be handled was not really very great, had also been overestimated."[23] The key point was that "NVN's adaptability and resourcefulness had been greatly underestimated."[24] The effectiveness of the strikes was further offset by an unanticipated result of the bombing: the North Vietnamese were highly successful in using the strikes to extract larger commitments of economic, military, and financial assistance from the Russians and Chinese.[25]

Secretary McNamara, according to the Pentagon history, "made no effort to conceal his dissatisfaction and disappointment at the failure of the POL attacks."[26] In January 1967 he testified before a joint session of the Senate Armed Services and Appropriations Committee that—

> I don't believe that the bombing up to the present has significantly reduced, nor any bombing that I could contemplate in the future would significantly reduce, actual flow of men and materiel to the South.[27]

Evaluation of Interdiction

During the course of the bombing of North Vietnam, a number of studies of its effectiveness were made. Two of the most important were carried out in 1966 and 1967 by a group of leading government-oriented scientists under the auspices of the JASON Division of the Institute for Defense Analyses.[28] According to the Pentagon history, the first study had a "powerful and perhaps decisive influence in McNamara's mind."[29] Both studies strongly criticized the effectiveness of bombing as a policy tool in the war effort. The 1967 JASON [not an acronym, named after the character in Greek mythology] study, for example, concluded that "the US bombing of North Vietnam has had no measurable effect on Hanoi's ability to mount and support military operations in the South."[30]

The studies found that the bombing had not reduced the flow of supplies to the Communists in South Vietnam. In fact—

> Since the beginning of the *Rolling Thunder* air strikes on NVN, the flow of men and materiel from NVN to SVN has greatly increased, and present evidence provides no basis for concluding that the damage inflicted on North Vietnam by the bombing program has had any significant effect on this

> flow. In short, the flow of men and materiel from North Vietnam to the South appears to reflect Hanoi's intentions rather than capabilities even in the face of bombing.[31]

Moreover, Hanoi's ability to support the war had not been decreased by the bombing. Rather, "its ability to sustain the war in the South has increased."[32]

> The failure of bombing to interdict the flow of men and supplies to the South is attributable to at least three factors. First, North Vietnam is an underdeveloped country, which makes her far less susceptible to the strategic effects of bombing. Second, the vast majority of material support for the war originates not in North Vietnam but in Russia and China. North Vietnam serves essentially as a conduit for the supplies. Third, the Communists have shown great resourcefulness and determination, while we have tended to overestimate the capability of our bombing.

Bombing an Underdeveloped Country

As an agricultural country, North Vietnam provides an extremely poor target for an air attack. In the words of the Pentagon history analyst—

> The theory of either strategic or interdiction bombing assumed highly developed industrial nations producing large quantities of military goods to sustain mass armies engaged in intensive warfare. NVN, as U.S. intelligence agencies knew, was an agricultural country with a rudimentary transportation system and little industry of any kind. Nearly all of the people were rice farmers who worked the land with water buffaloes and hand tools, and whose well-being at a subsistence level was almost entirely dependent on what they grew or made themselves. What intelligence agencies liked to call the "modern industrial sector" of the economy was tiny even by Asian standards, producing only about 12 percent of a GNP of $1.6 billion in 1965. There were only a handful of "major industrial facilities." When NVN was first targeted the JCS found only 8 industrial installations worth listing on a par with airfields, military supply dumps, barracks complexes, port facilities, bridges, and oil tanks. Even by the end of 1965, after the JCS had lowered the standards and more than doubled the number of important targets, the list included only 24 industrial installations, 18 of them power plants which were as important for such humble uses as lighting streets and pumping water as for operating any real factories.
>
> Apart from one explosives plant (which had already been demolished), NVN's limited industry made little contribution to its military capabilities. NVN forces, in intelligence terminology, placed "little direct reliance on the domestic economy for material." NVN in fact produced only limited quantities of simple military items, such as mortars, grenades, mines, small arms, and bullets.[33]

Moreover, such arms and munitions as were produced in North Vietnam were made in small workshops, which provided poor targets, rather than in larger, more vulnerable arsenals. "The great bulk of its military equipment, and all of the heavier and more sophisticated items, had to be imported."[34]

In short, North Vietnam's industry did not provide a rewarding target for an air attack. Meaningful targets were few, and those that existed were critical to neither the viability of the economy nor the prosecution of the war in the South.

> Much of the damage was to installations that the North Vietnamese did not need to sustain the military effort. The regime made no attempt to restore storage facilities and little to repair damage

> to power stations, evidently because of the existence of adequate excess capacity and because the facilities were not of vital importance.[35]

"The idea that destroying, or threatening to destroy, NVN's industry would pressure Hanoi into calling it quits seems, in retrospect a colossal misjudgment."[36] The idea, however, was based on an apparently plausible assumption about the rationality of North Vietnam's leaders, which according to the Pentagon history analyst, the U.S. intelligence community appeared to share.

> This was that the value of what little industrial plant NVN possessed was disproportionately great. That plant was purchased by an extremely poor nation at the price of considerable sacrifice, over many years. Even though it did not amount to much, it no doubt symbolized the regime's hopes and desires for national status, power, and wealth, and was probably a source of considerable pride. It did not seem unreasonable to believe that NVN leaders would not wish to risk the destruction of such assets, especially when that risk seemed (to us) easily avoidable by cutting down the insurgency and deferring the takeover of SVN until another day and perhaps in another manner—which Ho Chi Minh had apparently decided to do once before, in 1954.[37]

Experience, however, did not bear out this assumption. The North improved its air defenses, laid aside its economic development plans, and made necessary adjustments. Imports were increased to offset production losses; bombed facilities were in most cases simply abandoned; and large vulnerable targets such as barracks and storage depots were dispersed and concealed. The North Vietnamese appeared willing to accept the loss of the small industrial base rather than reduce their support for the war in the South.

The bombing and the strain of supporting the war in the South have caused considerable dislocation in the labor force of North Vietnam. By 1968, as many as 475,000 to 600,000 civilians including women and children were working to repair the damage done by the airstrikes, while another 110,000 military personnel were assigned to air defense duties.[38] Military induction standards were apparently also lowered, and there were reports of 15-year-old villagers being conscripted to fight in the South.

It appears, however, that the North has been able to meets its manpower needs. A study by the Systems Analysis Office of the Department of Defense reported that 90% of the North's manpower needs were met by normal population growth.[39] The same study found that the bombing also increased the supply of labor. Thirty-three thousand workers were released from their work by the destruction of North Vietnamese industry, and another 48,000 women were made available for work on roads and bridges in the countryside by their evacuation from the cities. Similarly, North Vietnam as an underdeveloped country had many underemployed who could be used to repair war damage without reducing production. Finally, an estimated 40,000 Communist Chinese were thought to be employed in maintaining North Vietnam's road and rail net. The Systems Analysis Office study concluded "it appears that the North Vietnamese government is not likely to be hampered by aggregate manpower shortages." [40] The Pentagon contribution to the NSSM 1 also held that "In spite of these extra demands, it appears that NVN has enough manpower to continue the war at the high casualty rates sustained in 1968."[41] The State Department contribution was more optimistic but concluded that "there is no evidence that manpower shortages in themselves were becoming acute enough to prevent Hanoi from continuing its policies."[42]

Bombing Vs. Foreign Aid

The second factor contributing to North Vietnam's ability to continue aiding the war in the South is the largest amount of military and economic aid received from Communist China and the Soviet Union. The second JASON study, submitted in December 1967, concluded:

> NVN has transmitted many of the material costs imposed by the bombing back to its allies. Since the bombing began, NVN's allies have provided almost $600 million in economic aid and another $1 billion in military aid—more than four times what NVN has lost in bombing damage. If economic criteria were the only consideration, NVN would show a substantial net gain from the bombing, primarily in military equipment.
>
> Because of this aid, and the effectiveness of its countermeasures, NVN's economy continues to function. NVN's adjustments to the physical damage, disruption, and other difficulties brought on by the bombing have been sufficiently effective to maintain living standards, meet transportation requirements, and improve its military capabilities. NVN is now a stronger military power than before the bombing.[43]

A study by the Systems Analysis Office of the Department of Defense reached a similar conclusion. "Over the entire period of the bombing, the value of economic resources gained through foreign aid has been greater than that lost because of the bombing."[44] The study concluded that North Vietnamese standards of living may have declined but that food supplies had been maintained with only a slight decline. Overall, "the North Vietnamese are not badly off by past North Vietnamese standards or the standards of other Asian countries."[45] With respect to the capital stock destroyed by the bombing—

> It is not certain that Russia and China will replace North Vietnam's destroyed capital assets through aid programs, thus absorbing part of the bombing cost themselves. However, they could do so in a short period of time at relatively small cost; if economic aid remained at its wartime yearly rate of $340 million and half were used to replace capital stock, North Vietnam's losses could be replaced in a year.[46]

Similar conclusions were also reached in the 1969 National Security Study Memorandum 1. "It is generally agreed that the bombing did not significantly raise the cost of the war to NVN. This was because production facilities outside of NVN were not targetable."[47] Estimates as of January 1969 placed North Vietnam's losses of capital stock, military facilities, and current production at $770 million. But economic and military aid from Communist allies totaled $3 billion.[48]

The key consideration so far as bombing policy is concerned, then, is the fact that North Vietnam serves as a funnel for the transit of military aid from other Communist countries to the Communist forces in the South. Attention should thus be focused on North Vietnam's capability to transport men and supplies to the South rather than on its ability to support the war economically.

The North Vietnamese transportation system is primitive and superficially appears highly vulnerable to air attack. But it has proved to be highly flexible and its capacity to air attack. But it has proved to be highly flexible and its capacity has greatly exceeded the demands placed upon it.[49] Because the North Vietnamese transportation system is based to a large degree on crude roads, trails, and waterways rather than on highways and railroads, it provides relatively few lucrative targets for air bombardment. This is particularly true of the southern half of North Vietnam and the trails through Laos. A March 1966 report by the CIA argued:

> The rudimentary nature of the logistic targets in the southern part of North Vietnam, the small volume of traffic moving over them in relation to route capacities, the relative ease and speed with which they are repaired, the extremely high frequency with which they would have to be re-struck—once every three days—all combined to make the logistic network in this region a relatively unattractive target system, except as a supplement to a larger program. A significant lesson from the *Rolling Thunder* program to date is that the goals of sustained interdictions of the rudimentary road and trail networks in southern North Vietnam and Laos will be extremely difficult and probably impossible to obtain in 1966, given the conventional ordnance and strike capabilities likely to exist.[50]

The debate as to the effectiveness of bombing in interdicting the flow of supplies from the North was reflected in the 1969 National Security Study Memorandum 1. The U.S. military command in Saigon (MACV) and the Joint Chiefs of Staff (JCS) felt that the bombing had succeeded, while the Department of State, CIA, and the Office of the Secretary of Defense (OSD) felt that it had failed. The debate over the attempt by MACV to block two key roads near the passes from North Vietnam into Laos in late 1968 illustrates the differences between the two views. According to the summary of NSSM 1—

> MACV finds it has effectively blocked these roads 80% of the time and therefore caused less traffic to get through. OSD/CIA/State agree that enemy traffic on the roads attacked has been disrupted. However, they point out that the enemy uses less than 15% of the available road capacity, is constantly expanding that capacity through new roads and bypasses, and our air strikes do not block but only delay traffic.
>
> Besides blocking the roads, our bombing destroys material in transit on them. JCS/MACV and OSD/CIA agree that we destroy 12% to 14% of the trucks observed moving through Laos and 20% to 35% of the total flow of supplies in Laos. To MACV/JCS, the material destroyed cannot be replaced so that our air effort denies it to the VC/NVA forces in South Vietnam. In complete disagreement, OSD and CIA find that the enemy needs in SVN (10 to 15 trucks of supplies per day) are so small and his supply of war material so large that the enemy can replace his losses easily, increase his traffic flows slightly, and get through as much supplies to SVN as he wants to in spite of the bombing.[51]

It seems that on balance the interdiction bombing of southern North Vietnam and Laos has made the North Vietnamese logistical effort more difficult, costly, and time consuming but that it has not prevented Hanoi from meeting the supply needs of the Communist forces in the South.

The northern half of North Vietnam, however, would seem to offer more lucrative transportation targets, particularly railroads and harbors. In 1966, approximately two-thirds of North Vietnam's imports arrived by sea and the bulk of the remaining third by rail from China.[52] Again, there was a sharp split between MACV and the Joint Chiefs on the one hand and the CIA and the Office of the Secretary of Defense on the other. MACV/JCS believed that if all imports by sea were denied and land routes through Laos and Cambodia were attacked vigorously, the North Vietnamese would be unable to obtain enough war supplies to continue. OSD and CIA, however, felt that the overland routes alone could provide North Vietnam enough material to carry on even in the face of an unlimited bombing campaign.[53]

The mining of North Vietnamese harbors and the current intensive bombing of the North should provide a test of these arguments. Because no reliable data is yet publicly available, it is impossible to judge the interdiction effects of this bombing. However, considering the previous adaptability of the North Vietnamese, it seems probable that they will adjust to the bombing and continue to support the war in the South, albeit at higher cost and with greater delay in the movement of supplies. The capability to wage large scale conventional warfare with armor and heavy artillery, as in the spring 1972 offensive, may be considerably reduced.

Adapting to Bombing

The third factor reducing the effectiveness of the bombing of the North has been the resourcefulness and determination of the North Vietnamese. During the massive bombing of their petroleum facilities, for example, they proved quite resourceful. Distribution was switched from bulk to barrels and decentralized without a major reduction in capabilities. The North has also adapted well to the continuing attacks on the transportation system. According to the Pentagon history—

> Several hundred thousand workers were mobilized to keep the transportation system operating. Miles of by-pass roads were built around choke-points to make the system redundant. Knocked-out bridges were replaced by fords, ferries, or alternate structures, and methods were adopted to protect them from attack. Traffic shifted to night time, poor weather, and camouflage. Shuttling and transshipment practices were instituted. Construction material, equipment, and workers were prepositioned along key routes in order to effect quick repairs. Imports of railroad cars and trucks were increased to offset equipment losses.[54]

The second JASON study concluded that because of such countermeasures, North Vietnam "has become increasingly less vulnerable to aerial interdiction aimed at reducing the flow of men and material from the North to the South."[55]

Coupled with the adaptability of the North Vietnamese has been a tendency to overestimate the capability of U.S. bombing. The first JASON study concluded in 1966:

> Initial plans and assessments for the *Rolling Thunder* program clearly tended to overestimate the persuasive and disruptive effects of the US air strikes and, correspondingly, to underestimate the tenacity and recuperative capabilities of the North Vietnamese. This tendency, in turn, appears to reflect a general failure to appreciate the fact, well-documented in the historical and social scientific literature, that a direct, frontal attack on a society tends [to] strengthen the social fabric of the nation, to increase popular support of the existing government, to improve the determination of both the leadership and the populace to fight back, to induce a variety of protective measures that reduce the society's vulnerability to future attack, and to develop an increased capacity for quick repair and restoration of essential functions. The great variety of physical and social countermeasures that North Vietnam has taken in response to the bombing is now well documented in current intelligence reports, but the potential effectiveness of these countermeasures was not stressed in the early planning or intelligence studies.[56]

The second JASON study concluded in 1967 that—

> because of foreign aid, and the effectiveness of its countermeasures, NVN's economy continues to function. NVN's adjustments to the physical damage, disruption, and other difficulties brought on by the bombing have been sufficiently effective to maintain living standards, meet transportation requirements, and improve its military capabilities. NVN is now a stronger military power than before the bombing and its remaining economy is more able to withstand bombing.[57]

Punishing the North

Although seldom stated explicitly in either memoranda or official statements, an implicit goal of the bombing has been the punishment of the North for its support of the war in the South. A relatively explicit statement of the goal was given by Secretary of Defense McNamara in 1967 in a list of what he considered to be the three objectives of the bombing campaign against North Vietnam: "To make clear to the North Vietnamese political leadership that so long as they continued their aggression against the South, they would have to pay a price in the North."[58]

The goal is often stated in terms of increasing the cost of the war for the North. A March 1966 CIA report argued for increased bombing of northern North Vietnam because it would inflict more pain on the regime and increase the cost of the war. They key argument was:

> The flow of military logistics supplies from the USSR and China cannot be cut off, but the movement could be made considerably more expensive and unreliable if authorization is granted to attack intensively the rail connections to Communist China and if the three major ports are effectively mined.[59]

As has been shown above, the bombing has caused severe damage and disruption to the domestic economy of North Vietnam. Many thousands of civilians have been evacuated from the cities or diverted to repairing damage done by the airstrikes. The civilian population has suffered considerably. National Security Study Memorandum 1 reports that—

> Individual citizens suffered many hardships. While the total supply of goods in NVN increased, individual standards of living declined. Food was rationed and consumer goods were scarce; and air raid warnings disrupted the lives of the populace and forced many to leave their homes. Moreover, it has been estimated that approximately 52,000 civilians were killed in NVN by US air strikes.[60]

While there is a natural desire to impose hardship on an enemy, such a goal seems unsupportable on either moral or policy grounds. The moral implications of mere retribution should require no explanation. By the same token, the high cost of the bombing to the United States in terms of lives and materiel makes such a policy undesirable. Simply raising the cost of the war to the North serves on policy end unless it has a pay-off in terms of impeding the ability of the North to support the war or increases the likelihood of the North's deciding to end the war. Hence, retribution is usually linked to interdiction or putting pressure on Hanoi's will. The preceding discussion has indicated, however, that the bombing has not stopped the flow of supplies to the South. The question then becomes what effect the bombing has had on Hanoi's will to continue the war.

Breaking Hanoi's Will

One of the most pervasive justifications for the bombing of the North is the belief that in some degree the bombing will put pressure on the Hanoi leadership to terminate the war. According to the Pentagon history of the conflict, this was the original purpose of the sustained bombing of the North, although the public rationale was generally put in terms of North Vietnam's capability to continue the war.[61] An interagency task force known as the NSC Working Group concluded in late 1964 that—

> The nature of the war in Vietnam is such that US ability to compel the DRV to end or reduce the VC insurrection rests essentially upon the effect of the US sanctions on the will of DRV leadership to sustain and enlarge that insurrection, and to a lesser extent upon the effect of sanctions on the capabilities of the DRV to do so.[62]

The contention that bombing would put increased pressure on Hanoi's will played a major role in the arguments of the JCS for the highly unsuccessful attacks on North Vietnam's petroleum facilities in 1966.[63] With the relative failure of bombing to achieve the goal of interdicting the flow of supplies south, the goal of breaking Hanoi's will, became more prominent. In arguing for continued bombing, presidential assistant for national security, Walt Rostow wrote in a 1967 memorandum—

> We have never held the view that bombing could stop infiltration…We have held the view that the degree of military and civilian cost felt in the North and the diversion of resources to deal with our

> bombing could contribute marginally—and perhaps significantly—to the timing of a decision to end the war.[64]

Although the reasoning is seldom explicit, the argument that the bombing would affect the will of Hanoi's leadership is generally based on three suppositions. First, the bombing would so reduce North Vietnam's capability to successfully prosecute the war that Hanoi would either sue for peace or substantially reduce the level of warfare. Second, the leadership would decide that the level of destruction visited upon the North Vietnamese economy was greater than the gain from supporting the revolution in the South. Or third, that the morale of the North Vietnamese population would so deteriorate that the leadership would be forced to seek relief from the bombing through negotiations or reduced support for the forces in the South.

Examination of the results of the bombing indicates that none of these suppositions have been borne out in practice. The bombing has made support of the war in the South more difficult and costly but has not reduced North Vietnam's ability to prosecute it. The damage to the North Vietnamese economy has been substantial and development plans have been postponed. But aid from Russia and China has more than offset the damage inflicted by bombing. In such a situation, it seems probable that Hanoi's relationship with her allies is more important than the bombing in the leadership's determination to continue the war. And according to the 1966 JASON study by government–oriented scientists—

> Hanoi's political relations with its allies were in some respects strengthened by the bombing. The attacks had the effect of encouraging greater material and political support from the Soviet Union than might otherwise have been the case. While the Soviet aid complicated Hanoi's relationship with Peking, it reduced North Vietnam's dependence on China and thereby gave Hanoi more room for maneuver on its own behalf.[65]

Available evidence indicates that the great hardships placed upon North Vietnam's population by the bombing and the cost of the war in the South have lowered popular morale but not to the degree that support for the war is threatened. Evidence of the deterioration of popular morale as of early 1968 came from reports of Spanish repatriates who lived in North Vietnam from 13 to 19 years, a decree on the "punishment of counterrevolutionary crimes," and the appearance of a widespread black market.[66] According to the CIA contribution to the 1969 National Security Study Memorandum 1—

> There were some indications in late 1967 and in 1968 that morale was wavering, but not to a degree that influenced the regime's policies on the war. The regime was quite successful, however, in using the bombing threat as an instrument to mobilize people behind the Communist war effort. There is substantial evidence, for instance, that the general populace found the hardships of the war more tolerable when it faced daily dangers from the bombing than when this threat was removed and many of the same hardships persisted. Concern about maintaining popular morale, and, in particular, discipline and unwavering support for the needs of the war appears to have grown markedly in the past year when most of the country was no longer subjected to

> bombing. Since the 1 November bombing halt over the entire country, Hanoi has put great stress on countering the widespread tendency of the people to relax their efforts. Concern of this kind is reflected almost daily in North Vietnamese publications and broadcasts as the regime has used exhortation, criticism, and the threat of coercion to sustain support for the needs of the war in South Vietnam.[67]

Similarly, in commenting on civilian hardships in North Vietnam, the military contribution to NSSM 1 stated:

> There is no evidence to suggest that these hardships reduced to a critical level NVN's willingness or resolve to continue the conflict. On the contrary, the bombing actually may have hardened the attitude of the people and rallied them behind the government's programs. Firm population controls and a steady flow of propaganda from Hanoi have been credited with helping to maintain support for the regime. There is some evidence, however, indicating that morale and support for the war in NVN has declined significantly since the bombing halt.[68]

The experience in bombing North Vietnam, then, appears to once again demonstrate that an attack by a clearly foreign power tends to increase support for the indigenous government and to increase social cohesion in spite of the hardships created by the war.

The persistence of the view that Hanoi's will can be broken by bombing seems inconsistent with what is known of the North Vietnamese leadership. Most of Hanoi's top leadership is composed of long-time revolutionaries who were intimately involved with Vietnam's struggle for independence from the French. Their struggle lasting over 30 years indicates tenacity and will not easily broken. Moreover, as both communists and nationalists, they apparently believe that they have a mission to liberate what they consider to be the southern half of their country. Their statements during the long period of negotiations leave little doubt that they think that time, international opinion, the weight of history, and their own commitment will bring them victory.

A convincing perspective on the effect of the bombing on Hanoi's will was provided by the 1966 JASON study:

> The indirect effects of the bombing on the will of the North Vietnamese to continue fighting and on their leaders' appraisal of the prospective gains and costs of maintaining the present policy have not shown themselves in any tangible way. Furthermore, we have not discovered any basis for concluding that the indirect punitive effects of bombing will prove decisive in these respects.
>
> It may be argued on a speculative basis that continued or increased bombing must eventually affect Hanoi's will to continue, particularly as a component of the total US military pressures being exerted throughout Southeast Asia. However, it is not a conclusion that necessarily follows from the available evidence, given the character of North Vietnam's economy and society, the present and prospective low levels of casualties and the amount of aid available to Hanoi. It would appear to be equally logical to assume that the major influences on Hanoi's will to continue are most likely to be the course of the war in the South and the degree to which the USSR and China support the policy of continuing the war and that the punitive impact of US bombing may have but a marginal effect in this broader context.[69]

Bombing as an Aid to Negotiations

Related to the belief that bombing would break the will of Hanoi's leadership is the belief that bombing would aid in negotiations with the North. Bombing was expected to play essentially two roles with respect to negotiations. These were expressed by Assistant Secretary of Defense John McNaughton in a 1966 memorandum: "The purposes of the bombing are mainly...b. To bring about negotiations (by indirect third-party pressure flowing from fear of escalation and by direct pressure on Hanoi). c. To provide a bargaining counter in negotiations (or in a tacit 'minuet')."[70]

The preceding discussion makes clear that the bombing of North Vietnam has not brought about a willingness of the North Vietnamese leadership to make fundamental negotiating concessions. Moreover, bombing appears to take second place to the military situation in the South in Hanoi's calculations. However, it appears probable that the desire to end the bombing played some role in the decision of Hanoi to accept the U.S. offer of negotiations in 1968. Such was the consensus of the national security agencies in the 1969 NSSM 1.[71] The bombing may, however, have contributed to the failure of other negotiating tracks, such as the 1966 contacts through the Polish representative to the International Control Commission, the direct contacts in Moscow in 1967, and the direct contacts in Rangoon December 1965–February 1966.[72] It thus remains a moot point whether the bombing contributed to the possibility of formal talks between the two sides.

No doubt, the bombing of the North represents a bargaining chip in negotiations, but its value is uncertain. In spite of its prominence in public statements by both sides, the uncertain role of bombing in the course of negotiations from 1965 onward, the relative ineffectiveness of bombing in either stemming infiltration or breaking the will of the North, and the predominance of concern with the course of the war in the South indicate that in terms of extracting major concessions, bombing is a bargaining chip of relatively low value.

Boosting Morale

A final purpose of the bombing of North Vietnam, according to Assistant Secretary of Defense McNaughton, was to sustain U.S. and South Vietnamese morale.[73] A similar view was echoed by Secretary McNamara in 1967.[74] To a degree this objective was achieved. The retaliatory strikes in 1964 and the sustained bombing begun in early 1965 probably contributed to some degree to boosting the morale of the hard-pressed South Vietnamese government. As the second JASON study found in 1967—

> There had been an appreciable improvement in South Vietnamese morale immediately after the bombing began and subsequent buoyancy always accompanied major new escalations of the air war. *But the effect was always transient*, fading, as a particular pattern of attack became a part of the

> routine of the war. There was no indication that bombing could ever constitute a permanent support for South Vietnamese morale if the situation in the South itself was adverse.[75] (Emphasis added.)

Conclusion

This study of the effectiveness of the air war against North Vietnam in achieving the goals set for it by those involved in making the bombing policy necessarily neglects many relevant considerations. These include civilian casualties, the international impact of the bombing, the risks of escalation and provoking Chinese or Soviet intervention, the costs of the bombing, captured airmen, and the consequences within the United States. But in so doing, the study places in a starker light the high hopes held out for the bombing and the small results actually achieved.

Throughout the war, the results of the bombing of North Vietnam have consistently fallen far short of the claims made for it. The bombing began with the expectation that it would break the will of the enemy—although many questioned its capability to do so. When Hanoi showed no signs of weakening, the rationale shifted toward interdiction, but this goal, too, proved unobtainable. Many suggested that this failure was because there were too many restrictions. If such targets as the North's petroleum facilities were attacked, it was argued, Hanoi's capabilities would be sharply reduced. But again, North Vietnam proved capable of adapting; the will of the Hanoi leadership held strong. Again, bombing failed to fulfill the promises made for it.

This study should contain two warning notes. First, the focus of this study has been on interdiction and strategic bombing of North Vietnam during the period 1965–1968. It does not consider tactical air support, which has been relatively successful in achieving its goals. Neither does it consider the current air war against North Vietnam, which is far heavier than previous offensives. No reliable information is yet available on its success or failure.

Second, the experience in Vietnam cannot be readily transferred to other situations. In overcoming the effects of the bombing, the North Vietnamese have had certain advantages which may not apply to other cases. The leadership has shown great tenacity and high motivation, as well as exceptional ingenuity and adaptability in coping with the effects of the bombing. The evident control and organization of the society, together with apparently high popular support have made possible this tenacity and adaptability. Equally important has been the willingness and ability of other Communist countries to provide sufficient military and economic aid. The location of North Vietnam has also been of considerable importance. Bordering on an ally, China, North Vietnam could not be blockaded; land transportation routes were available. Moreover, the proximity to China long tended to moderate U.S. escalation of the air war because of the fear of Chinese intervention. The common border with South Vietnam and the relatively unpopulated and heavily foliated border area with Laos facilitates infiltration and make interdiction bombing more difficult. The original guerrilla nature of the war long reduced the number of supplies which had to be infiltrated, thus reducing the burden on the North. And finally, the underdeveloped nature of the Vietnamese economy has provided relatively few valuable targets for bombing.

These caveats notwithstanding, this study calls into serious question the efficacy of strategic and interdiction bombing against a highly motivated guerilla enemy in an underdeveloped country. Bombing appears capable of raising the costs of war to an enemy in such a situation, but it cannot be depended on to weaken his will or to substantially reduce his activity by interdicting his supplies. Compared to the damage to U.S. prestige and the internal division created by the bombing policy, its meager gain must be seriously questioned.

Terms and Acronyms

AAA	Anti-aircraft Artillery
AFB	Air Force Base
AGL	Above ground level
Air wing	A large organization of squadrons that support the fleet command
Barrel Roll	Code name applying to U.S. armed reconnaissance and prebriefed air strikes against infiltration routes and facilities in northern Laos.
Bingo	Low on fuel
Blue Tree	Code name for *Rolling Thunder* photo-reconnaissance missions in North Vietnam of highway routes and military build-up areas.
Boltered	Missing the arresting cables on the carrier's deck and going around for another try.
CAG	Commander, Air Group
Call the Ball	The carrier pilot's radio call to the LSO on final approach, as he rolls into the "groove" and sights the ball "Meatball," the amber light in the ship's mirror which gives the pilot glideslope information. When it drifts low it turns red, requiring immediate attention. The pilot strives for a green light.
CAP	Combat Air Patrol
Capt.	Navy: Captain, O6 pay grade; one level below Rear Admiral; Marine Corps: O3
CARDIV	Carrier Division
CARQUAL	Carrier Qualifications. Includes pilots renewing their qualifications for carrier landings.
Cat	Catapult
Chief	Navy rate for senior enlisted Petty Officer
CIC	Combat Information Center

CINCPAC	Commander-in-Chief, Pacific
CINCPACFLEET	Commander-in-Chief, Pacific Fleet
Cmdr. (Cdr.)	Navy: Commander O5 level; Marine Corps: Lt. Col. Lieutenant Colonel, O5 level
CO	Commanding Officer
Corpsmen	Navy medic
Cross decking	Changing from one carrier to another
Crusader	Colloquial for RF-8A/G
CTF	Commander Task Force
CTG-77	Commander Task Group 77
CVW	Carrier Air Wing
Det./det	Detachment
Dirty, dirtied up	Preparing Crusader for landing by lowering landing gear, tail hook and raising wing
DMZ	Demilitarized Zone
DRV	Democratic Republic of Vietnam (South)
ECM	Electronic Countermeasures
ECMO	Electronic Countermeasures Officer
ELINT	Electronic Intelligence
Ensign	Navy: O1 level; Marine Corps: 1st Lieutenant (1st Lt) O1 level
Feet dry	Over land
Feet wet	Over sea
Flak	Bursting shells from anti-aircraft artillery
FNGs	"F—ing New Guys" rookie pilot or recent POW
FOGs	"F—ing Old Guys" senior pilot or long-term POW
Frag	Daily order of activities and assignments
Gig	Small boat
Hangar deck	Deck above water line where storage and maintenance of aircraft takes place.
Helo	Helicopter
Home guard	VFP-63's home-based squadron
Iron Hand	Operations against SAM and radar sites.
JCS	Joint Chiefs of Staff
Jink	The term that describes abrupt three-dimensional maneuvers to avoid gunners getting a good bead to shoot.
Knots (kts)	One knot is about 1.2 miles per hour
LSO	Landing Signal Officer mans a platform on the port side of the ship during recoveries and assists the pilot during landing aboard ship.
Lt.	Navy: Lieutenant, 0-3 level; Marine Corps: Captain, 0-3 level

Lt. (j. g.)	Navy: Lieutenant (junior grade), 0-2 level; Marine Corps: 2nd Lieutenant (2nd Lt)
Mach	Mach 1 is 761 mph at sea level at 59 deg. Mach 1 and more is supersonic.
MACV	Military Assistance Command Vietnam
MAW	Marine Air Wing
MCAS	Marine Corps Air Station
MiG	Mikoyan-Gurevich is a Russian aerospace and defense company.
Min burner	RF-8 had one mode of afterburner, On or Off. Later fighters had multiple stages.
Napalm	A jellied gas mixture that burned furiously.
NAS	Naval Air Station
NavCad	Naval Aviation Cadette—and officer in training
Net	Network
NVA	North Vietnamese Army
NVN	Democratic Republic (North) Vietnam or North Vietnam
OinC	Officer in Charge of a detachment
PC	Pneumatic control
Photomate	Colloquial for Photographer's Mate
PI	Photo Interpreter
POL	Petroleum, Oil, Lubricants
Port	Left side
POW	Prisoner of War
Pri-Fly	Primary Flight Control (carrier's control tower, the island, where the Air Boss resides)
P&W	Pratt & Whitney, manufacturer of J-57 engine
RA-3B	Two engine Heavy Photo jet
RAG	Replacement Aircraft Group, a specialized Navy squadron dedicated to all phases of training in a current fleet aircraft.
Recce or recon	Reconnaissance
Recover	Another term for land or trap aboard a carrier
Red Crown	The northern-most guard cruiser that controlled all air traffic in and out of North Vietnam.
RIO	Radar Intercept Officer (second seat of the F-4 Phantom)
Rolling Thunder	Code name assigned to reprisal strikes against NVN.
RVN	Republic of (South) Vietnam
R&R	Rest and relaxation
SAR	Search and Rescue
SA-2	Soviet surface-to-air missile
SAM	Surface-to-air missile

Sick bay	Medical department aboard ship
Skipper	Commanding Officer
Spads	A-1D/E Skyraider, a single engine propeller-driven attack aircraft
Squadronmate	Colloquial for squadron member
Starboard	Right side
SVN	South Vietnam
Tanker	Airborne refueler
Tap code	Communicating by a sequence of taps representing different letters in a matrix.
Task Group	Operational organization of military assets for a special purpose
TF-77	Carrier strike force, including all supporting ships and aircraft targeting infiltration.
TG-77	Task Group operations for Laos
Trap	Navy term for a successful carrier landing
USAF and AF	U.S. Air Force
VFP-62	Light Photographic Squadron 62
VFP-63	Light Photographic Squadron 63
VMCJ-1	Light Marine Composite Reconnaissance Squadron 1
VN	Vietnamese
WAC	World Aeronautical Chart is a type of aeronautical chart used for navigation by pilots
Waist	Refers to the angled deck catapult
WESTPAC	Western Pacific
XO	Executive Officer
Yankee Team	Code name for American missions over Laos involving attack, photographic, weather and electronics intelligence reconnaissance.

Source Notes

Abbreviations for Sources

BAPTVE 'BOMBING AS A POLICY TOOL IN VIETNAM: EFFECTIVENESS', A Staff Study Based on the Pentagon Papers, Naval History and Heritage Command, https://www.history.navy.mil/research/library/online-reading-room/title-list-alphabetically/b/bombing-as-policy-tool-vietnam.html#pre, October 12, 1972.

CHWW Col. H. Wayne Whitten USMC (Ret.), "VMCJ-1 AT WAR 1965-1966," written for this book and presented to the author.

HRYTO Historical Report, Yankee Team Operations.

Chapter 1: 1964–66: VMCJ-1 Photo-Reconnaissance and Electronic Countermeasures

1. Brigadier General Art Bloomer USMC (Ret.), 'Units 1 VMCJ-1 (1958-1975)', MCARA (Marine Corps Aviation Reconnaissance Association), webpage: mcara.us/VMCJ-1.php.
2. Colonel H. Wayne Whitten USMC (Ret.), 'Marine Composite Reconnaissance Squadron One (VMCJ-1) History', MCARA, website: mcara/VMCJ-1.us.
3. Colonel Denis (Deej) Kiely USMC (Ret.), 'The Road to War: Yankee Team and the Ho Chi Minh Trail', National Naval Aviation Museum: *Foundation,* vol. 35, (Spring 2014).
4. Ibid.
5. Ibid.
6. Ibid.
7. Ibid.
8. Ibid.
9. Ibid.
10. CHWW.
11. HRYTO December 1, 1964–March 31, 1965; Declassified U.S. Marine Corps Document No. 1201067096.
12. Ibid.
13. CHWW.
14. HRYTO December 1, 1964–March 31, 1965; Declassified U.S. Marine Corps Document No. 1201067096.

15. HRYTO April 1–June 30, 1965, July 22, 1965, Document No. 1201067097.
16. CHWW.
17. CHWW.
18. Command Chronology for the month of August 1965, Document No. 1201067103.
19. HRYTO July 1–September 30, 1965, Document No. 1201067098.
20. Ibid.
21. Col. H. Wayne Whitten USMC (Ret.), 'Operation Tally Ho: VMCJ-1's RF-8As and EF-10Bs Working in Concert.'
22. Ibid.

Chapter 2: 1964: VFP-63 Photo-Reconnaissance Over Laos and First Prisoner of War

1. Stanley Karnow, *Vietnam: A History*, (New York: Penguin Books, 1984), p. 43.
2. Ibid, p. 247.
3. Ibid.
4. Stanley Karnow, p. 368.
5. Ibid.
6. David S. Barry, 'Doomed to Repeat', *Philadelphia City Paper* (July 29, 2004).
7. Robert S. McNamara, *In Retrospect: The Tragedy and Lessons of Vietnam* (New York: Times Books, a division of Random House Inc., 1995), p. 128.
8. Ibid, pp. 128–29.
9. Ibid, p. 321.

Chapter 3: 1965: VFP-63 Support of Operation Rolling Thunder *Begins*

1. Dr. Mark Jacobson, 'Command and Control of Air Operations in the Vietnam War', Colloquium on Contemporary History, *Washington's Management of the ROLLING THUNDER CAMPAIGN*, No. 4, Naval Heritage and History Command (January 23, 1991).
2. Ibid.
3. Ibid.
4. Karnow, pp. 366–67.
5. Ibid, p. 368.
6. Robert S. McNamara, p. 208.
7. Ibid, p. 216.
8. Ibid.
9. Ibid, p. 321.
10. Jeannette Steel, '*After 5 decades, MIA pilot's wedding ring and bone fragments found in Vietnam fish pond*', *The San Diego Union-Tribune* (May 26, 2017).

Chapter 4: 1966: Operation Rolling Thunder *Intensifies*

1. Dr. Mark Jacobson, 'Command and Control of Air Operations in the Vietnam War', Colloquium on Contemporary History, *Washington's Management of the ROLLING THUNDER CAMPAIGN*, No. 4, Naval Heritage and History Command (January 23, 1991).
2. Ibid.
3. '*Naval Historical Summary Highlights*', Naval History and Heritage Command (January 1966).
4. Ibid.

5. Ibid.
6. '*Naval Historical Summary Highlights*', Naval History and Heritage Command (June 1966).
7. Ibid.

Chapter 6. 1967–68: Dangerous Skies Over Hanoi and Haiphong

1. Dr. Mark Jacobsen, 'Command and Control of Air Operations in the Vietnam War', Colloquium on Contemporary History, *Washington's Management of the ROLLING THUNDER CAMPAIGN*, No. 4, Naval Heritage and History Command (January 23, 1991).
2. Admiral James, 'Command and Control of Air Operations in the Vietnam War', Colloquium on Contemporary History, *Washington's Management of the ROLLING THUNDER CAMPAIGN*, No. 4, Naval Heritage and History Command (January 23, 1991).
3. Robert S. McNamara, *In Retrospect: The Tragedy and Lessons of Vietnam*, (New York: Times Books, a division of Random House Inc., 1995).
4. https://www.findagrave.com/memorial/84365363/milton-james-vescelius.
5. https://www.scopesys.com/cgi-bin/bio2.cgi?bio=V008.
6. https://www.findagrave.com/memorial/84365363/milton-james-vescelius.
7. http://www.rollingthunderremembered.com/rolling-thunder-remembered-21-september-1967-the-last-flight-of-lcdr-milton-james-vescelius-jr-usn/.

Chapter 7: 1969–72: The Final Years

1. Sarah Pruitt, 'Kent State Shootings: A Timeline of the Tragedy', www.history.com (May 1, 2020).
2. Victor P. Buckley LT, USN, "*Lucky Bag*," https://usnamemorialhall.org/index.php/VICTOR_P._BUCKLEY,_LT,_USN.

Chapter 8: Other Navy and Marine Corps Photo-Reconnaissance Aircraft

1. Greg Goebel, 'Air Vectors', www.airvectors.net/ava5.html#m3.
2. Greg Goebel, 'Air Vectors', www.airvectors.net/avf4_1.html#m8.
3. Greg Goebel, 'Air Vectors', www.airvectors.net/avskywar.htm.

Chapter 9: Summary and Conclusions

1. Cmdr. Peter Mersky, 'Vought's Long-Lived Photobird, *Air International*, 1987.
2. Ibid.

Appendix 1

1. Committee on Foreign Relations, 'Introduction', BAPTVE.
2. McNamara, p. 228.
3. Stanley Karnow, p. 458.
4. Committee on Foreign Relations, 'Bombing an Underdeveloped Country', BAPTVE.
5. Ibid.
6. Ibid.
7. Committee on Foreign Relations, 'Bombing vs. Foreign Aid', BAPTVE.

8. Committee on Foreign Relations, 'Breaking Hanoi's Will', BAPTVE.
9. Committee on Foreign Relations, 'Bombing as an Aid to Negotiations', BAPTVE.
10. Committee on Foreign Relations, 'Boosting Morale', BAPTVE.
11. Committee on Foreign Relations, 'Conclusion', BAPTVE.

Appendix 2

1. US Department of Defense, Office of the Secretary of Defense Task Force, Vietnam, *United States Vietnam Relations, 1945–1967* (Washington: Government Printing Office, 1971), IV.C.7. (a), "Volume I The Air War in North Vietnam," p. 3 (hereafter cited as *US–Vietnam Relations*).
2. Ibid., IV.C.3., "Evolution of the War: The *Rolling Thunder* Program Begins," p. 74.
3. CINCPAC 120205Z Jan. 1966, *ibid.*, IV.C.7. (a), p. 32. Sources are frequently not shown in the GPO edition of *US–Vietnam Relations*. But because the footnotes were recently declassified by the Department of Defense, they are cited in this study.
4. SNIE 10-9-65, July 23, 1965, "Communist and Free World Reactions to a Possible US Course of Action," *Ibid.*, pp. 10–11.
5. JCSM 41-66, January 18, 1966, *Ibid.* p. 32.
6. CIA SC No. 0828/66, "The Role of Air Strikes in Attaining Objectives in North Vietnam," Ibid., p. 17.
7. Analyst's comments, Ibid.
8. Testimony before Senate Committees on Armed Services and Appropriations, August 4, 1965, and House Committee on Armed Services, August 6, 1965, and Background briefing for the press, October 21, 1965, *Ibid.*, pp. 18–19.
9. Pentagon historian's comments, *Ibid.*, p. 138.
10. JCSM 810-65, "Air Operations Against the North Vietnam POL System," November 10, 1965, Ibid., p. 65.
11. Pentagon historian, Ibid., pp. 65–66, citing J-3 in collaboration with DIA, "Attack on the North Vietnam Petroleum Storage System—A Study," April 23, 1965 revised December 22, 1965.
12. JCSM 810-65, November 10, 1965, Ibid., pp. 66–67.
13. Memorandum for the Director, CIA, from Sherman Kent, for the Board of National Estimates, "Probable Reactions of the DRV, Communist China, and the USSR to US Air Attacks on Petroleum Storage Facilities in North Vietnam," November 27, 1965, Ibid., p. 68.
14. Pentagon historian's commentary and citations, Ibid., pp. 68–123.
15. SNIE 10-2-65, December 10, 1965, "Probable Communist Reactions to a US Course of Action," Ibid., p. 72. SNIE 10-1-66, "Possible Effects of a Proposed US Course of Action on DRV Capability to Support the Insurgency in South Vietnam," February 4, 1966, *Ibid.*, p. 76; and CIA SC No. 08440/66, "The Effect of Destruction of NVN Petroleum Storage Facilities on the War in SVN," June 8, 1966, Ibid., p. 123.
16. SNIE 10-2-65, December 10, 1965, Ibid., pp. 72–73.
17. Memorandum for the Director, CIA, from Sherman Kent, December 2, 1965, Ibid., p. 69.
18. SNIE 10-2-65, December 10, 1965, Ibid., p. 73.
19. DIA Special Intelligence Summary, NVN POL Status Report," August 1, 1966, Ibid., p. 141.
20. Ibid., p. 143.
21. Pentagon historian's analysis, Ibid., pp. 141–42.
22. Pentagon historian's analysis citing CIA SC No. 04442/67, "The *Rolling Thunder* Program, Present, and Potential Target Systems," Appendix A, January 1967, Ibid., p. 142.
23. Ibid.
24. Ibid.

25. Ibid. Also citing SNIE 13-66, "Current Chinese Communist Intentions in the Vietnam Situation," August 4, 1966.
26. USAF Historical Division Liaison Office, "USAF Plans and Operations: The Air Campaign Against North Vietnam, 1966," Ibid., p. 144.
27. Quoted in *The Washington Post*, February 15, 1967, Ibid., p. 145.
28. Institute for Defense Analyses Report, IDA TS/HQ66-49, "The Effects of US Bombing on North Vietnam's Ability to Support Military Operations in South Vietnam and Laos: Retrospect and Prospect," August 29, 1966, and IDA JASON Division, "The Bombing of North Vietnam," Vol. I, "Summary," IDA Log No. TS/HQ 67-217, December 16, 1967, Ibid., pp. 149–55 and *US–Vietnam Relations*, IV.C.7. (b), "Volume II: The Air War in North Vietnam," pp. 122–27.
29. *US–Vietnam Relations*, IV.C.7. (a), p. 149.
30. IDA, "The Bombing of North Vietnam," December 16, 1967, Ibid., IV.C.7. (b), p. 123.
31. Ibid., p. 124.
32. Ibid.
33. Ibid., IV.C.7. (a), pp. 54–55.
34. Ibid., p. 55.
35. IDA TS/HQ66-49, "The Effects of US Bombing," August 29, 1966, Ibid., pp. 152–53.
36. Pentagon historian's commentary, Ibid., p. 56.
37. Ibid., citing CIA/DIA, "An Appraisal of the Effects of the First Year of Bombing in North Vietnam," SC No. 08437/66, June 1, 1966.
38. Draft of National Security Council, "National Security Study Memorandum 1," 1969, in *Congressional Record*, Vol. 118, No. 77 (May 11, 1972), p. E5010 (hereafter cited as NSSM1). Another study put the total manpower diversion over a three-year period at 750,000. OASD (SA) Economics & Mobility Forces paper, "The Bombing—Its Economic Costs and Benefits to North Vietnam," January 2, 1968, attached to Alain Einthoven Memorandum for the Secretary of Defense, Subject: "The Economic Effects of Bombing North Vietnam," January 2, 1968, in *US–Vietnam Relations*, IV.C.7. (b), p. 130.
39. OASD (SA) Economics & Mobility Forces paper, "The Bombing," January 2, 1968, in *US–Vietnam Relations*, IV.C.7. (b), p. 130.
40. Ibid., pp. 130–31.
41. NSSM 1 in *Congressional Record*, Vol. 118, No. 77 (May 11, 1972) p. E5063.
42. Ibid., No. 76 (May 10, 1972), p. E5000. Emphasis in original.
43. IDA, "The Bombing of North Vietnam," December 16, 1967, in *US–Vietnam Relations*, IV.C.7. (b), p. 125.
44. OASD (SA) Economics & Mobility Forces paper, "The Bombing," January 2, 1968, Ibid., p. 128.
45. Ibid., p. 129.
46. "If the capital stock, is replaced, the economic cost to North Vietnam of the bombing will be the cumulative loss of output from the time the bombing began until the capital stock is fully replaced. Even this probably overstates the cost, however. Even if the pre-bombing capital stock were only replaced, it would be more modern and productive than it otherwise would have been." Ibid.
47. NSSM 1, in *Congressional Record*, Vol. 118, No. 77 (May 11, 1972), p. E5063.
48. Ibid.
49. Pentagon historian's commentary, *US–Vietnam Relations*, IV.C.7. (a), p. 55.
50. CIA SC No. 0828/66, "The Role of Air Strikes in Attaining Objectives in North Vietnam," March 1966, Ibid., p. 82.
51. National Security Council, NSSM 1, "Summary of Responses to NSSM 1—The Situation in Vietnam," in *Congressional Record*, Vol. 118, No. 76 (May 10, 1972), p. E4981.
52. CIA SC No. 0828/66, "The Role of Air Strikes," March 1966, in. *US–Vietnam Relations*, IV.C.7. (a), p. 82.

53. NSSM 1, in *Congressional Record*, Vol. 118, No. 76 (May 10, 1972), p. E4981.
54. *US–Vietnam Relations*, IV.C.7. (a), pp. 56–57.
55. IDA, "The Bombing of North Vietnam," December 16 1967, Ibid. IV.C.7. (b), p. 124.
56. IDA TS/HQ66-49, "The Effects of U.S. Bombing," August 29 1966, Ibid., IV.C.7. (a), p. 154.
57. IDA, "The Bombing of North Vietnam," December 16 1967, Ibid., IV.C.7. (b), p. 125.
58. Ibid., p. 123.
59. CIA SC No. 0828-66, "The Role of Air Strikes," March 1966, Ibid., IV.C.7. (a), p. 82.
60. NSSM 1 in *Congressional Record*, Vol. 118, No. 77 (May 11, 1972), p. E5063.
61. *US–Vietnam Relations*, IV.C.7. (a), p. 3.
62. NSC Working Group on Vietnam (Southeast Asia), "Section I: Intelligence Assessment: The Situation in Vietnam," November 24, 1964, pp. 6–8 (in State Department Materials, Vol. IV), Ibid., IV.C.2. (c), p. 10.
63. Pentagon historian, Ibid., IV.C.7. (a), p. 65.
64. Memorandum to Secretary of State Dean Rusk and Others from Walt W. Rostow, "U.S. Strategy in Vietnam," May 6, 1967, in New York Times, *The Pentagon Papers* (New York: Bantam Books, 1971), p. 574.
65. IDA TS/HQ66-49, "The Effects of US Bombing," August 29, 1966, *US–Vietnam Relations*, IV.C.7. (a) p. 153.
66. NSSM 1 in *Congressional Record*, Vol. 118. No. 76 (May 10, 1972), p. E4999.
67. Ibid., No. 77 (May 11, 1972), p. E5010.
68. Ibid., p. E5063.
69. IDA TS/HQ66-49, "The Effects of US Bombing," August 29, 1966, *US–Vietnam Relations*, IV.C.7. (a) p. 152.
70. McNaughton 2nd Draft, "Some Observations about Bombing North Vietnam," January 18, 1966, in McNaughton Book II, Tab DD, Ibid., p. 34.
71. NSSM 1 in *Congressional Record*, Vol. 118, No. 76 (May 10, 1972), pp. E4977 and E4986, and No. 77 (May 11, 1972), p. E5012.
72. "Negotiations, 1964–1968," a staff study based on the Pentagon Papers prepared for the use of the Committee on Foreign Relations, Study No. 4 (Washington, August 9, 1972).
73. McNaughton 2nd Draft, "Some Observations about Bombing North Vietnam," January 18, 1966, *US–Vietnam Relations*, IV.C.7. (a), p. 34.
74. IDA, "The Bombing of North Vietnam," December 16, 1967, Ibid., IV.C.7. (b), p. 123.
75. Ibid., p. 126.